MAXIMILIAN'S
LIEUTENANT

A Personal History of the
Mexican Campaign, 1864–7

ERNST PITNER

Translated and edited by Gordon Etherington-Smith
Note on the Mexican background by Don M. Coerver

I.B.Tauris & Co Ltd
Publishers
London • New York

For Dolly and Hubert

Published in 1993 by
I.B.Tauris & Co Ltd
45 Bloomsbury Square
London WC1A 2HY

A CIP record for this book is available from the British Library

A full CIP record is available from the Library of Congress

ISBN 1–85043–560–X

Printed and bound in Great Britain by
WBC Ltd, Bridgend, Mid Glamorgan

Contents

Maps

Preface

Some years ago my cousin Dorothea von Pitner showed me copies of letters and diaries written by Ernst Pitner, an ancestor of ours who, as an officer in the Austrian Army, had volunteered to go to Mexico in the Service of the Emperor Maximilian. The papers seemed to me to be of considerable interest, not only as an eye-witness account of some of the episodes in the drama of Maximilian's short-lived reign, but perhaps even more significantly as a record of the reactions of a young European officer at that period to a totally unfamiliar environment and people. On the advice of various friends, I was encouraged to translate the letters and diaries from their original German and to edit them with the addition of a commentary explaining the historical circumstances surrounding Pitner's experiences.

Unfortunately, the papers now preserved are only a part of Pitner's reminiscences. From evidence in what has survived of his writings, it is clear that some letters and diaries were lost in Mexico; and although it is believed that Pitner wrote about his experiences after his return to Austria, no such material has come to light. As far as we know, all the papers now preserved are those which have been handed down by the Pitner family.

I wish to record my thanks to the authorities in charge of the various State archives in Vienna, who have provided me with much useful information and with illustrations relevant to the period. The Austrian Institute in London have also been most helpful with information and allowing me to use their library.

Permission of the Mannheim gallery to reproduce Manet's

famous painting of the execution of Maximilian is gratefully acknowledged.

I am greatly indebted to Richard Lamb for much helpful advice and assistance in preparing the work for publication. Staff at I.B. Tauris have given me valuable help and advice with the publication of the book and my son-in-law, Harold Jones, has been most helpful in arranging for the preparation of the maps.

I wish to record my special thanks to Don M. Coerver of Texas Christian University for his advice on the Mexican background and for his valuable contribution reproduced below.

Finally, I wish to express my gratitude to my cousins Dorothea and Hubert von Pitner for their help throughout this enterprise, but for which this publication would not have been possible.

Gordon Etherington-Smith
London

February 1993

Introduction

In April 1864, Archduke Ferdinand Maximilian of Austria accepted the invitation, proferred by a delegation of Mexican notables, to become emperor of Mexico. This proved to be a fatal decision. For Maximilian had involved himself in a disastrous enterprise, which was to lead, in little more than three years, to his death before a firing squad on a hill near Querétaro.

Why Maximilian should have allowed himself to embark on such a hazardous venture is still far from clear. For us today, with the lessons of Vietnam, Algeria and Afghanistan fresh in our minds, the idea of imposing a foreign monarch by force of arms on a country half the size of Europe can be seen to have been hopelessly unrealistic – the more so since the country concerned already possessed a legally established government, recognized and supported by Mexico's powerful northern neighbour, the United States. The dangers of such an undertaking were indeed represented to Maximilian by a number of qualified persons, as well as by less expert friends and relatives (including his mother). But there were pressures, both political and personal, in the opposite direction. The French emperor, Louis Napoleon, the promoter of the project and embodiment of an army acclaimed for its success in the Crimea and in the recent battles against Maximilian's compatriots in Italy,[1] was at the height of his power. Inspired by visions of a region of French hegemony in Central and South America and spurred on by the urgings of his Spanish wife,

[1] In 1859 the French army, with only a little help from the Piedmontese, roundly defeated the Austrians at Solferino.

Eugénie, who was in sympathy with monarchist Mexican émigrés, Louis Napoleon commended the project to Maximilian in euphoric terms. Maximilian, an intelligent but somewhat impressionable prince, saw the enterprise as an outlet for his talents, which he felt himself to be denied in his native country, and was tempted by romantic imaginings of becoming the ruler of a utopian state in the New World. In this he was vigorously encouraged by his young and ambitious wife, Charlotte (daughter of King Leopold I of the Belgians and thus a first cousin of Queen Victoria), for whom imperial grandeur held irresistible attractions. Maximilian did experience moments of doubt before taking the final decision. In the end it was perhaps Charlotte's advocacy which tipped the scales.

The Maximilian adventure is a unique episode in nineteenth-century history, many aspects of which are relevant today. It throws into sharp relief the rivalries and designs which motivated the dominant powers in the late colonial era. It exemplifies, in a war whose characteristics have become familiar to us in more recent times, the difficulties faced by Western troops in an unfamiliar environment when confronted by determined local forces on their own terrain. And it presents an intriguing picture of the interaction of different cultural and national influences within Mexico itself and of the many colourful individuals from different countries who played a part in the drama.

One of these individuals was Ernst Pitner and it is his story, as told in his letters and diaries, which is the subject of this book. It is a simple account, told in a straightforward manner, of the author's experiences in Mexico, an account containing much that is trivial – the daily fare of military life – but interspersed here and there with a telling observation or humorous anecdote and combining to give an impression of the country and the period. It throws light on the personality of a young European in the middle of the last century – his tastes, his ambitions, his not inconsiderable sense of humour, above all his remarkable courage and fortitude. It also presents a vivid picture of conditions in Mexico at this time and of the people who came to be involved in one of the most extraordinary episodes of the century.

At the same time, it has to be recognized that Ernst's attitude to the country to which destiny had brought him and particularly its people hardly accords with present ideas of tolerance and humanity. He was contemptuous of his 'rebel' opponents, predominantly Indian, (even referring to them in the letters as 'riff-raff'), and on at least one occasion approved of the shooting of Liberals captured in combat.[2] His intemperate statements on this subject should be seen against the background of the general inhumanity of the war, the orders issued by the French High Command that prisoners were to be shot and the accepted standards of the age.

Ernst's experience has necessarily to be seen in the context of the wider developments surrounding it. Where necessary, I have delineated the background to the events in which Ernst was involved and have supplemented his own story with my own commentary to enable it to be seen in its historical context.

The foundations for the establishment of a monarchy in Mexico were to be provided by French military power. The first French troops were landed at Veracruz early in 1862 in a concerted operation with Spanish and British contingents, both of the latter, however, being speedily withdrawn (Britain's sole interest was to secure satisfaction of its financial claims against the Mexican government). But it soon became clear that the French had more far-reaching political objectives. Their numbers increased by substantial reinforcements, the French advanced into the interior and despite an initial setback at Puebla, whose stubborn defence by the Republicans should have served as a warning of what was to come, presently occupied Mexico City and much of the rest of the country (or at least its main towns), the Republican government of Benito Juárez meanwhile withdrawing to the far north, close to the American border. The country was then considered to have been made safe for Maximilian's installation as emperor. Under the agreement[3] concluded with him by Louis Napoleon, the latter pledged himself to keep twenty thousand French troops in Mexico for at least three years, to allow the Foreign Legion of some eight thousand men to remain indefinitely and to support the new empire whatever might happen – undertakings which he had no hesitation in breaking when it became expedient for him to do so.

It naturally suited Louis Napoleon that other countries should

[2] see below, p. 57.
[3] Convention of Miramar, 10 April 1864.

be involved militarily in support of Maximilian's rule and the Emperor Franz Josef's consent to the recruitment on Austrian soil of a corps of volunteers for service in Mexico (one of the few favours he showed his brother as the latter prepared himself for his new responsibilities) must have given the French emperor some satisfaction. The corps, together with its Belgian counterpart of some two thousand men, was to constitute an élite force, directly under Maximilian, which it was hoped would eventually form the nucleus of an imperial Mexican army. Under the agreement[4] reached between Maximilian and his brother the size of the corps was set at 6,300 men (in fact more than 7,000 were in Mexico by the spring of 1865). The force consisted of three infantry battalions, one regiment of lancers (Ulanen) and one regiment of Hussars (this unit, commanded by the dashing Count Khevenhüller, was unique in being composed entirely of Hungarians), as well as detachments of artillery and engineers and a military band. Volunteers, whether still in the Austrian army or not, had to have completed their military service in Austria, which meant that the men were at least thirty-one years of age. (However, officers received preferential treatment and, for example, Count Khevenhüller was recruited at twenty-four and Ernst Pitner at twenty-six.) All recruits undertook to serve in the corps for six years, after which they would be entitled to a free passage home. Officers would advance one rank on joining the corps and were guaranteed reinstatement in the Austrian army on completion of their contracted service in Mexico, but only in their old rank. Terms afforded to the men were somewhat less generous. Franz Josef had insisted that the entire cost of raising the corps should be borne by the Mexican government.

Men accepted for entry into the corps had to be of good conduct, preferably unmarried, not more than forty years of age, physically sound and of Christian faith (a further requirement for the fourteen Hungarians chosen to form Maximilian's personal bodyguard was the ability to grow a beard!). Bachelors were preferred, not only in order to avoid the cost of dependants, but also because it was hoped that many would marry and settle in Mexico. For officers the requirements were more severe: they must be of absolute integrity, robust good health and sound

[4] Convention between Austria and Mexico of 19 October 1864.

intelligence. All were expected to win respect and esteem for the corps by their discipline and good appearance.

Members of the corps were provided with a distinctive uniform, featuring a large, wide-brimmed felt hat with a coloured ostrich or goose feather, a dark blue tunic with red or brown trousers and a dark brown greatcoat or cape. The cavalry regiments wore green coats with crimson breeches and red or white caps.

Those who volunteered did so for many different reasons. Some of the men went simply for the excitement, out of wanderlust or for the sake of the material rewards which they hoped might be in store for them. But a fair number of others were unemployed and destitute individuals from the poorest parts of the Austro-Hungarian Empire – Bohemia, Silesia and Hungary – who seized the opportunity of escape from a miserable existence. There were also many impoverished Poles, who had fled to Austria after the failure of the uprising against Russia in 1863 (mostly enrolled in the Ulanen). All were subjected to a searching medical examination and many were turned down. Motivation among the officers, particularly those from aristocratic families, tended to be somewhat different. Many, like Ernst himself, went simply for the adventure and because of boredom and poor prospects at home. Others (Khevenhüller, for example) went to escape their creditors, others again because of unhappy love affairs or being involved in personal situations for which departure from home offered a ready solution.

But the way in which the corps was organized and the diversity of the elements composing it held the seeds of future trouble. The corps was supposed to be subordinate to only the Emperor Maximilian, but in practice it had to co-operate with the much larger French force, under Marshal Bazaine, in the conduct of operations against the Liberals. This led to much confusion – and increasing controversy and resentment – in relations with the French. The fact that the men in the corps came from so many different parts of the Austro-Hungarian Empire and were so diverse in language and culture was also a source of much difficulty. For it meant that there were cultural and linguistic divisions within the corps itself which impaired its efficiency. Many of its members were unable to converse not only with the Mexicans (whose auxiliary troops supported the Austrians in combat) but also with their French allies and even with some of their own comrades in arms. Furthermore, many of the Austrian soldiers, being hardened veterans of well over thirty (unlike the Belgians, who for the most part were untrained youths), were unruly characters difficult to control. They tended to be insubordinate and quarrelsome and their addiction to drink was a frequent problem for which their commanders devised severe punishments. For all these reasons the corps was never able to adapt itself to service in Mexico and as the military situation deteriorated and the condition of the men became harder their frustration tended to find expression in increasing indiscipline, quarrels and excesses.

The enrolment and marshalling of the volunteers took place in Laibach (Ljubljana) in Slovenia, from where they were despatched to Trieste for embarkation. Six ships had been chartered for the voyage and sailings took place at roughly fortnightly intervals from 19 November 1864 to 29 March 1865. A few volunteers had sailed from the French port of Saint Nazaire, among them Major Kodolitsch,[5] one of the senior officers of the corps, who was to make arrangements for the arrival of the troops in Mexico.

Among the volunteers was Ernst Pitner, a junior officer in the Austrian army. Born in Vienna in 1838, he came of a minor aristocratic family of lawyers, doctors, military men and civil servants. His father was a government official who had married Ernst's mother, Thérèse von Sommer-Sonnenschild, after the death of his first wife in 1834. Ernst's half-brother, Franz,[6] was a well-known painter. His cousin Max[7] was a naval officer, who commanded one of the warships in the Austrian fleet which defeated the Italians at the battle of Lissa in 1866 and became an admiral. Ernst was devoted to his mother, as is evident from the affection repeatedly and rather touchingly expressed in his letters, and was also much attached to his other relations, to whom a string of greetings was invariably included whenever he wrote.

After attending the military academy (*Kadettenschule*) in Graz, Ernst enlisted in the army as an ordinary serviceman (this was not unusual for future officers) in May 1859 at the age of twenty. He fought against the French at Solferino the same year, was decor-

---

[5] Alphons Freiherr von Kodolitsch.
[6] Franz Pitner, b. 1826.
[7] Max Pitner, 1833–1911.

ated for bravery and was promoted to second-lieutenant in October 1860. After other service appointments, which included two years in the navy, he volunteered for service in Mexico under the Emperor Maximilian in August 1864. His naval experience may well have contributed to this decision, for as commander-in-chief from 1854 to 1859 Maximilian had been outstandingly successful in revitalizing the Austrian navy and was widely popular in naval circles.

Note on the
Mexican Background

Since achieving independence from Spain in 1821, Mexico had laboured under the spectre of foreign intervention. Initially this fear of intervention was directed towards her former ruler who entertained delusions of reconquering the ex-colony throughout the 1820s. In July 1829 Spain made a half-hearted effort to retake Mexico, an invasion soundly defeated as much by climate and disease as by the prowess of the Mexican army. By the time Spain recognized Mexico's independence in 1836, a much more serious threat of foreign intervention was emanating from the north.

Since the late colonial period, authorities in Mexico City had been highly concerned about the security of Mexico's northern frontier. Efforts to colonize and fortify the area had failed for lack of resources. By the early nineteenth century, the expansionist activities of the United States increasingly threatened the northern region. The US acquisition of Florida in 1819, instead of satisfying expansionist ambitions, only focused them on the Mexican province of Texas. The Mexican response was to try to establish a 'buffer state' of American immigrants in Texas, a manœuvre that backfired completely when the buffer state turned into a beachhead. Efforts by the United States to purchase Texas in the late 1820s and early 1830s confirmed Mexican suspicions that the Americans were determined to acquire the region one way or another.

The outbreak of revolution in Texas in 1836 culminated in the loss of the area and the creation of the Republic of Texas. The annexation of Texas by the United States in 1845 led to war between the two countries with calamitous results for Mexico. US forces invaded Mexico, occupying the capital and imposing a treaty that involved the loss of approximately half of Mexico's national territory. Fear of US intervention would dominate Mexican thinking until the 1860s when it was replaced by the reality of another foreign intervention.

The problem of foreign intervention was the product of a host of ills afflicting Mexico throughout the first half century of its independence. Chronic political instability made Mexico a tempting target for countries interested in extending their control or influence. This instability was the end result of a number of factors: Liberal–Conservative competition, federalist–centralist tensions, church–state conflict, and a continuous strain of militarism.

Mexican liberalism was an uneasy blend of Enlightenment philosophy, Spanish reformism and admiration for the US model of political freedom and economic opportunity. The general goal of Mexican Liberals was to modernize Mexican society by introducing representative government and *laissez-faire* economics. The Liberals placed primary emphasis on political reforms, especially equality before the law; this led them to neglect basic social and economic problems and to overestimate their ability to legislate change in a traditional society. The Liberals were also handicapped by a longstanding factionalism that pitted moderate against more radical elements. Conservatives opposed representative government, favoured government intervention in the economy and opposed equality before the law. Defence of privilege was central to the Conservative philosophy, privileged groups being necessary for the proper functioning of society. Mexican Conservatism had a strong strain of monarchism which limited the Conservatives' political appeal and led to periodic efforts to 'import' monarchs from Europe. Cutting across Liberal–Conservative lines were the persistent opportunism and focus on personalities that characterized the era, often invalidating political labels.

The federalist–centralist controversy also contributed to Mexico's political instability. While this dispute was often seen as one phase of the Liberal–Conservative conflict, the issue transcended traditional political divisions. Regionalism had been an integral part of both the Hispanic and indigenous political traditions. While federalism was often equated with Liberalism, it could just as easily be invoked by Conservatives interested in preserving their own power at the local or provincial level. In its most extreme manifestation, the federalist–centralist dispute took the form of separatism. A trend toward centralism was a primary factor in the Texas Revolution of 1836; other separatist movements developed in the northern border states as well as Yucatán. This ongoing struggle between the centre and the periphery encouraged foreign meddling and ultimately military intervention.

Conflict between church and state was at the heart of the political instability afflicting Mexico. Church–state relations were often part of the broader Liberal–Conservative split as the position of the Catholic church in Mexican society became the most volatile political issue prior to 1860. In general terms the Liberals believed that the Catholic church was the principal obstacle to the modernization of society. Conservatives viewed Liberal efforts to curb the influence of the church as an attack on religion itself and actively supported the church's privileged position. A poor state confronting a relatively rich church further complicated relations. The historic political involvement and social control of the Catholic church made some sort of showdown with the Liberals unavoidable as they saw a secular state replacing the church in many of its traditional activities. The longstanding political alliance between the church hierarchy and the Conservatives would play a key role in the foreign intervention of the 1860s.

Political instability was also heightened by the unending contest for power among various military leaders. Militarism had been a growing problem since the late colonial period and had been accentuated by the lengthy struggle for independence lasting from 1810 to 1821. Mexico found itself saddled with a large group of military leaders determined to play a political role either officially or unofficially. The results were predictable: an endless series of rebellions, a high rate of turnover in the presidency (forty-four presidential administrations between 1824 and 1854), and a chronic drain on the treasury. Free from civilian control, the army viewed itself as the saviour of the nation and the repository of national honour. Although the military appropriated the role of national aribiter, it was unable to promote either political or financial stability. Militarism proved self-perpetuating and self-aggrandizing. The more the army intervened, the greater the degree of political instability; the greater the degree of political instability, the more likely the army was to intervene. The army had proved more adept at stirring up domestic politics than at defending the nation, a fact that did not escape those considering foreign intervention.

Political instability was closely linked with financial instability, further encouraging foreign interference and intervention. Mexico lacked the financial foundation upon which to construct a modern nation state. With a fiscal structure that depended too heavily on taxes on external trade, the Mexican government soon became involved in deficit-financing, borrowing from both domestic and foreign lenders. In an era when European governments were willing to use diplomatic pressure and even military force to collect debts owed to their citizens, foreign loans might very well lead to foreign intervention. Conservative and Liberal governments proved equally inept at meeting the financial crisis; both political groups were unwilling to attempt a major reform of the fiscal structure and continued a policy of incurring new debt to pay old debt. Foreign loans were a particularly sore point, with the conviction widespread in Mexico that the terms under which they were contracted were exploitative. While the terms were actually comparable to similar loans of the period, the real problem was the purposes for which the proceeds were being used: payments on earlier debts, military expenses, and administrative costs. The financial situation of the government put all administrations at risk both domestically and internationally.

The financial and political instability accelerated after the triumph of the Liberal revolution of Ayutla in 1855. The Liberals systematically set about to tear down what they perceived as the political, financial and social supports for the Conservatives. The Juárez Law, named after Minister of Justice Benito Juárez, attacked the privileged legal position of the Catholic church and the military by severely restricting the jurisdiction of ecclesiastical and military courts, a major step in the direction of establishing equality before the law. Minister of the Treasury Miguel Lerdo saw his name attached to a new law that forced corporate landowners (the church and Indian communities) to sell their property with a view to creating a new group of middle-class landowners. The maintenance of records relating to births, marriages, adoptions and deaths was transferred from ecclesiastical to civil officials. Even the fees charged by the church for spiritual services became subject to state regulation (the Iglesias Law).

These actions provided the background for a new Liberal constitution promulgated in early 1857. The new constitution incorporated the Juárez, Lerdo and Iglesias Laws and attacked the church's virtual monopoly on education by providing free public education. Although the Constitution of 1857 made no reference to religious toleration, it also did not establish Catholicism as the official state religion as all earlier constitutions had done. The Constitution also provided an extensive list of civil rights, including freedom of speech, press, petition and assembly.

Reaction to the Constitution of 1857 by Conservatives and the Catholic church was predictably hostile. The election of a moderate – Ignacio Comonfort – only briefly delayed a violent conflict between the Conservatives and the Liberals. The church was particularly bitter in its denunciation of the new constitution. The archbishop of Mexico not only denounced the provisions of the constitution relating to the church; he also railed against freedom of speech, press, assembly and education. Even the pope, Pius IX, publicly challenged the new constitution, declaring all constitutional restrictions on the church to be null and void. A Conservative coup opposing the Constitution but supporting Comonfort as president with extraordinary powers took place in December 1857. Comonfort – who saw himself as the moderator between Conservative and Liberal extremes – came out in favour of the coup, placing himself in the odd position of revolting against his own administration. Comonfort's continued efforts to mediate angered the Conservatives who overthrew him in January 1858, opening the way to a full-scale civil war.

The longstanding Liberal–Conservative dispute was now transformed into a three-year civil war known as the War of the Reform. With the conservatives controlling Mexico City and most major urban areas, the Liberals under Benito Juárez established an alternate government at Veracruz and waged guerrilla warfare in the provinces. The conduct of the war led both sides into fiscal and foreign policies that would open the way for outside intervention once the war was concluded. Mexico found itself with two governments, each claiming to rule and each running up bills that it did not have the money to pay. Financial problems led both Conservatives and Liberals into diplomatic negotiations that compromised Mexico's independence and sovereignty. In search of foreign financing, the Conservatives reached an agreement with the Spanish government that effectively resurrected some debt obligations going all the way back to the 1820s that had previously been considered cancelled. The Conservatives also contracted the notorious Jecker loan with French financiers that would play a key role in the French intervention in the 1860s. Financial problems pushed the Liberals into an equally questionable arrangement with the United States government. The McLane–Ocampo treaty of 1859 provided the United States with the right of transit across northern Mexico and the Isthmus of Tehuantepec in return for four million dollars, half of which would be retained by the United States to deal with financial claims by American citizens against the Mexican government. The United States was even granted the right to use its own forces to protect American lives and property in the two areas. Fortunately for the Liberals, the United States Senate – split by sectional differences – refused to ratify the treaty. The Liberals were also actively pursuing the sale of Baja California to the United States, another fund-raising scheme that was undone by the sectional controversy in the United States.

The War of the Reform pushed the Liberals into taking even harsher measures against the Catholic church. In the so-called 'Laws of the Reform' published in July 1859, the Liberals provided for the confiscation of all church property and the suppression of the religious orders. Later legislation made marriage a strictly civil matter and transferred cemeteries to secular control; religious toleration and separation of church and state were also officially incorporated into the Liberal programme. While the new restrictions proved difficult to enforce, they served to widen the ideological gap between the Liberals and the Conservatives.

While the first two years of the war went badly for the Liberals, during 1860 they enjoyed a series of victories, culminating in their return to Mexico City in January 1861. What Mexico needed most was a long period of peace in which to restore order to government and finance; what followed instead was another period of political and financial instability that would lead to another civil war and foreign intervention. The Conservatives – defeated militarily – still refused to accept the reform programme that the Liberals were determined to implement. The victorious Liberals increasingly fought among themselves over the moderate approach taken by Juárez. Overshadowing the disagreements about political philosophy was the seemingly intractable problem of the public finances.

The nation's finances had been in a state of disorder even before the War of the Reform. In addition to the destruction caused by the war, the conflict had also led to the collapse of the system of central collection of revenue; state governments attempted to retain control of federal revenue collection after the fighting stopped. Customs revenues – the principal source of financing for the central government – had been pledged to pay earlier debts and were not available to meet current expenses. Proceeds from the sale of nationalized church property also proved disappointing for the government. The dismissal of a large number of employees of the Ministry of the Treasury for co-operating with the Conservative government created further financial turmoil. Foreign creditors were pressuring the Liberal government to resume payments on debts, some of which dated back to the 1820s. The Juárez administration's plan for dealing with the crisis at first consisted of little more than promoting peace and trying to reduce military spending; more drastic action was needed to put Mexico's finances in order.

The possibility of suspending payment on the government debt had arisen even before the end of the War of the Reform. In May 1860 with the war still on Juárez had announced a suspension in payment on the foreign debt but quickly reversed his position, a move that led to the resignation of his minister of the treasury, Miguel Lerdo. After the war was over, the continuing financial problems of the Juárez administration soon revived the possibility of some kind of suspension of debt payment. Juárez and his cabinet originally considered the possibility of suspending payment only on the debt owed to Mexican creditors, a move that the government discussed with the Mexico City diplomatic corps. On 17 July 1861, however, the Mexican Congress passed legislation calling for a two-year suspension on payment of both the domestic and the foreign debt. Juárez and his advisors had long resisted such a move for fear that it might provoke some type of foreign intervention; the immediate result was that the major European countries broke off relations with the Liberal government.

The possibility of foreign intervention, including the importation of a foreign monarch, was as old as independent Mexico. The revolutionary plan of 1821 that had led to Mexican independence had called for the creation of a constitutional monarchy under a European prince. The monarchists among the Conservative group never abandoned the idea that the answer to Mexico's chronic instability lay in establishing a Mexican monarchy by importing European royalty. The project was given new life by the War of the Reform and the continuing political and financial instability of the Mexican government. This longstanding monarchist scheme, the suspension of debt payments and the imperial design of France's Napoleon III would converge to produce the French intervention and a new empire in Mexico in the 1860s.

The initial impetus for intervention was to come from Spain. As early as September 1861, Spain was threatening to intervene in Mexico but it delayed action, hoping that some type of joint European intervention might be made. Representatives from Spain, France and Great Britain met the following month in London where a convention calling for a tripartite intervention was signed. Under the terms of the agreement, the three countries would dispatch land and naval forces to secure key points along the Mexican coast. These forces would collect customs revenues which would be used to pay the suspended debts. The three countries specifically promised not to use the intervention to acquire territory, to gain any special advantage, or to try to influence the form of Mexico's government. The three signatories even invited the United States to participate in the intervention, an invitation rejected by the United States which was involved in its own civil war and which could scarcely sanction an action that violated the Monroe Doctrine.

Ironically, the Juárez government was most suspicious of Spain's intentions, particularly with the Spanish forces the first to arrive at Veracruz in December 1861. The landing of Spanish troops was unopposed, and in early January 1862 British and French troops landed. The allies attempted to allay Mexican fears by issuing a 'proclamation to the Mexican people', containing assurances that they were not there to conquer territory or interfere in the internal political affairs of Mexico. Less encouraging was the proclamation's reference to the desire of the intervening powers to be part of Mexico's 'regeneration'.

The principal ally of the Liberal government was the unhealthy climate at Veracruz which was already taking a heavy toll on the intervention forces. The allies wanted to escape the fever-ridden area around the city by moving their forces inland to higher elevations. For its part the Juárez government wanted to negotiate with, rather than fight, the allied troops. The result was the so-called 'Convention of La Soledad' in February in which Mexico agreed to permit the intervention forces to move inland in exchange for an allied promise to enter into negotiations and for renewed pledges that the expedition posed no threat to Mexico's sovereignty or territorial integrity.

The tripartite intervention had been a shaky alliance from the beginning. Great Britain in particular had been insistent that the intervention strictly adhere to its limited goal of debt collection, while France had shown a reluctance to pursue a negotiated settlement with the Juárez administration. Once the expedition had actually landed in Mexico, the diverging views of the different participants became more evident. Spain and Great Britain were not prepared to support the French demands on the Mexican government, which included payment of unproven financial claims. French representatives refused to negotiate with the Juárez government and were aiding in the return of leading Mexican Conservatives from exile. In April 1862 leaders of the Spanish and British forces – citing French violations of the Conventions of London and La Soledad – announced that they were withdrawing their forces, bringing the tripartite intervention to an end. The French forces, however, were to remain.

The unravelling of the alliance was hastened by the poorly concealed efforts of Napoleon III of France to replace the Juárez government with a European monarchy. Napoleon III had played an increasingly active role in European politics in the 1850s and was determined to resurrect the grandeur of the earlier Napoleonic empire. This resurrection would include a revival of the old Napoleonic scheme to extend French influence in the western hemisphere. Napoleon's choice for the Mexican monarchy was an Austrian archduke, Ferdinand Maximilian.

Maximilian, brother of Emperor Franz Josef of Austria, had served as commander of the Austrian navy and governor general of Austria's holdings in Italy. In this latter position Maximilian had proven too liberal to suit the taste of Franz Josef. With no realistic prospects of inheriting the Austrian crown, Maximilian was looking for an appropriate outlet for his political idealism. In this search he was aided by his ambitious wife, Charlotte, daughter of King Leopold of the Belgians.

As early as November 1861, Napoleon III was promoting Maximilian as the head of a new Mexican government. Prominent Mexican Conservatives were also actively recruiting the archduke for the imperial enterprise. Maximilian was keenly interested but wanted assurances of French support and Mexican approval for the scheme. The would-be emperor sought military and financial aid from Napoleon III and some indication of a popular sanction in Mexico for an empire. The Convention of Miramar, signed in March 1864, dealt with the military and financial relationship between Maximilian and Napoleon III. According to the convention, Napoleon promised to provide at least 25,000 troops until Maximilian could raise his own imperial forces; in addition, a Foreign Legion contingent of 5,000 men would remain in Mexico for at least eight years. Napoleon supported a loan of 200 million francs with the new Mexican government guaranteeing the interest payments; in addition Maximilian agreed to compensate the French government for the expenses connected with establishing his throne and to pay the expenses of all French troops remaining in Mexico after 1 July 1864. The French forces in Mexico, which had subdued most of the major urban areas, co-operated with the Mexican Conservatives to rig a plebiscite, which indicated over-whelming popular support for Maximilian's empire.

There were still two major items that needed to be addressed before Maximilian could depart Europe to take the Mexican throne: an agreement on his relationship with the Austrian monarchy and a discussion of church–state relations with the pope. While Emperor Franz Josef had originally expressed an interest in a Mexican throne for Maximilian, he later turned against the project and demanded that Maximilian sever all ties with the Austrian monarchy, including the renunciation of any claim to the crown or right to share in the family inheritance, if he accepted the Mexican title. In April 1864 Maximilian reluctantly agreed to his brother's demands in what became known as the 'family pact'. While the pact represented an effort to divorce Austria from the Mexican proceedings, it did contain one provi-sion of support for Maximilian's empire. Maximilian would be permitted to recruit a volunteer force of 6,000 Austrians for service in Mexico; it was this force that Ernst Pitner was to join.

Maximilian's efforts to settle church–state relations with the Vatican prior to departing from Europe were less emotional but considerably less conclusive. Maximilian and Charlotte visited the pope and received his blessing for the enterprise, but there was no formal agreement on church–state relations, something that Napoleon III had stressed should be settled before Maximilian's departure. Instead Pius IX and Maximilian simply agreed that a papal nuncio would be sent to Mexico to finalize church–state relations with the new imperial government.

By the time Maximilian and Charlotte arrived in Mexico in late May 1864, the French intervention had been underway for more than two years. French troops had subdued most of the major urban areas, had forced the Liberal government out of the capital, and had installed a friendly and pliable Conservative regime which invited Maximilian to become emperor of Mexico. The Juárez government had become an itinerant administration, pursued by the French and split by internal divisions. The liberals waged decentralized guerrilla war against the French, controlling much of the countryside but unable to inflict a decisive defeat on the invaders.

Maximilian's empire was soon mired in a stalemated military conflict, an intractable financial situation and deteriorating relations among the principal supporters of the empire. The guerrilla warfare of the Liberals continued to frustrate the French and Conservative forces. The financial situation worsened as Maximilian's lavish spending habits were added to the continuing economic problems of the central government. Both the French and the Conservatives were soon at odds with policies implemented by Maximilian. The separation of military control under the French and civil administration under imperial authority was a formula for bureaucratic disputes, with Maximilian and French Marshal François Bazaine regularly sniping at each other. More serious was the split between Maximilian and the Conservatives, who took strong exception to the emperor's efforts to impose a moderate brand of liberalism on the empire. The clergy in particular were outraged by Maximilian's refusal to repeal the anticlerical legislation of the Reform; especially disappointing was the emperor's rejection of demands for the restoration of church property. Maximilian's efforts to find a middle ground between the Conservatives and the Liberals resulted in the alienation of both groups.

Although beset with problems, the empire was at its strongest in late 1864 and early 1865 when Ernst Pitner embarked on his part of the Mexican adventure. Pitner came out of a military environment that had recently witnessed an Austrian defeat at the hands of the French in 1859 over Austria's presence in Italy. A predictable purge of the Austrian high command followed, but there was no rejuvenation of the armed forces. Military expenditures declined in the early 1860s, and the actual military establishment was considerably under its authorized strength. Prospects for promotion were correspondingly dim, and pay was poor, especially for junior officers such as Pitner.

The composition and organization of the volunteer corps was later to cause confusion and internal conflict. The corps reflected the ethnic diversity of the Habsburg Empire, complicating an already-difficult communications problem. Although experienced in cultural differences, most of the volunteers held feelings of superiority toward the Mexicans that were often hard to conceal. While the volunteers were nominally under the direct command of the emperor, they could not escape the dominant role played by the French forces, a secondary role that was not to the Austrians' liking. Trained in the conventional warfare of nineteenth-century Europe, the volunteer corps was ill prepared to deal with the guerrilla warfare that the Liberals had mastered after years of fighting the Mexican Conservatives and the French intervention.

Don M. Coerver,
Texas Christian University

Letters and Diaries

Letters and Diaries

Sea Voyage

The second ship to sail from Trieste, the *Brasilian*, was the one on which Ernst was travelling. He described the departure in his diary:

At ten o'clock on the morning of 1 December 1864, the embarkation began of the detachment of troops, 1,100 strong, to which I belonged.

The English steamer *Brasilian* was to carry us across the ocean.

The quay at which our steamer had moored was teeming with people. Driven partly by pity, but largely by curiosity, the good people of Trieste had gathered in their thousands to enjoy the spectacle of how one crammed 1,100 human beings – and volunteers to boot – into the frankly not very comfortably furnished compartments of our ship, and of how one could have succeeded in finding so many people who were minded of their own free will to exchange their good Austria for a doubtful future in a not very enticingly portrayed country.

A military band played us a few parting tunes and Lieutenant-Field Marshal Hartung and the officer corps of the Trieste garrison had also found their way to the landing stage to give us a final greeting.

The aforementioned general, not exactly a very warm devotee of our corps or of the whole Mexican enterprise, had not appeared at all at the departure of the first of our troopships, having instead undertaken a field exercise with the whole garrison.

There was general indignation over this. Both Austrian and Mexican officers openly expressed their opinion in a fairly unambiguous manner – and even the army newspaper was moved to report this offensive and inconsiderate behaviour, admittedly without comment, but nevertheless in a sufficiently intelligible way.

All these circumstances could have accounted for the fact that on the second and subsequent occasions His Excellency the Lieutenant-

Field Marshal appeared regularly at every departure of our individual troopships and favoured those who were leaving with a few gracious words.

Specially on my account, my good sister Marie had appeared with her husband, and my cousin Max with Mathilde and a few more of the latter's relations.

In addition, however, causing me no little embarrassment, there also appeared the larger feminine part of the German theatrical company 'Fürst', which happened to be in Trieste at the time, to greet me before our departure.

I entertained the latter as far apart from my assembled relations as possible and almost ran my feet raw to reach now one, now the other party and to calm their agitated spirits.

But finally nothing remained for me but to put an end to the matter – I said goodbye to everyone and went on board, continuing to wave from there in both directions with my handkerchief until, to the strains of the Austrian national anthem and continued applause and shouts of hooray, we gradually began to distance ourselves further and further until finally we lost sight of the beloved coastline, perhaps for ever.

Ernst had written to his mother on the morning of his departure.

Trieste, 1 December 1864, 5 a.m.
My precious, deeply beloved Mother,
When you receive these lines, I shall already be far from the homeland and my kinsmen and thereby has been fulfilled what has already for a long time in my private moments been a mature decision.

Indeed, its execution only cost me an effort because I foresaw the pain which I would thereby be causing you, my dear, good Mother.

The infinite spiritual fortitude with which you avoided everything which could have made going more difficult for me was admirable and I thank you for it with my whole heart.

Be assured that everywhere you will be my holiest and most constant remembrance and believe me that I will assuredly miss no opportunity of giving you detailed and frequent news of me.

I am disconsolate that it is not yet possible today for me to tell you in detail about the last few days, but you can hardly imagine how rushed I am day and night, so that I positively long to be on board at last in order to be able to collect myself and rest there.

I spent the whole of yesterday on board my ship attending to the loading of the baggage, the powder, the internal arrangements, etc. Then I had to go to Maria and Max for just a few minutes; then I went to the station to await the evening train from Vienna; then wrote home; later at two hours after midnight the troops for our ship arrived from Ljubljana – these too I had to meet and billet, and then I went back home immediately in order to write to you.

Enclosed you will receive my photograph, in everyone's opinion it is a decided success and it will, I hope, give you pleasure. In a few days Ludwig* will send you two more copies, which were not finished yesterday.

Now, hard though it is for me, I must still trouble you with one last request.

For the bill for my stay in the hotel here was so high that, believing as I did that I was staying at state expense, I was very unpleasantly surprised and really embarrassed when I was told that I could only draw on the billeting allowance of 35 gulden a day for this and I had to borrow another 15 gulden from Marie in order not to embark without a penny.

I beg you most earnestly to return this money to poor Marie on my behalf, for she really cannot do without a farthing, however much she would like to.

Forgive me, dear Mother, for not sparing you such requests even in my farewell letter, but Marie will tell you that it is not my fault and that only the niggardliness of our public purse has put me in this embarrassing position.

And now that I have told you this too I bid you again farewell, my precious, angelic Mother; forgive me all the sorrow and worry, which I have always caused you.

Let us hope that fate will not be persistently unfavourable to me and perhaps an opportunity may yet come of thanking you by deed for the great sacrifices you have made for me.

You will receive news from me from all the stations where we shall take on coal. I myself will expect a letter from you on arrival at Veracruz. Herzfeld† is at present in Trieste and will remain here for another month, so write to him, remind him of his purchase and enclose the letter to me.

A thousand kisses to little Max,‡ the other brothers and sisters, friends and acquaintances – may they remember me now and then, as I will always remember them. Goodbye again, dearest Mother, farewell,

Your Ernst

* Ludwig Fuchs, Marie's husband.
† Baron Stefan Herzfeld, a friend of the family, who was to go to Mexico later as adviser to Maximilian.
‡ Ernst's younger brother, aged thirteen.

Ernst recorded in his diary:

> The first hours of our voyage passed somewhat tediously.
>
> Each of us was still more or less under the impression of the departure from our country which had just taken place and, dejected and silent, we sought to arrange and settle ourselves in our cabins, which were not exactly spacious.
>
> What, then, may have been the feelings of the unfortunate men when they came to see the areas which were to be their accommodation for a period of forty-six days!
>
> Nevertheless the *Brasilian* was the best equipped of all six transport steamers, for unlike on the other ships the men were not accommodated in bunks resembling coffins, but in simple plank beds and hammocks.
>
> Our journey along the Italian coast was accompanied by the most beautiful weather.
>
> On the evening of 3 December we passed Cape Santa Maria di Leuca and during that night, while crossing the Gulf of Taranto to Cape Spartivento, we had so fresh a north-west breeze that all on board who were not hardened against seasickness had to pay their tribute to it.
>
> At the first dawn on the morning of 4 December everyone was on deck so as to be able to admire with their own eyes what could be the most beautiful part of our journey.
>
> To the left, in mist, lay the Sicilian coast with Etna only partly visible; to the right the rocky coasts of Calabria with the little town of Reggio, renowned from Garibaldi's landing in 1860.
>
> And immediately thereafter, as we came further into the narrows, the Mexican flag, with the same colours of white–red–green which we in Austria had always fought against and always hated* – and which we had now to learn to love! – was hoisted at our main mast.
>
> What indeed may the local fishermen have thought, when they saw our steamer – with their national colours on the mast and a thousand people on deck – all attired in almost the same fantastic manner as the partisans of their favourite compatriot† in the year 1860?
>
> But between then and now lies Aspromonte‡ and who knows how the same people think of their liberation hero today?
>
> Meanwhile the sun had come out fully and we were approaching the town of Messina and with it the northern exit from the narrows. The

---

* They were hated because they are also the Italian colours.

† Garibaldi.

‡ The battle at which, after only a few shots, Garibaldi was wounded in the foot and taken prisoner by the troops of Victor Emmanuel in 1862.

sight before us was truly magnificent. In the manner in which it was offered for us to see, Messina presents the most beautiful picture imaginable. Everything illuminated, everything turned to gold. Then the citadel, the mountainous background and some sixty to seventy larger sailing ships coursing in the narrows, three to four of them actually in Scylla and Charybdis and only moving forward with the help of their boats and of the most strenuous rowing – all of this together so unusually beautiful and picturesque that it is hard to extinguish it from one's memory.

Having traversed the Straits of Messina, we still saw Stromboli smoking in the distance and then travelled the whole day down the Sicilian coast. At the fall of darkness the Palermo lighthouse became visible, only to disappear soon afterwards from our eyes, truly sufficiently satiated that day with the beauties of nature. Everyone went to rest and next day the coast had long disappeared.

They reached Gibraltar on 9 December. Writing to his mother, Ernst describes his first view of the Rock:

On the 9th of this month at midday we ran into Gibraltar under a violent headwind. The view of the fortress, from afar as well as from very near, has been described so often and is so widely known that I will only touch on it briefly. To the traveller proceeding from east to west a huge rock appears in the middle of the sea and only connected with the Spanish mainland by a barely visible spit of land, falling on that side vertically and therefore unsurmountably and levelling out towards the sea to end in a lighthouse. Opposite is the African coast and the so-called Monkey Mountain. The town is built to the west of the rock and the impression of this mighty bastion of the English was, at least for me – and perhaps because of the bad weather – a grim one.

We had to wait until nearly five o'clock in the evening for permission from the governor, Lieutenant-General Lord Codrington, to set foot on land and then had to make great haste, for the gates of the fortress are closed at half past five and from that hour one can neither enter nor leave until the next morning.

The Austrians were well received in Gibraltar. The governor, on whom Ernst called with a deputation of his fellow-officers, was welcoming and afforded them all facilities to view the sights of the city, including the famous fortifications (which, Ernst says, were very interesting, but 'in my opinion do not today correspond to their reputation'). They also visited 'Crystal House or the so-called *Palacio de Cristal*' which, Ernst found 'of the greatest interest for me and most of my comrades'.

Ernst commented to his mother:

> The town is overflowing with troops: six regiments of the line, one brigade of artillery and riflemen from the garrison and the handsome boys in their bright red uniforms and tunics made a very favourable impression on me. But with them a great deal is still very much a continuation of old times. The officers are all rich people; every regiment has its club and every stick of furniture in it belongs to the officer corps. All the plates and dishes are of heavy silver, the servants dressed in smart liveries. In a word, an establishment without equal in all European officer corps. Almost every one of the gentlemen serving with the infantry here keeps two or three horses of his own.

They were lavishly entertained by the English officers, some of whom Ernst found very pleasant.

> English officers of the 15th Regiment invited us to breakfast and to dinner the same evening. Unfortunately Captain Kropatsek of our artillery did not behave on this occasion in the manner which would have been desirable with such distinguished officers as these English are. His subsequent resignation, moreover, is related to this affair.

Ernst does not disclose the nature of the captain's misdemeanour. Despite this *contretemps*, however, the evening

> went off very pleasantly. The dinner and the wines were delicious, the atmosphere was relaxed and even though we had no language to converse in and could only make ourselves intelligible to each other in a most miserable way the conversation was very animated, particularly towards the end of the dinner.

Ernst was critical of the inns and hotels and of the high cost of almost everything in Gibraltar. But he took a favourable view of the Spanish ladies:

> I cannot let this opportunity pass without acknowledging that the appearance of the Spanish women, whom I saw in Gibraltar for the first time in large numbers, made the most favourable impression on me and that in this respect I was filled with the pleasantest hopes and

expectations for Mexico, always presupposing, that is, that the Spanish race has been preserved there in the same way to its advantage.

Writing to his mother, Ernst mentions that in Gibraltar he had had news of the Austrian officers in the troop ship which had preceded theirs.

They were similarly all well and in good heart. From this you can judge the groundlessness of the childish gossip, which was spread around about the manner of our transportation. Our accommodation is certainly not comfortable, but it is also not really such as to kill one and if an epidemic should break out, which may God forbid, it would not be less dangerous on a ship that was not so fully laden.

While the Austrians were still in Gibraltar a violent westerly wind got up and several ships in the harbour were torn from their moorings. As a result the Austrians were no longer to go on land – a fact which Ernst found not altogether unwelcome from a financial point of view, given the high cost of everything in Gibraltar and the exorbitant prices charged for their transport to and from the shore. In these unfavourable conditions the *Brasilian* sailed on 14 December and very heavy seas were encountered for about ten days. Ernst wrote to his mother:

Forgive me if, when you open this letter, my handwriting appears less regular than usual, but it is almost a miracle to write as I am doing . . . I had to break off the letter begun five days ago, for I was so giddy from the violent movements of the ship that I was incapable of continuing. Until today there was no question of writing. Continually a violent headwind and high seas. Now and then tragi-comic positions, nothing stays firm that is not fastened. At table one has to carry the plates in one's hand in order to spill as little soup as possible; meanwhile plates, bottles, glasses, large serving dishes etc. slide down irresistibly and a chaos of meat, broken crockery and wine covers the floor at almost every midday meal. It is just the same in the cabins. One has to be glad to keep oneself in bed and as a result of the continual frenetic clinging our periods of rest are pretty tiring.

Furthermore during the night all kinds of things fall literally on to one's head. The trade wind which has been expected for eight days has so far remained firmly absent and so has completely nullified the calculations of our maritime comrades in distress . . .

You can imagine that we had many cases of seasickness, for

immediately outside Gibraltar harbour, which is anyhow bad, a wild dance began. At Tarifa lighthouse, for good measure, a Spanish coastal battery fired briskly at us because it believed that we were not flying a flag; in fact we had one overhead and so paid no heed to the blank warning salvoes and only when the shot fell quite near us in the water did we hoist an enormous flag, visible to any blind man . . .

Yesterday, the day before Christmas, we passed the Tropic of Cancer and are in the tropics. It is very hot, the nights are pleasant. Since yesterday the constellation of the Southern Cross is visible in the sky. Yesterday we also enjoyed the magnificient spectacle of a falling meteor such as I have never seen. A sudden illumination of the horizon, as with strong lightning, preceded the occurrence and thereupon a shining luminous star, appearing perhaps to be twelve times the size of the Evening Star, fell down in a long arc.

Yesterday [25 December] we saw from far off a whale or rather the column of water which it blew out. This is a rare occurrence in these regions and today a flying fish flew through an opening in the turret, where it was killed and prepared for preservation by one of the officers . . .

In general our people have held out fairly well against seasickness, although we had to pass a hard test. At times the situation was really very funny and this was particularly the case at table and sometimes at night. For two days we have had practically no wind! . . .

Today, 26 December, we bathed in large tubs on the front deck and allowed ourselves to be thoroughly showered by the pump. The day before yesterday, in the evening, the previously announced little Christmas Eve entertainment for the men took place. Instead of a Christmas tree, a sort of framework in the form of a chandelier was put together out of cords, which were wrapped in coloured rags and hung with various trifles such as cigars, pieces of silver and vouchers for wine, brandy and claret. The whole contraption was then hoisted up the gaff-sail mast and the men had to climb up on a rope. The one who happily reached the top could take a piece, but the one who didn't get there was, of course, laughed at. Later the men manufactured quite nice Christmas trees for themselves out of brooms, decorated with all sorts of things, and they made very successful transparencies with witty sayings. In the evening we sent up a few rockets, let off fireworks, drank punch and dispelled boredom as decorously as possible. Yesterday on Christmas Day we had a big dinner at which champagne flowed copiously and innumerable toasts were drunk. Of course this cost us nothing, for the French company which is carrying us provides all these luxury drinks as an extra out of courtesy . . .

Yesterday morning [27 December] a man of my company died of

typhus. It was the first case of this kind on board; the state of health of the rest of the men is highly satisfactory. A few hours later the poor devil was sown up in a hammock and, with a bag of sand and iron at his feet, committed to the ocean. The major recited a short prayer over the corpse, which was covered with the Mexican flag, made the sign of the cross and it was over. A short address to the men, ending with three cheers for the emperor, brought the sad ceremony to a close . . .

On all other days on which the weather did not foil us we passed the time by playing *écarté*, eating, drinking, sleeping and quarrelling. This last occupation was, I would affirm almost with certainty, one of the most frequent, for there were many heterogeneous elements on board and living so close together caused many a bad quality of some individuals, which until then had slumbered unsuspected, to awaken and assert itself to the detriment of us all . . .

The last four days have offered nothing of interest. Sky and water and the same again, this monotony being broken only occasionally by flying fish rising in swarms and keeping above water for 100 to 150 paces and, the day before yesterday, by the renewed appearance of a whale, which repeatedly sent up its column of water . . .

Tomorrow is the last day of this year, an important one for me, and with this day a large part of our journey will also end. For on Sunday, 1 January 1865, we arrive in Martinique, where we will stop for about four days before going on to Santiago de Cuba, where we will only stop one day and then travel to Veracruz, for which we will require about another eight days from there.

How often I have thought of you, my precious Mother, as well as of the other dear ones, you can imagine. I was so convinced that you too have all remembered me now and then that this thought came to compensate me for the separation.

You have my most affectionate and warmest wishes for the New Year, belated, it is true, but they were in my heart and had sprung from my pen at the right time, and only the great distance has meant that they are not with you on time. Warmest kisses to dear Franz . . . I would also like you to ask Mathilde whether there is still no prospect of my winning a ring.* She will know well enough what is meant . . .

We have just measured the temperature. Today (31 December) at midday the thermometer showed 26 degrees Réaumur in the shade and 40 degrees in the sun. You can imagine that this is not exactly very agreeable, for even the extended awning does not give us much shade. We are therefore all looking forward to our arrival in Martinique. The

---

* Apparently Ernst had made a bet that Mathilde was pregnant and was to win a ring if proved correct.

captain promises us that, if the weather remains clear, we shall have sight of the island today towards evening. My little Monkey,* who is much liked here on board, also seems to be greatly looking forward to *terra firma*. I hope that I shall be able to get the poor hound over safely, for he has stood up well so far. The noise and confusion on the first day of landing did not permit this.

Ernst wrote to his mother on 10 January 1865:

Forty-two days have passed since I left Trieste and in a few days we shall have arrived at our preliminary destination, shall at last be able to exchange the ship for firm land and shall, we hope, learn something definite about our next assignment, our pay – in a word, about the many things as yet unknown to us. I shall take up my travel notes where I ended in my last letter.

On the 1 January, New Year's Day, at eleven o'clock in the morning we ran into Martinique and this time moored directly on the quay and could therefore, unlike at Gibraltar, go ashore without expense. The island, which belongs to the French, is charming and from the moment of its beholding offers a European so much that is strange that one can hardly see and look enough. A more abundant vegetation you cannot easily imagine. Coconut palms, aloes, cacti and goodness knows what other plants and strange trees, unknown to me, cover the whole islands down to the sea. At the shore whole troops of negroes and mulattos awaited our arrival in order to sell us their coconuts, pineapples, bananas and other fruits at derisory prices. An enormous pineapple costs four kreuzer, a similar coconut the same. One gets a hundred oranges for one franc and even so the natives consider that we are cheated. French soldiers, the naval infantry, hailed our infantry from the top of the fort with vigorous hurrahs, which we returned in a similar manner. A few minutes sufficed for us to make ourselves as spruce as could be so that we could set foot again on land, which we had been denied for eighteen days, in a worthy manner and not fail to make the most favourable impression on the black population. Before leaving the ship we amused ourselves on deck with twelve negro boys, who swam round our ship like fishes and asked us to throw coins into the water. With remarkable virtuosity they dived down every time and always succeeded in bringing up the coin, which they stored in their mouths, until finally their mouths were full of the copper money which the delighted audience had thrown down to them.

Apart from the French military, their families and a few industrial

---

* Ernst's pet dog.

and Creole families resident there, Martinique is inhabited almost entirely by mulattos and negroes. To these should be added a few thousand Chinese, East Indians, coolies etc. There are only two larger places on the island, namely St Pierre, the capital, with 30,000 inhabitants, and the military colony, Fort de France, where we were, with some 15,000 inhabitants. After we had wandered around for some hours in the latter place and, among other things, presented ourselves to the governor, we decided to make use of the beautiful day and the time at our disposal and visit the capital, St Pierre. We took the steamer, which went there and back once a day, and after two hours' journey found ourselves in the very nice little town. The impression on the traveller is much the same as in Fort de France: strange faces, pretty Creole women, etc. But in addition we had a following of at least two hundred black street urchins who, just as at home, cheekily crowded round us, screamed, whistled and even let off crackers in our faces. As it was already evening when we arrived we could not use the time as we would have wished, but could only endeavour to use the last of the daylight to see what was most notable in the whole town, the Jardin des Plantes. The sight of this alone makes the whole journey worth while. I cannot describe to you the magnificient impression which is evoked in the European by this assemblage of all the tropical plants of the earth. It is, as I say, unique. Furthermore we had the not exactly agreeable, but nevertheless exciting awareness that to complete its tropical character the whole Jardin des Plants swarms with all sorts of poisonous snakes, as indeed this form of life is very prevalent in Martinique generally and therefore occasioned very careful behaviour on our part. On returning from our exploration of the town we dined very well and astonishingly cheaply at the Hôtel des Bains, slept excellently and returned to Fort de France the following morning. Just this little trip by water along the coast of the island provides one with the infectious pleasure of being able to admire the extraordinary vegetation. And only when one has seen with one's own eyes all that thrives here is one no longer surprised at the idleness and indolence of the working class. A few banana and coconut palms easily feed a whole family, and when this rabble has earned enough in two days of the week to be able to buy itself a few bright rags and satisfy its greatest needs, not even God Almighty could persuade it to work the remaining five days, even for the highest pay.

All our men were allowed to land at Martinique and billeted in the Desaix barracks. The poor devils were delighted to be able to step on to firm land again and, to my surprise, they behaved unexpectedly well. Nothing outrageous occurred and when we re-embarked not one of our 1,200 men was missing, whereas of the Belgian contingent of

360, five men remained behind drunk and had finally to be picked up by our people and brought on in our ship. This Belgian battalion happened to arrive in Martinique while we were there, but left a day before us. Their people are far worse disciplined than ours* and there was general amazement among the French in Martinique that we were able in so short a time to form a well-disciplined unit out of such mixed elements. As the officers also had to be on duty in turn with our men at the Fort it fell to me to spend twenty-four hours there and I was very interested on this occasion to hear from the mouth of the fort commander, a French captain, details about Mexico, which had to be right since he had been in all the fighting there for two and a half years and had only been posted to Martinique a few months previously.

We remained on the island until eleven o'clock on the morning of the 5th. We idled away the time at our disposal in the usual way, looked at everything that was noteworthy and were again heartily glad when we sailed again at the aforementioned time to hasten directly towards our future destination, for because of the arrival of a tender of the Compagnie Générale de Transports Atlantiques no stop was to be made at Santiago.

Our crossing of the Caribbean Sea passed without hindrance. On the morning of the 9th we sighted the island of Jamaica and passed all day along the north coast of the island, without, however, being able to see the island of Cuba situated further to the right. On the 10th a strong north wind got up, which became so powerful on the 11th that we were afraid that it would greatly delay us in our passage through the Yucatán Channel. Everything danced around again as merrily as before Gibraltar, and even I rendered the sea its tribute for the first time, though only momentarily and without significantly interrupting my continued well-being. Yesterday, my saint's day, passed in the same manner and only today came complete calm and the most beautiful weather. We passed through the above mentioned strait yesterday at two o'clock in the afternoon and have been since then in the Gulf of Mexico, confidently hoping to arrive in Veracruz on Sunday the 15th – the long journey of 7,300 sea miles will then be almost over. I hope you will have received my second letter, whose arrival I only announced to you for the end of February, already in the first days of that month and I shall have this letter ready to be conveyed immediately to the mail-boat in Veracruz, as it may possibly not have left there yet. If I am no longer able to do this, however, and should the letter therefore have to wait until the next steamer, you will receive the evidence of our

---

* There was general criticism among the Austrians of the poor quality of the Belgian troops who, though of good physique, were considered too young and poorly trained. Many were to be killed in an engagement at Tacambaro.

arrival and news of all the novelties which await us there with this letter, as I will then open it again and continue it.

And so, dearest Mother, I now provisonally end this letter, embracing you a thousand times and as always asking you to greet most warmly on my behalf and kiss all dear relations and friends. Again goodbye and ten thousand kisses from your grateful and sincere son

Ernst

Ernst wrote again from Veracruz on 16 January.

Although when I closed my last letter to you a few days ago I hardly expected to be again beginning a few lines to you today, chance has so ordained that I can do so. We arrived here yesterday at two o'clock in the afternoon. General Thun,* who was awaiting us here, ordered the immediate disembarkation of the men, which accordingly took place at once. I, who in my previous life in the army have regularly had the minor misfortune during garrison changes in strange places of always being the first to be on duty, received the order to remain on board with thirty men and to maintain a twenty-four-hour watch there, which had to continue until the complete disembarkation of the contingent. Willy-nilly I took up my disagreeable duty and at eleven o'clock this morning had worked off twenty-three hours of it when suddenly the *nortes* (north wind), which is so greatly feared here, got up and began to blow so strongly that all communication with the shore became impossible. In consequence I have as yet still not been relieved, have not up to now set foot on land and am faced with an excellent propect of kicking my heels here on board, perhaps for eight days, like a prisoner, in utter solitude. Hugo Thoren,† who, as you know, had already been in Veracruz for a month, also came to meet us immediately on the ship and it is thanks to him and a few other officers who were already here before we came that I have at least learnt the main news in all haste – for if these people had not told us everything straight away, red-hot, my present annoyance and my impatience at finding myself imprisoned here would no doubt be even greater. The main question concerning pay has resolved itself quite favourably. As a second-lieutenant I receive a fixed monthly salary with billeting allowance of 75 pesos or 150 gulden in silver. Added to this are another 27 gulden in respect of marching supplement and foraging allowance,

* General Count Franz Thun-Hohenstein, commander of the Austrian Volunteer Corps (not to be confused with his cousin, Count Guido Thun, Austrian Minister in Mexico).
† An Austrian Cavalry captain, who had travelled out with Major Kodolitsch some weeks before.

so that altogether I receive about 180 gulden a month, a sum with which one can live very comfortably in Austria, but which here is not in the slightest degree over-generous, considering the enormously inflated price levels prevailing. Fortunately our occupation is not at all, as in Austria, an indolent garrison life, on the contrary we shall soon be so busy tbat all expensive items such as restaurants, theatres etc. will automatically cease. In Veracruz the ordinary cost of admission to a theatre is 5 gulden and for a simple midday meal our officers pay, as I heard this morning, 4 gulden in silver. Similarly a passably smokable cigar costs around 30 kreuzer. Furthermore the smallest coin in current use here, the real, is equal to 27½ Austrian kreuzer in silver and the most ordinary manual workers certainly earn 10 to 15 gulden a day. For instance, one pays 4 gulden for a boat from the ship to the shore – in Austria 20 kreuzer suffice to travel the same distance. But all these things have nevertheless not surprised me in the slightest, since one was of course sufficiently prepared for this, indeed imagined far worse after the exaggerated stories of others.

In a few days my battalion will march from here to Orizaba, where it will remain for two to three months to organize itself. The 1st battalion will do the same in Jalapa and the 3rd in Puebla. For the time immediately, ahead, if you think of me, seek me in your mind in Orizaba, a little town at the foot of the 1,700 metre high mountain giant Citlaltepetl. The climate there is healthy, the country charming, the vegetation exceptional.

After the various units of our corps have organized themselves, everyone will set out on the march to Yucatán, the southernmost province of the empire, where according to all reports a strong hand is needed to disperse the guerrillas and for the complete subjection of the country. Altogether the political state of the country does not seem to be nearly as promising as is affirmed by the press in Europe, and the greatest pessimists in this are the French themselves, who maintain that there is not much more to be achieved with this decimated and corrupted population. As against this, we and all the others want to hope for the best, for it would be a terrible moral defeat for the emperor to have to withdraw again from here and, if it comes to this, we shall certainly not be wanting to support him.

Veracruz, which up to now I have only seen through a telescope, presents itself to the beholder exactly as it is to be seen in all drawings. The houses with the flat roofs, the many Gothic churches, cupolas and minaret-like towers, also the For San Juan d'Ulloa, which I pictured to myself as being much more impressive, as it has now almost become a ruin. The familiar vultures, which are as native to Veracruz as to other Mexican towns, fly around in hundreds and they seem so much at home that one can almost regard them as the pigeons of Saint Mark's. Of my relief there is today as yet nothing to be seen, for although the wind had already dropped considerably I am nevertheless still unable, despite the most assiduous searches with my telescope, to discover anyone ashore who might come to release me. So there is nothing left for me but to resign myself in patience for the time being. To receive a message from you here, dearest mother, would certainly make me very happy; however, I rather doubt that I shall, for the letters despatched to me by Herzfeld in the service mail will very probably find their way to the capital first and only reach me afterwards, which will certainly cause a delay of ten to twelve days. Altogether I shall be much worse off as regards news from you than you from me. For I am always able to write to you by the regular mail, whereas your letters may perhaps have to look for me for months and over the whole of Mexico. I shall give this letter to the captain of the ship with which we came here, so that he may post it in Liverpool. In this way you will soon have news of me.

Unfortunately I must now close this letter, as I have just been informed that my long awaited relief is arriving. I cannot let the boat wait and must pass the letter sealed to the captain, so will end now.

Many warm kisses and embraces to all. Write to me soon and at the old address, directed to Orizaba.

Goodbye precious, dear Mother, remember often your faithful son,

                                                            Ernst

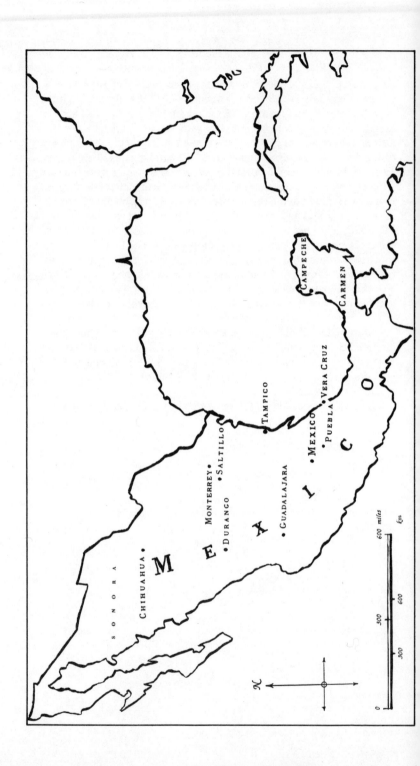

Land of Conflict

The country which Ernst now experienced for the first time was very different from his native Austria. A vast territory extending over thousands of square miles from its long border with the United States to the tropical jungles of Central America, it had seen the flowering of ancient cultures of remarkable sophistication created by its original Indian inhabitants. Conquered by the Spaniards in 1519, Mexico was ruled for three hundred years as a Spanish dependency known as 'New Spain'. During this time the country as a whole was stable and prosperous and the society created by the Spanish conquerors attained new heights of intellectual and cultural distinction. In due course, however, dissatisfaction with political and social conditions fostered by the new ideas inspired by the French Revolution gradually gained currency and a desire for independence began to manifest itself.

Pressure for change came mainly from the Creoles, the white descendants of original Spanish immigrants, who constituted about 15 per cent of a total population of some eight million, as against 1 per cent Spaniards (gachupines), 30 per cent of mixed race (mestizos) and about 54 per cent Indians of various tribes. Despite their small number, the gachupines still dominated Mexican society at the beginning of the nineteenth century, exercising virtually unrestricted political power and occupying most of the top positions. This was bitterly resented by the Creoles, who considered themselves no less qualified to govern than the Spaniards and, encouraged by the success of the American colonists in winning independence from Britain, wished to see Mexico similarly ruled by its own people, rather than by distant bureaucrats in Europe. They objected to the privileges enjoyed by European Spaniards in their own country. And, reacting to the liberal ideas reaching the territory in an increasing flow from across the Atlantic, they were beginning to seek the removal of at least the most extreme political and social inequalities existing in Mexico.

Stirrings of a desire for independence were encouraged by the political decline in Spain after the death of Charles III in 1788 and further strengthened by France's occupation of the country during the Napoleonic Wars. What had previously appeared as the near-divine source of all authority and the mainspring of colonial rule was now seen to have feet of clay. Nevertheless, the first two attempts to throw off Spanish rule – that of Miguel Hidalgo y Costilla, an obscure Creole parish priest, in 1811 and the sub-sequent rising led by another parish priest, the mestizo José María Morelos, in 1812 – ended in failure. But it was significant that Hidalgo's appeal was to the downtrodden masses of Indians and mestizos who flocked to his banner in tens of thousand – the first time these communities had figured as a major political force. Hidalgo's concern for the common people brought a new element into Mexican politics and the popular dimensions of his movement dealt the colonial system a blow from which it was never to recover. Also significant and a foretaste of things to come was the political programme announced by Morelos in 1813, which called for the establishment of a republic, universal suffrage without distinction of race, the abolition of privilege and the expropriation of large estates, including those of the church.

A deplorable feature of the fighting between rebels and vice-regal troops was the increasing cruelty on both sides. Atrocities and pillage became a common occurrence and the excesses of the belligerents set a precedent which was unfortunately to be mir-rored in the brutality of much of the turmoil of the next hundred years.

Independence was finally achieved in 1821, when the Creole establishment commissioned a young officer of conservative sym-pathies, Agustín de Iturbide, to command their troops against the viceregal government. The latter having capitulated, Iturbide seized the leadership of the new regime, proclaimed Mexico an independent kingdom and, failing to find a suitable monarch for the Mexican throne, had himself recognized as Emperor Agustín

I. He was, however, unable to control a highly unstable situation and was soon overthrown by a group of former guerrilla leaders together with a certain Antonio López de Santa Anna, who was to exert a baneful influence on Mexican politics for the next thirty years. The new junta declared a republic. Iturbide was banished and, on his attempting to return to the country a few months later, was unceremoniously shot.

The decades following Iturbide's successful insurrection saw a marked deterioration in political stability, public order and general well-being. The Creoles as a class were now in control, but proved incapable of giving the country the leadership and reforms which it needed to meet the requirements of its new situation. The old social structure was kept largely in place, but without the support of a government with the power or the will to maintain it. The mass of the population had been subjected to centuries of despotic, if paternalistic, rule, and the nation had no experience of the new democratic forms which various governments sought to introduce. Despite the good intentions of some individuals, the nation fell prey to the ambitions of unprincipled adventurers, and inefficiency, corruption and violence dominated public life. Power was exercised by a succession of military leaders with a sufficient following and the money to pay their armies. The country was heavily in debt, revenue collection was inefficient and commercial activity was seriously affected by the disorders prevalent in many regions.

Political debate naturally centred on how the new Mexico should be governed. It involved, in the main, the competing claims of those advocating Conservatism on the one hand and Liberal policies on the other. The Conservatives favoured the interests of the big landowners, the maintenance of traditional privileges and property rights, support for Roman Catholicism in the enjoyment of its unique status and a centralized, monarchical system of government. The Liberals advocated democratic, republican and federal institutions and were divided between the *moderados*, who were prepared not to force the pace of social change, and the *puros*, who included in their ranks former associates of Hidalgo and Morelos and stood for more radical policies. The efforts of sincere and qualified reformers, however, tended to be frustrated and nullified by the arbitrary intrusion in the nation's affairs of self-seeking military leaders, of whom Santa

Anna was one of the most unprincipled and persistent. Changes of government were generally brought about by unconstitutional means, the favoured technique being the *pronunciamiento*, a statement of policy by the aspiring general. A state of near-anarchy prevailed and governments succeeded one another with bewildering rapidity (thirty changes in as many years). The most important event of the first three decades of independence was the disastrous war with the United States, ending with the occupation of the capital by American troops in 1847 and involving the surrender of more than half of Mexico's territory. But more significant in many ways was the outrage felt by all Mexicans at the violation of their territory. The experience bit deep into the Mexican soul and horror of foreign aggression became a component of the nation's psychology which was to make itself felt in the years to come.

The position and power of the church had remained virtually unimpaired. It possessed vast wealth and enjoyed privileges which to a large extent rendered it immune from outside interference. Moreover, it still commanded the respect and devotion of the mass of the population, who looked to the clergy to protect them from exploitation by their overlords. Nevertheless, conditions in the church had declined and its members no longer possessed the integrity, dedication and self-sacrifice which had animated some of their predecessors. Criticism of the church and calls for a reduction of its wealth and privileges began to be voiced in radical circles, but such was the inherited strength of its position that some time had to pass before it could be challenged.

Soon after the mid-century, however, an important political change took place. A Conservative government, headed once again by the ubiquitous Santa Anna, was replaced by a Liberal administration bent on political and social reform. The new ministry, headed initially by Juan Alvárez and subsequently by Ignacio Comonfort, included as minister of justice Benito Juárez. A Zapotec Indian, Juárez had risen to the post of governor of Oaxaca, which he had held for five years. The new government had the support of a large number of young Liberals who, profoundly dissatisfied with the existing state of affairs, wished to see radical changes, including a reduction of the power and privileges of the church. Many came from among the mestizos,

who were beginning to challenge the near-monopoly of office
hitherto reserved to themselves by the Creoles. Immediately on
taking office the government embarked on a series of drastic
reforms, including the abolition of the privileges of the clergy and
army and the sale of church property. The new legislation,
however, encountered widespread opposition, both among the
many devout Catholics in all communities and among the Indians,
whose communal lands were to be expropriated. The ensuing
turmoil escalated into a bitter civil war, involving much bloodshed
and lasting for three years. The Conservatives had the better of
the fighting in the early stages, thanks to the leadership of three
able generals – Miguel Miramón (who succeeded to the presidency
of the Conservative government in 1859), Leonardo Márquez and
Tomás Mejía, the first two Creoles and the third an Indian. But
the Liberals, whose political leaders were of demonstrably higher
quality than those of their opponents, eventually prevailed and in
1861 the Liberal government, now headed by Juárez, returned to
Mexico City. Juárez was recognized both by Britain and the
United States, but was immediately faced with severe financial
difficulties. He had already, while the war was still in progress,
decreed the confiscation of all remaining church property and the
dissolution of the monasteries – a measure which, by stopping the
flow of church funds to the Conservatives, may well have helped
him to final victory. But now the proceeds of the sale of ecclesiastical property were exhausted, the government was in desperate
need of funds to keep the machinery of the state in motion and to
service the massive foreign debts incurred by previous administrations. Juárez decided that he had no option but to declare a
two-year moratorium on payments to his creditors. This provoked
a sharp reaction from the three governments having substantial
claims against Mexico – Great Britain, Spain and France. On 31
October 1861, representatives of the three governments met in
London and signed a convention agreeing to the despatch of a
joint expedition to Mexico with strictly limited aims. It was in
these circumstances that troops of the three countries landed at
Veracruz in December 1861 and January 1862, and opened yet
another chapter in Mexico's turbulent history.

Veracruz was Mexico's principal port and it was here too that
Ernst now landed. The place was important not only as commanding the main route to the capital, but also because it was there

that substantial customs dues, which provided most of Mexico's national revenue, were collected. On arrival the French had taken control of this important source of income, thereby depriving Maximilian's government of its use. Until then the whole area had been controlled by Juárez and the local population was generally in sympathy with the Liberals. It was an area where the deadly yellow fever, the so-called *vómito negro*, was widely prevalent.

Ernst wrote to his mother from Orizaba on 28 January 1865:

Dear, beloved mother,
I have been in my temporary garrison station for two days and now, having more or less overcome the exertions of several strenous marches and of a garrison inspection which as usual was inflicted on me right at the beginning, and having also settled myself tolerably in a room or should I say depot without windows, I will set about giving you a full account of my further experiences since Veracruz. Of this latter place I can tell you little that is of particular interest, but since I know that you wish to learn everything I shall begin by describing my accommodation there at the Hôtel de Paris.

Imagine a crumbling, dirty tavern with one upper floor, the rooms without windows, light only obtainable through a door. Everything in a state of utmost squalor, and you have a picture of this fortunately most inferior hotel of Veracruz. Unfortunately all the other hostelries were already filled to overflowing and I, who because of the storm had been delayed several days, as you will know from my last letter, got what was left. Also it is not the custom here to give each guest a room and so it came about that I was parked in a chamber with nine beds which, apart from myself and two other unfortunate officers of the corps, were occupied by a travelling company of Italian harpists. The beds themselves are simple campbed frames and instead of a mattress ordinary canvas is laid over the stretchers. On this instrument of torture we slept.

In Veracruz I found the Austrian frigate *Novara*, in which one of my best friends, Naval Lieutenant Kern, was sailing. You can imagine how much this meeting, 7,300 miles from home, gladdened me.

I also listened to my favourite opera, *Un Ballo in Maschera*, performed by a very good Italian company on the day of our departure.

Unfortunately every pleasure in this country is made more difficult for one by the considerable expenditure that it causes. Thus merely to enter the theatre costs 2½ pesos or 5.50 florins.* Nevertheless there is

* 1 florin = 1 gulden = 0.45 pesos.

much exaggeration when this point is discussed in Europe. When all is said and done, one manages well on one's pay here in spite of the high cost of living, which is unfortunately impossible at home.

The theatre in Veracruz is quite pretty; the boxes are not separated from one another, but adjoining, as in Renz's circus. A multitude of pretty ladies fills all the rooms. But unfortunately I made the observation, also confirmed to me from many quarters, that the noted courtesy of the Mexican ladies was not so pronounced and a Frenchman, who was certainly very experienced in this matter, said 'elles sont excessivement bêtes et extrèmement froides'. Let us hope that it is not the same everywhere. It is true that one finds no welcome here and one of the main reasons could be our being foreigners. The French here are hated like the devil and we too are not regarded with much friendliness. Altogether one has no idea of the ignorance of the middle class. I will not speak of the Indians, the *gente sin zazoa**. But I even heard more respectable people ask, for instance, whether Emperor Maximilian was also emperor of Austria or whether he was the son of the Austrian emperor. In a word, they know nothing and also do not care about anything; altogether they seem to regard the whole government as only a short, unsustainable interregnum. Even if this attitude is incorrect, the emperor still has a very difficult task and only his exceptional energy and iron will can succeed in bringing order to this chaos. The insurgency is far from being suppressed. The very strong position of Oaxaca to the south west of Orizaba is even now being besieged by the French. One wants to catch the whole pack alive, for among the defenders are more than a thousand French deserters, who are the most dangerous guerrillas in this country.

Us they may still leave to take breath here for a few more weeks, but then we will certainly go further into the country, for in the north, in Sonora, and in the south, in Yucatán, there is still an immense amount to be done and 200,000 men would not be too many to pacify the country quickly and without much bloodshed.

On the morning of the 22nd my battalion went (from Veracruz) with the train to Camerón, which we reached towards midday. A European can hardly have an idea of what a train in these parts is like. The crossposts are short and long, lying higher and lower, and instead of bridges there are only scaffoldings of beams leading over the deepest ravines and *barrancas*.† The whole contraption sways and tosses around, as on a bad country road – downhill to make one's ears hum, uphill with immense slowness. At the same time the engine whistles and jolts pitifully. In front it has a sort of plough to hurl away all the stones,

---

* 'People without reason'.
† Gullies

logs etc. which are deliberately laid on the track. Very often this plough is also applied to an ox grazing or walking peacefully on the railway. There is not a line-keeper's hut to be seen and on arriving at the station one frequently has to whistle several times for a man to come to change the points.

Camerón is a small Indian village with huts made of reeds, or occasionally of wood, and is of importance solely as the starting point of the railway, which runs inland for some twelve German miles. At the place where we left the carriages there was a simple wooden cross with approximately this inscription: '3 Compagnie du Régiment Étranger tuée le 24 avril, 1863, dans le combat de Camerón'. We were just at the spot where, two years before, the above-named company of about sixty men was attacked by 800 Mexicans and, after being called upon four times to surrender and having always refused, met a hero's death with its three officers. When I was at the cross, I remembered clearly having read of this incident.

In Camerón we camped in the open. At seven in the evening it began to rain and it rained until the afternoon of the following day, when we arrived at Paso Del Macho completely soaked and fortunately found a bed in a *posada*.* Next day we marched to Potrero, not really a place, but only a coffee and sugar plantation. On the 25th we set out for Córdoba. This place, a small town of 3,000–5,000 inhabitants, is of no further interest and only the country from Potrero as far as Pahín is deserving of comment. Far and wide tropical jungle and, here and there along the route, plantations of coffee, sugar and maize. That is the part of Mexico where one most frequently encounters the tapir, the creature half-way between a pig and an elephant. Big game, parrots, monkeys, eagles, vultures, pumas and goodness knows what other animals are said to exist here in large numbers and so in every house, for instance, one finds four to six parrots, which run about like chickens in the courtyard and in the passages. It is hard to imagine how bad the roads are and, although the government has for years spent much money on it, the highway is destroyed again ever year by the enormous waggons, loading up to five tons and harnessing twenty or more mules, which ply between Veracruz and Mexico,† and also by the effects of the monsoon. Whole blocks of rock, which are washed down, often cover the road in all directions for a quarter of a mile and it is amazing how much effort is needed here to move goods and luggage forward.

At one place on the way we found seventy-four large and smaller bronze bells and also four or five enormous metal cannon lying on the

* Inn.
† Mexico City, the capital.

ground. We learnt that three or four governments had already sold the bells to different people, from whom the succeeding government took them back, denying its predecessor's right to sell the bells. They come from confiscated church properties and at present provisionally belong to a Prussian subject. In every place there are several dissolved monasteries and these are at present the barracks of our men. Here in Orizaba the troops are lodged in as many as six or eight different churches and you can imagine how disapprovingly many a cleric or bigoted idiot regards us for desecrating by our presence the venerable monasteries of Carmen, San Juan, De Dios and whatever they are all called.

Orizaba, a town of about 24,000 inhabitants, lies in a pronounced rocky depression and the country round it is extremely beautiful and picturesque. A particularly splendid sight is the Pik of Orizaba, only the highest part of which is visible, completely covered in snow. It is also thanks to this Pik that we experience damnable cold at night and towards dawn, so that one is very happy if one is well provided with proper winter clothing.

On our arrival every officer received a billet slip together with the advice that the person providing the billet would probably pay for the officer in an inn rather than provide him with lodging, as they do not like to see foreigners in their houses. So it happened to me also and after a long search a room according with local standards, in most primitive condition, was discovered for me. At home any day labourer would object to occupying it, but here my billeting sponsor has to pay the innkeeper 1 peso or 2.20 gulden daily for it. In spite of all this I have arranged it in a tolerable manner and am very well and satisfied.

We have arranged a system under which we breakfast in the morning, have a substantial lunch at eleven o'clock and have dinner at six, for which we pay about 20 pesos or 45 gulden. A manservant looks after the laundry, which is very expensive here. The other things, such as boots and clothes, are left to be dealt with in the company and as one is already home at eight o'clock, one has enough money left over to be able to provide sufficiently for one's other requirements.

I am sorry that at present there is no visible prospect of getting to Mexico. I would very much like to deliver my letters of introduction in person, since otherwise they completely lose their value. The letters to the Kuhacsevichs* I have entrusted to a messenger of the emperor for him to deal with. He travelled here from Trieste with us and will

---

* Officials at Court: Jakob von Kuhacsevich was treasurer in the imperial household and his wife was Lady of the bedchamber.

already have delivered them. Those to the Bombelles* and Schaffers,† however, I intend to send to Mexico by a more suitable opportunity or, if this is lacking, on my account with an accompanying letter.

For three days I cannot get round to ending this letter. Troops come and go and all day long one is kept on the hop. Most unfortunately they have saddled me with the job of town major of my battalion in Orizaba for the duration of our stay here. As a result I am almost constantly on the run and busy from five o'clock in the morning till nightfall, as I have to find quarters for the arriving troops and officers and see to their messing, which in God's truth is no small task, for the providers of accommodation try in every way possible to evade their duties.

Yesterday, with the proceeds of my warm civilian clothes, I bought myself a horse complete with bridle and saddle.

I sold the clothes, having worn them for six months for 30 florins more than they had cost me new in Europe. I obtained about 84 florins in silver for them and am delighted with this transaction, as one only realizes here how difficult the transport of every unnecessary ounce of weight becomes. Moreover the clothes would certainly have been ruined on the many marches in the pasteboard trunks which let the water in . . .

You, precious Mother, I kiss and embrace a thousand times. Remember me much and often and be assured that no day passes without my thinking of you and my kinsmen just as often.

Goodbye, dear Mother, be embraced and kissed once again by your grateful son,

Ernst

Ernst wrote again to his mother from Orizaba on 24 February.

Beloved Mother,
Soon a month will again have passed since I last wrote to you and although quite a lot has happened since then directly affecting our corps, I am nevertheless in the same spot and am still town major in Orizaba.

I have received your last two letters of 14 December and 9 January and they really made me happy, for only when one is so far away, completely separated from all one's dear ones, does one learn to appreciate the true worth of news from home. So in future send letters

---

* Count Charles de Bombelles was an old friend of Maximilian with a high position at Court.
†Karl Schaffer was a court official.

only through the consulate-general, since after all this, it seems to me, is the surest way.

On the tenth of this month, in the evening, as we were sitting in the coffee house, we were surprised by two telegrams from Puebla. The first notified us that our troops had brilliantly celebrated their debut at Tesiutlan in the vicinity of Jalapa. Two of our companies stormed the place, which was defended by 1,400 Mexicans under General Ortega, and drove the enemy away, taking from him more than a hundred prisoners, many arms, his money and countless horses and mules. The second telegram brought us the sad news that a very dear friend and comrade of mine, Captain von Halsinger, son of the senior medical officer in Vienna, had fallen while entering the place at the head of his company. Lieutenant-Colonel Kodolitsch, too, was lightly wounded and on the 20th Count Herberstein was shot in the chest. Of the other ranks we lost about forty men dead or wounded. You can imagine that this somewhat marred our pleasure over the first victory.

Two days later the division, to which I also belong, received the order to leave immediately the same night and to drive away the guerrillas who were assembling in the neighbourhood of Jalapa. I immediately asked to be relieved of the post of town major, which was granted, and joined my company; and on the night of the 14th around midnight our column, whose departure was kept very secret from the population, marched off. All the officers were mounted. I myself had exchanged my first, not very brilliant, horse for a splendid grey stallion, who cost me all my savings, including the first horse – about 400 gulden. Of course I rode him and so we left on a pitch-dark night and marched that day, with a single rest-stop of four hours, until 10 o'clock at night – twenty-two hours on the march. While encamped at Canada, which was the name of the village where we were, we were informed by a courier of the hussars that yet another company, a mountain battery and fifty hussars from our corps were following to support us. The next day we marched to San Andrés, Chalchicomula, where we joined with the promised reinforcement. While on the march I was commanding the vanguard when it was suddenly reported to us that a large hacienda to the left of the road was occupied by the enemy. I was ordered to attack immediately and advanced with my column. And indeed we sighted many people, horses, etc. in the distance. As it was difficult for the men to advance on the ploughed land, however, I decided first to reconnoitre on horseback, the more so as at first glance it did not look so dangerous to me. With revolver in hand I rode up at a gallop and became very disappointed when I discovered in the supposed enemy only servants and Indians from the hacienda who, standing in groups, gaped at us passing. I withdrew very dissatisfied and we reached the next station without interference. We learnt there to our great regret that the real enemy had already run away and that we could therefore do no better than return to Orizaba. After two very arduous marches over two mountains of over 7,000 feet we reached Orizaba again in good order, but quite exhausted. I myself was quite all right during the whole time except for a few small beetles which had crept into our laundry and clothes during the various night stops. But unfortunately my grey had suffered far more and he will probably be lost to me, as he has collected a very unpleasant throat inflammation, catarrh, etc. Should this happen, the expedition will have cost me all of 400 florins in silver. Hardly agreeable. As the fortress of Oaxaca had surrendered during these days the hopes in my last letter of a siege of that place had evaporated. You can hardly imagine the isolation and complete ignorance, even of events occurring in the immediate neighbourhood, in which one lives here. Far and wide no trace of a European newspaper and consequently no idea of conditions at home. Do not forget to inform me of the most important developments in this respect in your future letters. We too are very ill informed regarding the course of events in Mexico and only know that there is still a good deal of work to be done.

I have sent Frau von Kuhacsevich the letter of introduction I was carrying and a bonnet which Marie gave me for her, together with a letter from myself asking her to pass the remaining letters to the addressees and seek their good offices on my behalf. I indicated my little worries and wishes to her in this letter, but have so far received no message or reply and so I imagine that it is the same with her as with all other people, who at a distance of so many thousands of miles care damned little about former female friends and their interests. However that may be, it is certainly not of vital importance to me and I can get on without outside assistance.

In the inn in which I am staying there is a German family on their travels, namely a young man with an eighteen-year-old wife, and, with only a door separating us, I now hear that she is in process of becoming a mother. The poor girl cries and moans dreadfully and so I am reminded of good Marie who, let us hope, has by now survived the ordeal. Since we happen to be on this subject I will stay with it a moment longer to convey to dear Mathilde herewith my warmest congratulations and a compliment to myself for being so observant in foreseeing the course of events and winning a ring for myself.

I do not think we will stay long in Orizaba and if, as seems probable, my battalion is moved to Puebla I will probably ride to Mexico straight away in the first days, as it is only fourteen miles away and I must go there whatever happens. From here the journey is just too far for me, as it is about another thirty miles. The different items of news which you have given me interested me very much and, judging from their fairly unambiguous significance, left a disagreeable impression . . .

As I have already told you, Monkey is here and is as well as circumstances permit – indeed in a certain respect better off than I, for he has formed a liaison, which seems to occupy him a great deal, as he runs around all day long and does not come home any more. Unfortunately I have not so far been able to do the same and I am therefore very envious of him. Let us hope that this will change with time.

Goodbye precious, good Mother, be most affectionately and warmly embraced and think often with love of your grateful son

Ernst

I am breaking this letter open again in order to inform you that I have just received a very friendly letter from the corps. It tells me that the emperor has sent Schartzenlechner* packing back to Europe because of his shameless behaviour.

On 2 March the battalion received orders to proceed to Puebla. Ernst notes in his diary:

The five weeks which I spent in Orizaba had no great appeal for me as far as company was concerned, for I did not get to know a living soul and was bored to distraction. An attempt made with all the energy at my command to woo my recalcitrant neighbour, a charming young woman without a husband, was to my dismay a complete failure and I was just in the process of despairing of myself and of the whole female element of the population of Orizaba when happily the aforementioned order to leave for Puebla reached me. A further attempt of mine at the eleventh hour to saddle Lieutenant-Colonel Delavigne with my sick grey was equally unsuccessful, but the latter offered me almost by force a loan of 80 pesos, so that I could still buy another horse in Orizaba. Although I did not need a loan for this, my evil spirit nevertheless led me to accept Delavigne's offer. I bought myself another horse – from a certain Mr Sota, a splendid rough-coated black – and still had more than 110 pesos in my pocket, but lost them and another 80 pesos to Captain Laszlo in a little game of Macao on the march in Canada!

The march from Orizaba to Puebla is rather difficult. After the first stage, Aculcingo, one has to cross the so-called *cumbres*. The road crosses the first mountain in twenty-one serpentine bends, the second in eighteen, and the Canada station lies 1,000 metres above sea level.

* Sebastian Schartzenlechner, scheming and unprincipled ex-valet of Maximilian, who became for a time his private secretary in Mexico.

At Puente Colorado the road to Oaxaca via Tehuacan turns off. From Aculcingo the road is nothing but sand and marching is infinitely difficult for the men.

2 March   Aculcingo
3 March   Canada
4 March   Palmar
5 March   Halfway to Acacingo
6 March   Acacingo
7 March   Amozoc
8 March   Puebla

On our arrival at the latter place we were met by General Count Thun, who inspected us, and the company was given the assignment of occupying the forts of Loreto and Guadelupe.

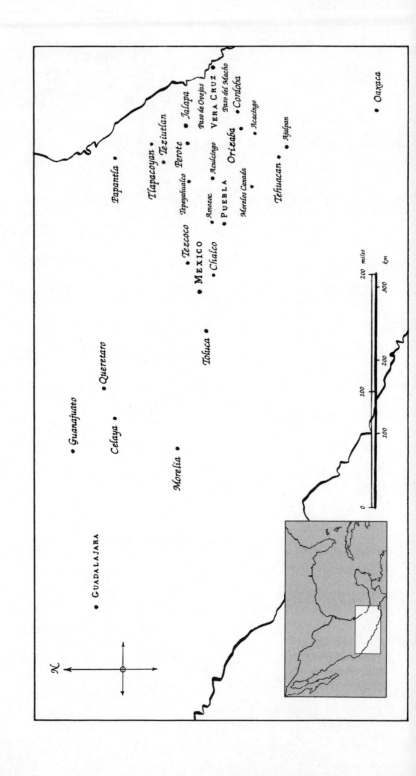

A Funny Kind of War

Puebla, second only to the capital in importance, was to be the headquarters of the volunteer corps and its operational base. Strategically situated within a region comprising the states of Puebla, Mexico, Querétaro, and Guanajuato, which at this time was firmly controlled by the government – although not immune to occasional forays by the Liberals – it also commanded the vital route linking Veracruz and the capital. The original intention of the French was that the volunteer corps should be responsible for operations within the region, as well as in adjoining areas to the south (Oaxaca, Yucatán), thereby releasing them to carry the pacification effort to the extensive and largely uncharted regions of the north, to which the Juárez government and a large part of its forces had withdrawn. The area of responsibility thus delegated to the corps included, to the north-east, the Sierra del Norte, a wild and precipitous mountain region inhabited only by Indian tribes. The French, having failed to pacify the Sierra, advised against trying to control it; but the Austrians, emboldened by the ambitious and adventurous Major Alphons von Kodolitsch (who was to command the corps in its last days), took a contrary view and in a series of operations in which Major Kodolitsch played a leading part had won control of the area by January 1866. But it was not to last and as the general military situation deteriorated the Austrians were forced to abandon successive positions and had withdrawn from the entire area by the following December. Except for his brief excursion to Jalapa in February 1865 Ernst was not himself involved in this sector of the fighting, but it absorbed most of the energies of the volunteer corps during the whole Mexican campaign.

Besides the political causes of the disaster in Mexico, a significant factor in the disastrous campaign was the failure of the Europeans to appreciate the magnitude of the physical task before them and the nature of the war they would have to fight. The French, who had been able to impose their will on native populations in North Africa, thought they could do the same in the very different circumstances of Mexico. But for this their resources were totally inadequate. Even with the 9,000 men of the Austro-Belgian corps, the French army of some 28,000 could never hope to subjugate a rugged country half the size of Europe and enjoying the active support of the United States. And without military dominance there could be no administrative control, an essential pre-requisite of successful counter-insurgency.

The fighting, too, was of a kind to which the Europeans were not accustomed. The Austrians, no less than the French, expected to engage the enemy in set-piece battles reminiscent of Solferino and even Austerlitz. In fact they found themselves involved in a very different kind of warfare, against an elusive enemy. The Liberals were always careful to avoid major engagements with imperial forces unless possessed of overwhelming superiority. Their preferred method was to make lightning raids on weakly held positions or to lure their opponents into ambushes. Since their forces were mostly cavalry they possessed great mobility and their losses tended to be comparatively light, whereas the casualties suffered by the Europeans, although fewer in aggregate, were, because of their limited numbers, relatively much more damaging. The Liberal troops, despite their slovenly and unkempt appearance, were tough and capable of remarkable endurance. Moreover, in addition to the armies headed by individual Republican generals, whose numbers waxed and waned with the changing fortunes of the war, countless irregular bands, roamed the countryside, more interested in plunder than politics. Such bandit groups would appear from nowhere, attack and pillage poorly defended targets and then melt into the countryside. Their activities aggravated the general state of insecurity.

Inevitably, as the fighting continued, the imperial forces found themselves increasingly reduced to holding a few important towns, but unable to control the surrounding countryside, which lay open to the Liberals. They had lost the initiative and from now on were on the defensive. The linguistic and cultural barriers that divided them from the population also made it difficult for the Europeans to secure local co-operation. The Liberals, moving freely throughout the countryside, could more readily secure support, if necessary by the use of terror. Equally the Europeans – again partly for linguistic reasons – had difficulty in working in harmony with the Mexican auxiliaries who were attached to all their fighting units. Many of these troops had been press-ganged into service, were capable of fighting courageously but, not surprisingly, were liable to change their allegiance if it suited them to do so. That is why, as soon as the military balance was seen to be moving in favour of the Liberals, support for their cause increased at an accelerating pace.

Much of the war was fought with great brutality on both sides. This was particularly the case after Maximilian had been persuaded by the French in October 1865 to publish a decree* ordering the summary trial – and virtually certain execution – of Liberals taken prisoner in the fighting. The inevitable result of this ill-considered act (which was to contribute to Maximilian's own execution, as it formed one of the main charges brought against him at his trial) was to intensify the brutality on both sides. The Austrians, however, who had been inclined to treat their prisoners humanely, were told by Maximilian to ignore the decree. The Austrians as a whole fought with dash and courage, although perhaps not always with great skill.

Ernst wrote to his mother from Puebla on 13 March:

Puebla is a handsome town of about 80,000 inhabitants, built in a very regular manner, the houses mostly of one to two floors, decorated with bright colours, frescoes and inlaid faïence ornamentation, and presents a strange, friendly appearance.

But in his diary he wrote:

Puebla itself gave me the impression of a town which was attractive, but dead and completely under the influence of a clerical party not

---

* Decree of 3 October 1865. Bazaine had already by 10 April ordered his commanders to shoot all 'guerrilla leaders' captured out of hand.

very favourably disposed to the government. Bigotry is said to be in fullest flower here.

Ernst's letter to his mother continues:

Anyhow, it is just as boring here as in all the other places in this country. I was therefore not displeased to be assigned, immediately on the day of our arrival, to the Fort Loreto which dominates the town, where I was on twenty-four-hour duty, alternating with another officer. In the fort there are three captured generals, among them Díaz,* the former commander of the fortress of Oaxaca captured by the French, twelve colonels and twenty-two lieutenant-colonels of the Mexican army, all prisoners of war. The strict surveillance of these people is entrusted to us and although this duty is said to be disagreeable and is full of responsibility, it is not without a certain interest, as there are some very interesting personalities among them.† But in general these senior Mexican officers are riff-raff, such as it is hard to picture to oneself in Europe. I tell you only that in the case of four-fifths of our captured staff officers one would hesitate in Europe to make them corporals.

However, I do not think that we will stay here long, for there is constant unrest in the surrounding countryside and we receive reports almost daily of more or less bloody smaller engagements and skirmishes, which our detached companies in the neighbourhood of Jalapa and Perote have to endure. The enemy here has a peculiar and, for him, very practical method of fighting. Large units of from 400–500 men can hardly ever expect to encounter these fellows in the open, even if they were four times as strong. But, hidden behind all kinds of objects, they will discharge several vigorous salvoes, which cost us many men, and then run away as fast as they can. If, on the other hand, a small unit – for example a company or half a company – is somewhere on its own, we can be sure that there will be an alarm almost every night. This is tiring and causes many casualties – since someone or other always cops it – and achieves nothing. In these circumstances the most effective system is to leave the fellows undisturbed so long that they feel safe in some place or other and then to surround them completely, catch them and string them up. In this way one rids oneself of this rabble most easily and with the least bloodshed.

* Porfirio Díaz, probably the ablest Republican commander and later President of Mexico; notwithstanding the 'strict surveillance' mentioned by Ernst, he escaped soon afterwards.
† In his diary Ernst lists Díaz as one of the 'decent' officers.

Ernst wrote in his diary:

After two days in the fort we made the sad discovery of a desertion plot in the company, in which an NCO and also my former batman were involved. As a case had already occurred in the company in Orizaba of four men deserting simultaneously, as a result of which martial law was of course then proclaimed immediately, the recent case acquired a much more serious and, for the company, naturally not very favourable significance. The ringleader, Rifleman Worrel, tried to hang himself while under arrest, but was prevented in time from doing so.

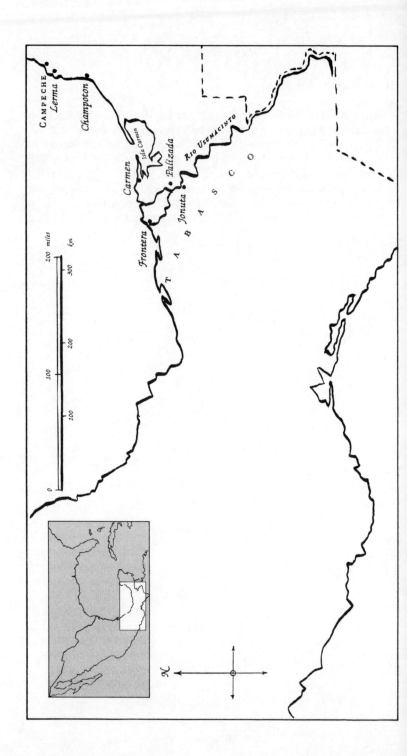

Success and Sadness

Ernst had expected to remain in Puebla with his company for some time at least. But fate willed otherwise. Early in 1865 it was decided to send a small Austrian force under Captain Hedemann and First Lieutenant Bideskuty to the Yucatán peninsula in the extreme south, which was then only lightly held by the French. The coastal population in and around the main cities had voluntarily declared their allegiance to the empire, but the area was subject to incursions by Liberal bands of Indians from the interior. The purpose of the operation was therefore seen as being primarily political: to show the flag and promote confidence among the people; but a secondary objective was to cut supplies to the Liberals from neighbouring Guatemala and British Honduras, while also dealing with any threats that might develop locally. In the expectation that the Sierra del Norte would soon be completely pacified, it was planned that the whole corps should be moved to Yucatán in the autumn (proof, if such were needed, of the totally unrealistic view of the overall situation taken by the government – or, more probably, the French). Meanwhile Ernst took part in two successful operations against the liberals and was decorated for his bravery. But no further progress in operations was made in the ensuing months, while the Austrians suffered heavy casualties from the deadly yellow fever. As the fighting quality of the force had been seriously impaired by the impact of the disease, the troops were thereupon withdrawn from the area.

Ernst wrote in his diary:

On 15 March I was summoned by a service note to Major Pollak, who informed me in a mysterious manner that I had been selected to take part as company officer in the highly honourable mission which the 2nd Company had been charged to carry out in Yucatán. Our mission, Major Pollak said, was more of a diplomatic than of a military nature and the aim was for this loyal province, which was unquestionably devoted to the emperor, to be conquered morally – where there was still a need for it – by our irresistible amiability. Major Pollak seemed very surprised when he did not discern in my long face the expression of joy which he probably expected to be produced by his announcement. To a few modest questions on my part as to how long this honourable exile might last he returned the consoling answer, that it could well last one to two years. On hearing this I hastened to bid the aforementioned personality a fond farewell, in which I alluded to the faint possibility that a visitation of yellow fever might prevent me from being able to behold his amiable giraffe-like figure again in this world. Although he called me a pessimist, my fears were nevertheless subsequently confirmed in that I was confidentially informed that the purpose of our diplomatic mission was really only to observe to what extent European troops and immigrants can resist the unhealthy climate of the *Tierra caliente* in the monsoon. A pleasant mission!

Ernst expressed his feelings to his mother in somewhat similar vein:

There [in Yucatán] we will remain detached and alone and must pacify the province, in which the Indians still cause great unrest, to the best of our ability. Since, however, Yucatán has an extent of 2,000 miles and a company only has 150 men, this could become quite a difficult task and we will very probably have to confine ourselves to conquering the province morally by our amiability . . .

In one respect this new expedition gives me much pleasure, since I will get to know another country, completely foreign to me and, so they say, quite different from conditions here. I am told that one has a splendid time there, according to ideas here, since the people are very sociable and convival. On the other hand, I am annoyed to be relegated so far from the fount of everything in Mexico, where they will then bother all the less about us. Moreover, there is no prospect of an early departure and so it is very probable that I shall roast there for one to two years. The country is completely flat and the highest point is 200 feet above sea level, whereas here in Puebla we are over 7,000 feet. Since, moreover, Yucatán lies much further south, there will probably not be many cool days in the year there. But the climate is bearable. It is true that yellow fever is also indigenous, but much less prevalent than in Veracruz . . . Only, dear, precious Mother, continue to be courageous and reassured: it is not as awful here as people at home in Europe imagine and, God willing, we shall see each other again, healthy and well, in a few years . . . As for comfort, one has to renounce it here in every respect from the first. I have not known a bed for the last three weeks and will probably have to do without one for as long again. Here one has to lie down to sleep on one's back with one's clothing on and nothing to cover one. But one gets used to it.

The diary continues:

I was offered a choice of travelling to Veracruz with the stagecoach and awaiting the 2nd Company there, or of joining the 7th Company, which was just marching from Puebla to Tesiutlan. I chose the latter alternative for two reasons, firstly because I wanted to take my horses with me and secondly because I wanted to get to know the part of Mexico unknown to me north of the Pik of Orizaba.

Early on the 17th we marched off, after General Thun had on this occasion, too, wished me farewell and much luck in this not exactly very agreeable expedition.

On the 18th we halted in Amozoc. On the 19th we came to Napolucan, where we found the Ulan squadron of Döring, whose officers at our arrival were just chasing a horse – and fortunately did not catch it. In the evening we allowed ourselves to be enticed to a little Macao game at which Krikl lost 600 pesos, Metternich, Soga and I 100 each and Ludovici 60 pesos to Döring, to whom 960 pesos had thus fallen as from the sky. I forgot to mention that I sold my grey in Puebla to the Monkey Commission for 70 pesos. As a result of the occurrence I have mentioned the proceeds found their way into Döring's pocket instead of Delavigne's.

On the 20th we marched to San Ildefonso. I decided during the march to turn off to San Inandelos, which place lay five leguas* off our route and where my friend Thoren was. As I was completely independent of the company I carried out this plan and arrived there and gossiped a lot with Thoren, who incidentally appeared to have had enough of Mexican service and sketched out all kinds of return plans. At two o'clock on the afternoon of the 21st I rode away again in the company of Thoren, Malburg and Thurneissen and also of two Mexican lancers in order to rejoin the 7th Company, which had meanwhile marched to Tepeyahualeoc. The officers accompanied me to half-way and the lancers to the stage, where I arrived at 6 o'clock in the evening and found everyone alarmed on my account, as I had already been

* 1 legua = 2.6 kilometers.

missed too long. In Tepeyahualeoc we also met First-Lieutenant Hanke, who was escorting First-Lieutenant Preiss to Puebla. On the 22nd we reached Perote, where I met First-Lieutenant Manzano, First-Lieutenant Bideskuty and several other comrades and spent the day with them. The 6th Company arrived there the same day on the way to Jalapa, while the 7th Company turned off to Tesiutlan. Riding out from Perote on the 23rd, I left the 6th Company to make the march in the prescribed two stages while I joined a passing troop of Mexican cavalry who were riding the same route in one stage. It was raining in torrents and, soaked to the skin, I arrived at five o'clock in Jalapa, where I found all the gentlemen, except for a few who kept house for themselves, assembled at dinner in the hotel. I was received in a very friendly manner and I stayed in Jalapa until the morning of the 27th, when my new company began the march to Veracruz and Campeche. Jalapa was much to my liking and I do not think I am mistaken in remarking that several of our other gentlemen, too, cannot have had a bad time there. At least throughout the last three days my amiable Captain von Hedemann wore a really miserable expression, as though he were leaving behind the entirety of his Indian – let it be said pretty material – aspirations. In Jalapa I also sold my little black horse to First-Lieutenant Mannsi for 112 pesos (thereby making 42 pesos) and paid my debt to Delavigne out of the proceeds.

The march from Jalapa to Veracruz was decidedly unamusing and it was again our amiable Captain – presenting, as he rode at the head of his faithful, the most comic sight imaginable – who provided us with the only material for hilarity. Rosinante,* a dun mare captured at Tesiutlan, small, most miserable and in foal to boot, almost allowed our friend Hedemann, while riding, to use his feet for walking as well. The saddle, saddle-cloth, bridle, in short everything on the horse was in the most pitiable condition – all of it, be it said, pieces of booty from Tesiutlan. Hedemann himself had feverishly wound an enormous sash round hat and clasp, had a huge field-bottle hanging at his side and altogether had such a melancholic and half sleepy expression that, with all respect and deference, one could not refrain from laughing out loud at the sight of him . . .

We set out from Paso de Ovejas at two o'clock in the morning and reached Veracruz at ten o'clock that night. Bideskuty and I rode ahead from Santa Fé to let it be known in Veracruz that we were arriving one day early. As we had heard rumours in Sante Fé of there being guerrillas in the neighbourhood, we were constantly on the look-out, riding at a fast trot with revolver in hand. But we did not encounter so much as a cat and arrived safely in Veracruz.

* The name of Don Quixote's mount.

Our departure was fixed for the afternoon of 31 March and we were to be transported by the propeller-driven French corvette *Forfait*. On the morning of the 31st I went aboard the frigate *Novara* before all the others in order to greet my dear friends from Austria, who were shortly to begin the return journey – perhaps for the last time in my life: for although I am not at all a pessimist or hypochondriac, it is nevertheless certain that one requires much luck and a damned good constitution to withstand for six years all the vicissitudes which our corps has to face in this country and return to the fatherland unscathed.

We put to sea at four o'clock in the afternoon and on the morning of 2 April we lay at anchor twelve miles from Campeche, as one could go no nearer to the coast because of the shallow water. The officers of the *Forfait* were generally quite friendly. But with the exception of the commander, Capitaine de Frégate Potestas, and of the midshipman Minier, I found the others not very engaging and quite of a pattern with the other officers of this nation, who according to my standards are pretty good soldiers, but not at all gentlemen.

In the afternoon a number of gentlemen from Campeche came on board our ship in order to carry the company ashore in the shallow-draught vessels they had brought with them. This was achieved at half past ten at night and with the band playing we made our entry into the town, already competely asleep.

The *Forfait* remained off Campeche for a few more days and when the commander, accompanied by a resident of Campeche, Mr Mac-Gregor, and a few other gentlemen, went to board his ship to leave, it so happened that the boat sank and the whole crew, exposed to all the terrors of a death by drowning in mid-ocean for twelve hours and fighting the elements, remained afloat for a sufficient time to be rescued by a fishing boat which happened to be passing by. Only one gentlemen, the head of the French military dispensaries in Veracruz, was drowned. Mr MacGregor was dangerously ill for several days as a result of the extreme fatigue and the searing heat of the sun. It was only on Capitaine de Frégate Potestas that the affair seemed not to have had the slightest effect, for although also badly sunburnt he stayed up for several hours after returning to his ship, eating, walking about on deck and giving his orders. In the water too Potestas is said to have shown throughout an admirable presence of mind and, although not a swimmer, nevertheless to have maintained the greatest composure . . .

In general we were very well received here and, as I think I can not inappropriately mention, have won general esteem by our reserved, well-behaved, courteous and yet at the same time firm demeanour. No one is more impressed by the decent behaviour of officers than the

Mexicans, for they are used to regarding their military as the lowest caste of the land and the native officers as a horde of rough and knavish riff-raff, not much better than robbers . . .

Here in Campeche we – and especially I, as the one most fond of company – visit the houses of Mr MacGregor, blessed with thirteen children, Mr Precier, with fourteen children, Mr Ferrer etc., etc. At the beginning of May the family Gutiérrez d'Estrada* arrived here from Mexico – and this is really the most respectable family I have yet encountered in this country. Three unmarried, pretty and pleasant daughters are also calculated to make a visit to this house a pleasure and I cannot deny that I could easily be shackled to this house – if I knew which of the daughters pleased me best.

Quietly as the month of April passed, May and June were to be turbulent for our company. Already soon after our arrival our worthy, but somewhat timorous and pessimistic prefect had made various allusions to possibly impending *pronunciamientos*,† Juárez machinations etc. and left us, who then did not yet know Mr Rámoz, in a state of some alarm, or shall I say increased vigilance. Nevertheless the month of April, as I have said, passed perfectly peacefully. In the first days of May, however, news was received from the governorate of the town of Carmen that a certain Arevale had landed on the island of the same name as the town with a band of sixteen to twenty adventurers and was trying to bring about a uprising of the population, pretending to be one of the dissident generals and chargé d'affaires. This put our prefect into a state of deathly fear and Hedemann, who takes a personal pleasure in reinforcing the poor devil in all his fears, was equally assiduous in magnifying the importance of the matter; and so it was decided to send forty men from our company with First-Lieutenant Bideskuty and Second-Lieutenant Schmidt to Carmen to restore law and order. Arevale was clever enough to clear out in good time and took a ship to Champotón, where no opposition whatever was shown to him, but on the contrary a number of men from the population joined his troop, and where he extorted 600 pesos. One day later he left Champotón, plundered ranches in the vicinity, was dangerously wounded by a servant in one of them, but in spite of all this gave the slip to our detachment, which reached Champotón two days after Arevale's departure. After occupying this small town for eight days our men were relieved by Mexican troops and on 20 May the whole 2nd Company was again united in Campeche.

---

* José María Gutiérrez d'Estrada was an elderly Mexican monarchist, who had played a leading part in persuading Maximilian to accept the crown.
† Declarations of allegiance – or, more commonly, of a change of allegiance – by political or military leaders.

On the 24 May, however, a further report was received from the bay saying that 200 liberals from the direction of Tabasco had invaded the territory of Isla Carmen and rapid support was desirable and necessary. It happened that I was sent on this new expedition with a detachment of fifty men.

The day before, on the 23rd, the sad case had occurred that First-Lieutenant Bideskuty had been obliged by the insubordination of Section-Leader Lankitsch to shoot him with his revolver. Drinking and disobedience had become prevalent generally, but particularly among a certain clique of higher ranks, all former officers, to such an extent that it became very necessary to bring the matter to a decisive end. The outrage which resulted in Lankitsch's death also led to the permanent degradation of a certain Junior-Rifleman Stepp and the condemnation of Patrol-Leader Rästle to degradation, loss of medals and five years' imprisonment in San Juan d'Ulloa. These aforementioned deterrent examples had a very favourable effect on the company and I set out by ship for Carmen with my detachment on the night of the 24th completely reassured as to the morale of the men.

Ernst described the expedition in a letter to his mother:

I hardly believe that any of our units in the corps can have experienced greater difficulties in the past months than we have . . .

In the second half of last month [May] I received the order to proceed with fifty men of the company to the island of Carmen, where according to hearsay 200 dissidents were believed to have landed. Packed like sardines in a small sailing boat, we set out the same night and arrived at our destination after a twenty-four-hour journey. I had our craft moored alongside the French naval steamship *Brandon*, which was stationed there, in order to enquire about the state of affairs; I learnt that the rumour of an insurgent landing was indeed false, but that a detachment of guerrillas was present a little further away from the island of Carmen, at Chiltepec, and that an expedition for their expulsion was being prepared for the very next morning, in which I was invited to take part. As you can imagine, I accepted with pleasure and so we set out again by ship at dawn a few hours later, the column consisting this time of some fifty Mexican auxiliaries, fifty Austrians and thirty French sailors. The latter were in a tiny little steamboat and we and the Mexicans were towed by this steamer. In this way we again spent another day on board ship, exposed to the most scorching sunlight, and at ten o'clock at night we arrived at the mouth of the Río Usumacinto or Río de Tabasco. Six nautical miles upstream, at the place called Frontera, a French gunboat and a

Mexican steamer are anchored: they levy toll for the account of the imperial government on all ships going to the town of Juan Bautista, while the same ships have to pay a second toll into the hands of the rebels on arrival at the aforementioned town. I should have mentioned before that the whole state of Tabasco is still in the hands of the liberals. You can imagine what trade conditions are like if all ships have to pay the toll, which is already enormous, twice over.

As our small steamer could not tow the two sailing boats with our troops upstream against the strong current and the wind had completely dropped, we decided to leave the two ships lying at anchor at the mouth of the river and that we officers should go on alone with the small steamer in order, on arrival at Frontera, to obtain information from the French gunboat *Tourmente* about the insurgents who were supposed to be in Chiltepec.

It was half past seven at night and we were all more or less fatigued by the heat of the past day and thinking of nothing else but an evening meal on the *Tourmente* and going to sleep when suddenly, as we sailed close to the river bank, we were greeted with intense small-arms fire. As it was pitch dark and the sailors' weapons as well as our own were stowed below deck our situation in the first moment of surprise was not exactly agreeable. Fortunately, however, we were already close to the two big warships and, observing our embarrassment, the Mexican steamer sent a few rounds of grape-shot into the shrubbery on the river bank, which immediately cleared it of the enemy. On board the *Tourmente* we learnt that by chance the whole band for which we had been looking in Chiltepec had been in Frontera for two days and had thus saved us half our journey. The commander of the *Tourmente* told us that we had arrived very opportunely, as he himself had been too weak to disperse the infiltrators on land without depriving the ship of its necessary crew. We held a council of war and decided to disembark and attack at dawn. For this purpose, however, the ships anchored at the river mouth with their troops had first to be brought up and the Mexican steamer received the order to do this. As it was already one o'clock in the morning we could only leave towards half past two, as the Mexican steamer needed one and a half hours to get up steam.

As we went downstream we were again greeted with a rain of bullets, to which we replied with a few rounds of grapeshot; and the same occurred when, dawn having already broken, we came up again with the troops. Then, however, I had already positioned my men along the bulwark and we replied with a vigorous rifle and grapeshot fusillade and thereupon disembarked as quickly as possible, attacking the places simultaneously from different sides. We met with hardly any resistance; the beggars ran away ignominiously and only their commander rode towards us half drunk, but rapidly took his leave when I sent a bullet after him, which unfortunately missed. In the pursuit a few of the enemy were brought down, thirty-two deserted and claimed they had been forcefully conscripted, the rest – about forty men – escaped to Jonuta, where a certain Prast was in a fortified position with 600 men. During the next two to three days we were constantly on guard – at night awaiting an attack in a fortified position, in the morning and during the day making expeditions into the interior to attack possible stragglers or deserters from the enemy, of whom some, it was reported to us, were in hiding in the different *ranchos*. In fact we found no one, but made all the more interesting discoveries in regard to the strangeness of this truly magnificient tropical country. For example, we would set out at two o'clock in the morning to raid and search a *rancho*. No one was allowed to utter a word or smoke during the march. Silently, in pitch darkness, with an Indian as our guide, we made our way into the bush. One could only go in single file and each man had to keep hold of the next to be sure that the column stayed together. Then, in what was otherwise the stillness of the night, there came the really amazingly powerful roar of a kind of large monkey, which is indigenous there in large numbers and whose roaring is heard over two to three leguas. At last we arrived at a *rancho* to the barely perceptible breaking of the dawn; in a trice it is encircled, and then the sight of all the faces of these Indians, overcome with sleep and startled, is so unusual and striking that it remains unforgettable although it is difficult to portray.

The following days passed in this way, and when we had finally convinced ourselves of the complete absence of the enemy we set out, to my great satisfaction, on the return to Carmen. I say satisfaction, for during the whole time I had never been out of my clothes at night and slept in brotherly companionship with two other French officers on a billiard-table in the coffee house of the place, the latter having been, I may say, completely deserted by the inhabitants. In front of our door was the improvised entrenchment and behind it lay our men, exposed to the bites of millions of bloodthirsty mosquitoes.

On the night of the 30th we finally reached Carmen again, where meanwhile a plan for a further larger expedition against Pallizada and Jonuta had formed in the mind of the French commander. The latter congratulated me on the success of the aforementioned small affair and informed me that I could remain in Carmen without further ado to await the other part of my company there, which was due to arrive hourly under the command of Major X with the two other officers in order to participate in the larger expedition against Prast in unison with 230 Mexicans and 70 Frenchmen.

Ernst reports this arrival in his diary and continues with some character sketches of his fellow-officers:

Next day, 1 June, my whole company did indeed arrive in Carmen despite the anguished protestations of the good prefect of Campeche, who could not at all understand why no one was remaining there for his defence. Hedemann was malicious and merciless enough to encourage the poor man in his apprehension, for when the latter said that if the Liberals got there he would certainly be killed, Hedemann replied laconically, 'Without doubt', whereupon the poor devil in his fright is said to have broken out in beads of sweat.

Anyhow, Hedemann, who in spite of his phlegmatic nature can be *mauvaise langue* in the highest degree, is happy to avenge himself on other people in return for all the teasing to which he had been subjected on our part for his healthy appetite, his butterfly behaviour and his no small egoism. Altogether Hedemann is an eccentric and incidentally one of the luckiest people on earth. Although not endowed with an excessive devotion to duty, his reputation in this respect at corps headquarters is nevertheless first class. His attainments have always found recognition – two decorations already adorn his chest and one or two are still in prospect for him. He inherits legacies, finds rich partners, always – though he persistently denies this – has a splendid appetite and never loses his temper. Moreover, he amuses himself here, where everyone is bored, by chasing after butterflies, caterpillars and worms all day long, which he carefully preserves and of which he already possesses splendid collections, whose purpose it is in time to gain him an honourable place among scientists. For Hedemann plans in a few months to return to Europe, where a seat in the Danish Upper House and the Dannebrog* await him; and he will also assuredly bring to a conclusion a matrimonial negotiation now in progress, the proceeds of which, as well as a wife, could amount to some 2–300,000 pesos. But what is wonderful and special about this otherwise exceptionally pleasant, cultured and estimable comrade is just the fact that all these things, which seem to be just castles in the air, come to fruition with him, for he was, as I have said, born under a lucky star.

We the other officers of the company have far less to record in the way of particular strokes of luck. Of my own ill fortune in the military career I hardly need to speak at this stage. All who know me are aware that I was not particularly favoured by fortune. First-Lieutenant Bideskuty, it is true, cannot complain in this respect, but equally has nothing particular to bring to notice, and Schmidt, who is also no boy

* Danish order of chivalry.

Left. Ernst Pitner in the uniform of the Austrian volunteer corps. *Below*. The arrival of the volunteer corps in Veracruz, Mexico. (Photographs this page in possession of the Pitner family, from the Pitner archives, Vienna.)

Above. Members of the Austrian volunteer corps. *Below.* Portrait of the Archduke Ferdinand Maximilian as Commander of the navy before the Mexico episode. Pastel by Georg Deker (1819–94.) (Photographs this page by permission of the Heeresgeschichtlichen Museums, Vienna.)

Above. Photograph of
Charlotte, wife of
Maximilian. *Below*.
Portrait of the Emperor
Franz Josef.
Watercolour on paper,
1868, by the artist Franz
Pitner, half-brother of
Ernst Pitner.
(Photographs this page
by permission of the
Heeresgeschichtlichen
Museums, Vienna.)

Above. Ernst Pitner wearing Mexican uniform. In late 1866 the Austrian volunteer corps had been dissolved and the remaining volunteers, who had chosen to remain in Mexico rather than return to Austria, joined the Mexican army and adopted Mexican uniform. Watercolour by Franz Pitner, 1868. (By permission of the Heeresgeschichtlichen Museums, Vienna.)

Below. Photograph of Princess Engalicheff, wife of Ernst Pitner. (Photograph in possession of the Pitner family, from the Pitner archives, Vienna.)

any more, has seen many years of service and has this month, by the skin of his teeth, brought it to Lieutenant First Class.

Our characters differ in the highest degree and our heterogeneous ideas would surely have led to serious conflicts had we not all been in possession of good hearts, which simply do not allow tension to exist for long between us.

The doctor, who as a Prussian is the scapegoat of us all, is a profoundly good person equipped with a gigantic amount of patience and his few faults are rooted in his Prussian nature and are therefore to be forgiven as being innate and inherited.

Of my many faults I am fortunately fully conscious. I am somewhat quarrelsome and arrogant, very quick-tempered and consequently often unjust, irritable in party games when I am losing, and inclined to rejoice rather too noticeably when I am winning; I am, as far as my own convenience is concerned, a little egoist. With this honest confession, however, I consider myself to have won, apart from the merit of candour, also the right to pass an honest judgement on my other two comrades and I ask them, in case it should come to their notice, to accept it as an expression of opinion intended only for myself and not for their ears.

First-Lieutenant Bideskuty is still very young: that is no fault and the consequences arising from this circumstance will diminish to his advantage with every day that passes. One of his truly major faults, however, particularly in an officer, is too great a softness of his nature, which immediately paralyses every surge of energy through the reaction which sets in. Politeness is never and in no way harmful so long as one does not in some way compromise oneself thereby, and that one does not continue to greet people who have already behaved rudely and tactlessly to one with the same mawkish amiability. I am certainly no partisan of boors and hate all brutality, but I believe that, particularly in this country, one wins public esteem for oneself far more quickly and certainly if one calmly and energetically rebuts every encroachment of the inhabitants here, demands appropriate satisfaction and in the aftermath either distances oneself completely from such individuals or at least always deals with them on the coolest footing. Bideskuty's politeness is, however, in many cases exaggerated and certainly has not always been repaid to him in the same measure. I will here refer only to the case where we escorted López* for embarkation in parade order, when on another occasion we were delivering biscuits to the Mexican troops and I, when I enquired personally about the delivery, was treated impolitely by all the officers. I will mention further the

---

* Presumably Miguel López, the officer who was to betray Maximilian.

similar ocurrence when Schmidt in Champotón was literally insulted by the Mexican Second-Lieutenant and finally I recall our reception after the return from Jonuta when, despite cannon shots from the station tender, the esteemed *agentemiento* neither received us nor provided beds for the poor wounded, but on the contrary even complained because we fetched these ourselves from the hospital. My various little disputes with Bideskuty I will only mention in passing, believing that these left no ill will against each other in our hearts and ascribing the blame here in equal measure to both parties.

Quite the opposite of Bideskuty is Schmidt. In his many good and bad qualities the latter is a true replica of a soldier of fortune. He and Bideskuty both have equally good hearts in quite different covering. Whereas the latter is extremely polite towards everybody, Schmidt is excessively rude to all the world without exception, whether it be by word, gesture or look and I must admit that, if I had the choice of the two qualities, Bideskuty's politeness would be many thousand times preferable to me. Schmidt hates and despises all that is Mexican from the start and treats them accordingly. He is against the whole world and therefore terribly inconsiderate even towards us; he often causes us the greatest embarrassment through his casual behaviour towards others and he neglects his person, so far as its exterior is concerned, in the most incredible manner. His clothing in quarters is always the same: just a shirt, otherwise he is completely naked, never wearing shoes, and even here in Lerma he crosses the square in a kind of sandals without stockings. Schmidt is informed about many things and is talented. But when he thinks he knows best – and this happens not infrequently – he allows himself to be convinced neither by printed books nor by a hundred contrary opinions, but sticks obstinately to his often completely incorrect viewpoint. Money does not have much hold on any of us. But certainly on Schmidt least of all; and when perchance he has some – which, be it said, occurs very rarely – he never makes sensible use of it. To buy some shirts, socks or a jacket for a few thalers would not occur to him in his wildest moments; on the other hand it is a matter of indifference to him to toss out quantities of money in gaming or in any way that amuses him. Finally, Schmidt cannot be induced to write to his poor parents, whom he has not so far provided with a line of news since he came to Mexico, although their thirteenth letter arrived here only recently. To try to change something in his character would be completely wasted effort. When spoken to he either does not answer at all or else asks rudely to be left in peace; consequently nobody says anything to him any more. Yet with all these characteristics Schmidt is, in my opinion, the most self-sacrificing comrade and the most faithful heart in the world. He would give his last shirt for others – if it were not already torn and useless. At the same time Schmidt is a courageous soldier, although he bothers somewhat too little about leading his men, whom incidentally he does not treat very politely, which is also why, I believe, he is not very well liked among the other ranks.

This is our quintet and I believe that everyone who may happen to see these lines and who knows the personalities as I do will judge me to be right in many things. Should I, however, have made a hasty judgement in one or the other direction, I ask forgiveness in advance of the person thereby affected.

After this somewhat lengthy digression concerning our domestic circumstances I will continue my diary, which ended with my telling of the reunion of my detachment with the main body of the company on the island of Carmen.

The 1st, 2nd and 3rd of June were spent organizing the expedition to be undertaken against Palizada and Jonuta.

A detachment of 230 Mexicans under the command of Lieutenant-Colonel Traconis, the 2nd Austrian Rifle Company, 130 men strong, and seventy sailors from the warship *Brandon*, 430 men all told, with two four-pounder hauled naval cannon belonging to the French formed the expeditionary column, whose overall command Capitaine de Frégate Joignière assumed. After a speech addressed by the latter to the troops, in which in the usual French way there was much deceit, reference was made to the sad period of 1859* and the brilliant era of today, which sees Austrian and French armies fighting for the same cause, then, after mutual esteem was emphasized and both emperors cheered, we embarked in eight sailing schooners and the little so-called 'steam-canoe' and sailed punctually at midday on 3 June.

On 4 June, the anniversary of Magenta,† we anchored in the so-called *boca escondida* of the Río de Palizada and remained there during the day, Austrians and French in peaceful unison. In the evening we continued the journey and at two o'clock on the morning of the 5th I was disembarked with forty men in order that we attack Palizada on land together with the Mexicans, while the other troops went on and were to arrive there at the same time as us.

Ernst wrote to his mother:

This march was one of the most arduous that I ever made. The land route is completely flooded for months in the year and boats ply on it;

* When the Austrians were defeated by the French in North Italy.
† A battle which the Austrians lost to the French in 1859.

the rest of the time it is a swamp. We waded continuously from two to eleven o'clock in the morning either above our ankles in the awful stinking swamp or in reeds eight foot high, crossed three small branches of the river up to our shoulders in water, holding ammunition and weapons over our heads, our boots battered, tortured by mosquitoes, our feet raw – truly no pleasure. On the way we saw a number of small lakes, which never dry out completely, and alligators of the most varied sizes, particularly at dawn, when they all swam around on the surface. One lay right next to our path and only withdrew when prodded with the guns, probably frightened by the number of people surrounding him. We encountered many snakes of the most poisonous kind, which, however, fortunately always depart first, and saw herds of at least a thousand wild horses and horned cattle, which remain in the open year in, year out, and in case of need are caught by their owners with lassos. Finally, we arrived dead tired at Palizada, where we learnt that on getting word of our approach the enemy garrison, consisting of sixty mounted men, had withdrawn to Jonuta the same morning, but only after they had exacted a levy of 2,000 pesos from the place. The ships arrived in Palizada at the same time as we did and we spent the night there and started for Jonuta on the morning of the 6th. At four o'clock in the afternoon, at a sudden bend of the river, we saw before us a fortified position, in the middle of which the Mexican Republican flag was fluttering. Continuing a few hundred paces, we were showered with a hail of projectiles of all kinds. We had surrounded our deck with sandbags in the form of a bulwark and energetically returned the cannon and small-arms fire of the enemy, while still continuing on our way. Having arrived at 500 paces from the enemy's fortification we let the ships run up to the bank and landed our men under the most enormous difficulties. The side of the bank rises upwards for several fathoms and as we clambered up with every imaginable exertion the beggars shot at our heads. In order to get to land more quickly and believing that it could not be deep so close to the bank, I jumped into the water and sank completely, but was already on land the next moment, unfortunately with a wet revolver. As soon as only a few men were together above, we threw ourselves into the brush and stormed forward with a roar of 'Hurrah!' as if instead of six men, 200 were there. In this way we succeeded in intimidating and later, when our men had completely disembarked, in totally defeating the much stronger enemy. We lost six dead and about thirty wounded, but the enemy many more, for we had the satisfaction of throwing no less than fifteen of his dead into the water as food for the alligators and many more dead, as well as wounded and prisoners, were brought in later. We then occupied the stronghold, in which we found the marks of our well-aimed cannon and rifle shots, left 230 Mexicans behind in Jonuta as garrison and left on the seventh day to return to Carmen, where we arrived on the 8th, remained for a few days to recuperate and finally, as already mentioned, returned to warlike Campeche again on the 13th . . .

. . . we are still somewhat run down after our recent exertions. In the last three weeks I have spent fifteen days afloat on small river craft, packed in with the other ranks without being able to sleep and exposed to the most intense heat from the sun during the daytime. The other seven days we spent on land, undertaking the most tiring marches in the swamplands, often up to our shoulders in water, bitten to pieces by millions of mosquitoes, without good drinking water and adequate food and in battle with the enemy on two occasions.

But all these little vexations were outweighed a thousandfold by the interest of the expedition. Everywhere in that country there are multitudes of the most enormous crocodiles, monkeys, panthers, snakes etc. I shot three large alligators from the boat and on land I killed two big monkeys. In the last few days I certainly saw some 500 crocodiles. For if one looks carefully one can observe such an animal asleep on the banks of the rivers every fifty paces or even more often, looking like a log of wood.

Tomorrow or the day after the company will return to Campeche quietly and at leisure and I must say that I am looking forward to leading an idle life again for a few weeks.

Ernst noted in his diary: 'Meanwhile the rainy season had begun and with it the unhealthy time of the year.'

He continued to his mother:

We have in the house here a veritable menagerie of monkeys, parrots, flamingos, egrets and dogs (including Monkey), all acquisitions of the last weeks. On 24 May I thought of you continually and together with other officers, one of whom was also celebrating his birthday just then and whom I told that it was also yours, I drank to your health and to our seeing each other again soon. The local prefect has just been here with the commander of the Mexican troops in Campeche to inform us that the 230 Mexicans, whom we left behind as a garrison in Jonuta, had been attacked by the enemy, 600 strong, and were urgently asking for reinforcement. For this purpose 100 men have already left from Carmen and the prefect is asking Captain von Hedemann to send fifty men from our company along as well, since the presence of European troops has an immensely favourable influence on the spirit of our Mexican auxiliaries. Unfortunately this time it is not my turn and First-

Lieutenant Schmidt will go instead; I shall remain quietly in Campeche and console myself that at least I shall not be roasted by the sun on those abominable sailing boats, but can enjoy tranquillity here . . .

For the Trieste relations who know the former Naval Lieutenant Shaffer, now Mexican Lieutenant-Colonel and aide-de-camp to the emperor, I report that in Orizaba during the emperor's last tour he fell in love with the daughter of a certain Brenca, who possesses 40 million pesos. The emperor himself asked for the girl's hand for Schaffer and her father consented. What tremendous luck! . . .

On my return [to Campeche] I became somewhat unwell and had to keep to my bed – or rather hammock – for several days. The unhealthy climate of Palizada and Jonuta and the marshland of the region had brought on another attack of the old fever. Thanks to my strong constitution I suffered only a few days of continuing lack of appetite, of vomiting up everything I ate as well as a fairly severe headache. Before my illness I had accepted an invitation to a shooting excursion in the interior and it so happened that the moment for carrying out this project came just at the time when I was still rather unwell. In order not to leave the gentlemen who had invited me in the lurch and because our doctor recommended a little change of air as being not disadvantageous, I went off and had no cause to regret it, as I recovered completely during the nine days of my absence and had some very interesting experiences. The property of the gentleman, whose wife is a Gutiérrez d'Estrada, lady-in-waiting to the empress, lies approximately twenty-six leguas, that is eighteen German miles, from Campeche in the interior and the area which he calls his own measures over a hundred leguas in circumference and consists, like the entirety of Yucatán, of tropical jungle. To ride through the middle of it is the most interesting thing you can imagine. Everywhere the path is only one to two feet wide and the overhanging branches form an immense avenue of foliage, which is always covered over, and one has alternately to stoop and parry with one's hands in order not to be struck in the face and scratched to pieces by the thorns and branches. Despite that, one continues forward at the fastest pace through thick and thin. Constantly one meets game crossing the path – stags, roebuck, masses of wild boar and all varieties of birds of the strangest kind. In the *rancho* of Mr Arigunaga we took a few hours of well-earned rest, for we covered the aforementioned eighteen miles in one stage and in about sixteen hours with the same horses. The next day there was a wild boar hunt, the second day a water hunt and on the third day a tiger hunt – the latter unfortunately without result, although a large number of these animals exist there. It is not, however, the species of African and Asiatic tiger and is really more of a panther than a tiger, but has the latter name here and it would have pleased me immensely to have shot one . . .

I recollect that I am to give you news of another person, namely one named Kepler, about whom you enquire so assiduously.

Unfortunately I have no idea how things stand with this individual, since in Yucatán I am so far from the rest of the corps that it is not possible for me to gather information about him. But to reassure his mother you can tell her that from the time of the corps' arrival in Mexico, 1 Company has been in the capital as the emperor's guard of honour, that it has never so far fought against the enemy and that it is certainly better off than all the other units of the corps. Unless, therefore, an accident were to befall the son in the natural course of things, which is unlikely, it is only due to laziness on his part if he has so far not written . . .

You mention in your last letter, no. 10, a newspaper article which speaks of a diplomatic mission in Yucatán. Since then you will surely have observed that there have certainly been more diplomatic missions than ours, unless we have entered an age in which envoys conduct their disputes with knife and revolver instead of with the pen . . .

This concludes all the newsworthy material I have been able to assemble for you and I hope that you are not dissatisfied with the fullness of this letter. You also ask me about some other matters, which can easily be answered. For example: Who makes my boots? Since people here wear boots just as elsewhere in the world, there is a profusion of shoemakers, which, however, fortunately I do not need, as our company cobbler does the job just as well and far more cheaply. My grey, about whom you have repeatedly asked me, I have sold, since he never properly regained his strength, at a considerable loss – 180 florins – but on the other hand I made 120 florins on the sale of my second horse before I went to Yucatán, so that the one almost made up for the other.

Ernst continued in his diary:

On my return [from the shooting expedition] the fever came upon me more violently than ever. I had to vomit all the time, could eat nothing and was very miserable. Although I am now better, yesterday, 26 July, I again had an attack.

But other much sadder events have since taken place. The bad season has given rise to a yellow fever epidemic among our men, who are not used to the climate, to which ten men have already succumbed in the shortest time; it was particularly the days 25–26 July which carried off eight of our men, the last five in a period of twenty hours.

On the 22nd the company marched to the village of Lerma two miles from Campeche. With the fresh air and light duty we are hoping that things will improve for the company, and indeed until now we have had no new cases of sickness, for the two men who were carried from Lerma to hospital in the town had already brought the seed of this terrible disease out with them.

A young, decent and talented soldier of my company, Patrol-Leader Spannkraft, was also buried yesterday and I cannot let this opportunity pass without committing to paper, for myself and possible readers of these lines, a touching poem which has come into my hands and which he composed a few days before his death!

> Lonely stand I and abandoned,
> Far the joys for which I yearn,
> Never can the pain be fathomed,
> Homewards as my thoughts return.
> Longing do my gazes wander,
> To the east so far away,
> By the sea that beckons yonder,
> Homeward would I make my way.
>
> See this sun its rays bestowing,
> Beats on me so strongly down,
> All these palms and meadows glowing,
> Now for me no charm do own.
> Now my heart longs for the courtyards,
> Where the Danube dwellers stray,
> To the land of golden vineyards,
> Homeward would I make my way.
>
> There where every flower is hiding,
> From its sweetness greetings brings,
> In the trees each bird abiding,
> In familiar accents sings.
> That is where all things are lovely,
> Even sorrow and dismay,
> There will fortune smile upon me,
> Homeward when I make my way.

A. Spannkraft,
Campeche, 17 July 1865

A second poem addressed to his sweetheart, who lives here, was written by Spannkraft two days before his death, when he was already seriously ill with yellow fever. The paper was found under his pillow and I copied it as well.

To Carmen

Willst come to me once more, my dearest,
With thy angel's face so bright,
Call me still thine own, with fairest
Eyes to shed their heavenly light.

Deep with love my heart is stricken
Love begetting sweetest pain,
From this wound t'will ever sicken,
Never can be whole again.

But willst thou, thy love bestowing,
Grant my prayer, O sweetest maid,
Then my tears shall cease their flowing,
All my longing be allayed.

If spring flowers I may not gather,
Then for ever let me be,
If breath fails me, seek another,
Brighter star to shine on thee.

Tolls the bell for me tomorrow.,
Dearest, do its message take,
For it tells with sounds of sorrow
That a loving heart did break.

How sad we all are about the poor boy I need not say; among the others who died, too, there were several who on account of their abilities, their character and their good behaviour were highly esteemed by us.

The rainy season starts here at the end of May or the beginning of June and lasts until the middle or even the end of September. All the dangerous illnesses of this country develop in this period, during which the air is filled with the harmful vapours and miasmas rising from the earth. Although a torrential downpour occurs every day with almost unfailing regularity between three and seven o'clock in the afternoon, flooding all streets, alleys and paths, the earth is still so desiccated from the dry months that in most places a few hours' sunshine causes the water to evaporate again. On the other hand regular pools are formed, the emanations from which cannot be very conducive to health. There are innumerable mosquitoes and just now at half past three in the morning, during a sleepless night, I am getting a frightful visitation from them. The other insects, too, multiply enormously during this period: interesting at night are the thousands of fireflies, which fly around everywhere. But they are smaller than those in Veracruz.

We officers are reasonably well off here in Lerma; we are lodged tolerably and eat as usual. We receive frequent visits – unfortunately almost always terribly boring for us – from townspeople, who descend on the house already at six o'clock in the morning and only leave us at five in the afternoon; apart from the fact that our wine and other provisions suffer severely as a result, we are embarrassed by this and, with a few exceptions, not greatly enchanted by such attentions.

I have hired a horse for the duration of our stay here and ride almost every evening to the town, eat my ice, make visits or go to the theatre and then quietly return home. The good citizens of Campeche cannot grasp this and insist on assuming that some other reason, some love affair, in other words, motivates these rides of an officer. Were the people of Campeche able to read in my heart or my diary they would be convinced that this is not the case. Mr Arigunaga, whose wife is a Gutiérrez daughter, seems to be particularly disturbd about this, for he asks all the time whom I am courting and to whom I am going, although he knows very well that I chiefly frequent the family of his mother-in-law. It seems to me that he would not be very enchanted to get me as a brother-in-law.

On 29 July Ernst wrote to his mother:

Yesterday I received your letter no. 12 of 6 June with the greatest joy. At the same time it caused me great disquiet, for in the first place my letters seem to reach you much more uncertainly than yours to me, as I have had all of these so far; and secondly, it seems, as you are so concerned for my life, that terrible things are being given currency among you people in Vienna about conditions here. For your consolation I can assure you that all this is not true and although the new empire may not appear fully consolidated, even to the greatest optimist, conditions have without question already improved substantially in the short time of our presence (I do not say because of our presence). In our corps there are a multitude of decayed universal geniuses, former officers who were once respectable but now completely deteriorated individuals, who came here with high hopes and on their way encountered little money, but instead many hardships and bullets. All these people feel disappointed and write letters of lamentation home, which in turn circulate everywhere and finally, smartened by the pen of some journalist or other, appear in some Viennese newspaper for the illumination of Mexican conditions. These are the general sources of horror stories which at present circulate in Austria about this poor country . . .

It seems to me that I am the only one who continually has, even if fortunately not the yellow, still the cold alternating fever, which I already mentioned to you in my last letter. In fact it left me alone for the last eight days and I was beginning to think that I had recovered when I again had a severe attack yesterday. The illness is not dangerous, it is true, but it is associated with a very stubborn stomach catarrh, which on the days of the feverish attack induces such continual and violent vomiting, that one is enormously weakened by this. I have already applied to be transferred to a detachment of our corps stationed in the interior of Mexico, as our doctor considers a change of air to be necessary. The good thing about my sickness is the assertion of the doctors that sufferers from the cold fever do not get the yellow fever and this consolation compensates me for the disagreeable hours, which my condition causes me . . .

Yesterday evening quite suddenly we saw many of the dangerous animals of the country, though in a harmless state. The fishermen caught an enormous shark, which they left for some time on show on the shore for the amusement of the public; and our soldiers caught a cobra and a rattlesnake, which they killed and brought to us. In addition we also trod on a few scorpions; of these, as of snakes, there are masses here, which does not exactly constitute one of the country's attractions . . .

In Campeche one even gets fruit ice, of course produced artificially with the ice machine, but nevertheless cold and refreshing: This is what has the most attraction for me in Campeche, whereas the good citizens of the town are determined, quite erroneously, to find the explanation of my rides there in some passionate love affair.

Ernst wrote in his diary:

On the 29th I had a particularly severe attack of fever, which almost made me fear that I had contracted yellow fever. The same symptoms, violent head and back pains. Nevertheless by yesterday, the 31st, I was able to ride to Campeche again and visit Gutiérrez.

Yesterday, too, the last volunteer who had been ill with yellow fever, Ziska, died in the hospital at Campeche. The poor devil had already got over the yellow fever and perished from its consequences, several open wounds turning gangrenous. He was also a very decent man.

Today, the 1st, the male nurse Jagun Hanisch, who until then had behaved with exemplary courage in defiance of all dangers, also went to the hospital in Campeche stricken with yellow fever, after he had tirelessly nursed all our sick people day and night up to Ziska's death and only reported to the company yesterday after the hospital became empty. Let us hope that he will get well.

Until yesterday we have had to record one man murdered in the month of May, two men fallen before the enemy in June, and thirteen men dead from yellow fever in July – that is sixteen men lost since our arrival here in Campeche, exactly ten per cent.

This evening the doctor brought us from the town a letter from Perote. Major Bernard writes to Hedemann fully about events in the corps of which we were still unaware and about the commencement of hostilities against the Liberals under Ortega in the Sierra de Zacapo-axtla. Right at the end, before the termination of the letter, Bernard seems to have received the sad news of the fate of our second Ulan squadron, which probably fell into an ambush and was partly broken up and partly taken prisoner. Captain Count Kurzrock* fell then. Captain Count Sternberg was captured and First-Lieutenant Sega wounded. Fortunately victories were won in other places and Captain Sala captured a position of the enemy.

Today, 2 August, I am celebrating a very boring birthday, which I am marking for myself simply and solitarily – though also somewhat arbitrarily as head of our household – with a somewhat choicer breakfast. At table I remembered my good mother, who is no doubt often thinking of me in the same way today, and Captain Hedemann proposed a toast to her health, in which we all happily joined.

Ernst wrote in his diary:

10 August, at sea off Veracruz

On Friday the 4th I was in the theatre in Campeche when I met Dr Campos after the first act, who told me that he had just been sent for to Lerma, where our doctor, Dr Neubert, First-Lieutenant Schmidt and a few men had recently been stricken by yellow fever. As I had left Lerma only two hours before I was doubly alarmed to hear this and went home immediately. Hedemann and Bideskuty were still up and confirmed the matter to me. Hedemann immediately gave me the order to go to Puebla as courier and to organize the transfer of the company from the *Tierra caliente*† to the highlands. He said he was counting on my gift of the gab, which, however, was further strengthened by the fact that on the 4th six men and on the 5th five more went down with yellow fever and the company would perish if no remedy were found.

At midday on the 5th I embarked on the miserable ship *Strigg Hercules*. Even after four days we cannot enter Veracruz because of

* Count Karl Kurzrock-Wellingsbüttel, murdered in cold blood after being taken prisoner.
† The torrid region.

the calm, but have had to swan around outside the harbour. I am terribly bored, quite without anyone to converse with; the captain is a negro, the company a hundred pigs which are to be sold in Veracruz for the Ferrer concern, and in the meantime are making an awful lot of noise. There are masses of sharks here and I shot at two of them today. When the wind drops they become so familiar that they come right up to the ship's side and the surface of the water. Our bosun also cleverly harpoons a number of other fish.

Rest and Recuperation

On 23 August Ernst wrote to his mother from Mexico City:

I can begin these lines to you today with confidence, for I know that with them I shall be relieving you of great anxiety on my account. Although I only indicated in my last letter that the state of health of our company in Campeche left something to be desired, you will not have been pleased by this. Unfortunately it was in reality far worse. In a few days many of our people died and when on August another two officers and fifteen men of the company suddenly went down with yellow fever I was ordered to go to Mexico [City] as a courier to convey the critical state of our people. Although pretty debilitated by the cold fever, I was nevertheless glad to get away from Campeche and I covered the trifle of 380 leguas or 280 German miles, which is the distance from there to the capital, in twelve days, of which I spent seven at sea. On land I used the stage-coach and no one in the world can imagine what a journey between Veracruz and Mexico in these excruciating vehicles in the rainy season can signify. One is continually thrown about, getting stuck in mud, having to get out and walk. And always with a revolver in hand, for the stage-coaches are now robbed more often than ever, though usually only when carrying peaceable travellers, who are not determined to defend themselves. I would much rather travel four weeks on our railway than three days in such stage-coaches. In front of the coaches, in which nine people are seated, up to eighteen or twenty mules are harnessed (the same number of horses would be no use, as they draw much less well and tire more easily).

On passing through Puebla, where I arrived at ten o'clock at night and left again at four o'clock the next morning, I learnt that I had been decorated with the Order of Guadelupe* for the affair in Jonuta. Late

* The order of Guadelupe was founded by Agustín de Iturbide, who won independence from Spain in 1821, and revived by Maximilian.

at night the order and diploma were brought to me at the inn. On arriving in Mexico on the morning of the 17th I carried out my mission and the company was immediately recalled by telegram – that is to say a French steamer was ordered telegraphically to proceed from Veracruz to Campeche to get the company. It will be temporarily stationed in Orizaba. I took four weeks' leave so as to see something of Mexico.

Ernst wrote in his diary:

The journey was very pleasant as far as the company was concerned, for it so happened that Naval Lieutenant Greaves, Midshipman Salvini, Commissioners Lochner, Eloin, Ressegnier – all old acquaintances – were also travelling. The route, on the other hand, was appalling and indescribable. Mud three feet deep, having to get out continually and always the revolver ready.

In Mexico Herr and Frau von Kuhacsevich were very friendly to me. I took food with them very often, but had to abstain from all other social gatherings because of my very shabby clothes, which were all I had with me, and I only visited our own and the Italian minister. Otherwise I was pretty well, except for the first days after my arrival, when I got the fever again. But as far as morale was concerned I suffered considerable depression, for my continued ill luck at cards pursued me there too and I lost a not inconsiderable sum.

On 30 August I learnt from the newspapers of the death of my poor friends Neubert and Schmidt, as well as of many decent people of my company. Two of the leading riflemen, namely Randhartinger and Pesch, and then also the good Zeilner, are dead and fifty-eight men of the company succumbed within a few days to that terrible illness, from which heaven had this time mercifully preserved me. I am very much saddened and distressed by this, for I was very fond of the company and we lost our best people. A few pages earlier, as we still sat undiminished in Campeche, I described the characters of our five-leaved clover* and today we are reduced to two, for poor Bideskuty, too, is no longer with the company, but is in Puebla at the prefect's, awaiting his fate because of the affair with Lankitsch.† I can say with a clear conscience that I have neglected nothing to present the whole matter as favourably as possible for Bideskuty in every way.

Ernst wrote to his mother:

* The 'quintet' of Ernst's brother officers – pp. 70–73 above.
† See above p. 67.

The town [Mexico City] is very attractive and I would say it had the quality of a great city if the ill-paved streets and certain other things did not strike the eye unpleasantly. My fever is unfortunately not yet quite mended and although it did not appear at all on the way here from Campeche I have already had it here very severely several times, but am at present well again . . .

I have already been to the Kuhacsevichs' several times. She and he are extremely kind to me and it is very pleasant for me to have found such agreeable company here. A further benefit arises for me through their repeated invitations to meals, whereby I am saved the horrendously expensive inns. My lodgings costs nothing, as I have gone to stay with a good friend, Captain Fünfkirchen . . .

The emperor left this morning for eight to ten days, escorted by a squadron of hussars. The corps under General Thun is still sitting in the Sierra Negra without making contact with the enemy, who wisely remain hidden in the mountains. On the other hand, the whole of the rest of the country is laid bare and our single detachments are attacked and eliminated. This is what happened to poor Count Kurzrock.

Ernst wrote again to his mother from Mexico on 3 September:

My poor brave company, whose recall here from Yucatán I brought about, has been for a few days in Orizaba, where I too am to report after the end of my leave . . .

The company will now be left quietly in its garrison station for an extended period of rest and recuperation, about which I too am not in the least displeased. As you know, I am here without my luggage and without a servant and since in consequence I do not have my better uniforms with me I cannot attend very many social occasions, as one cannot set aside the customary conventions everywhere. Regardless of that, I have had myself introduced to the Italian minister here, who keeps a very pleasant establishment, which I frequent from time to time. The Austrian Minister, Count Thun, also invited me to a meal once and if I have nothing else in view I visit the Italian opera. In a word, one could exist if life were not just rather too dear. I dine at the Kuhacsevichs' every other day and this always saves me considerable expense.

A few days ago we had a remarkable spectacle. Because of the fact that Mexico lies in a valley and has very deficient drainage, the continuing rain had caused a flooding of the town such as had not been seen for years. It was like in Venice, but unfortunately the gondolas were lacking and, as the streets stood three feet under water, one had to wade around with water over one's belly. As I only have one pair of boots here this experience did not do my cold fever an exceptional amount of good. But although I ran around with wet feet for three days, I nevertheless remained quite well. All shops, coffee houses etc. stood at least two feet under water and the damage was considerable. Now everything is all right again, as it has fortunately not rained for the last three days.

Ernst wrote again to his mother from Orizaba on 21 September:

For a few days I have been in Orizaba again, the place in which I spent the first six weeks of my stay in Mexico. This town was specially chosen as the station for my poor company to enable it to recuperate in this healthy and splendid climate after the recent terrible times. I cannot describe to you the sadly joyful feeling it gives me to see again my friend Captain Hedemann and the men on my arrival here. But nearly all the people whom I knew particularly well and who were particularly prized by me on account of their helpfulness and good qualities are not here. Apart from Captain Chief Doctor Dr Neubert and First-Lieutenant Schmidt, all three leading riflemen and a further fifty-five men – that is sixty people in all – succumbed to yellow fever in a few days. It was only here that I learnt the names of all the dead and you cannot imagine how sad it made me to hear that almost half the company had fallen victim to that disease. I have all the more cause to be pleased with fate, which so graciously let me slip through this time, and, that said, as a good soldier I must also strike the whole sad episode from my memory.

It was only after I had left Mexico on the 8th that I began to see all the ravages that the downpour of rain, which I mentioned to you in my last letter, had wrought. Immediately on arriving outside the town barrier we had to leave the stage-coach and exchange the vehicle for a ship for a distance of two hours since the road between the lakes of Tezcoco and Chalco was completely flooded by the rising waters of the two lakes. Later we again got into another vehicle waiting for us on the other side of the water, but had to get out countless times as the mud was more than three feet deep and the carriage repeatedly got stuck in it. On the 9th I arrived in Puebla and remained there – detained by various private and duty matters – until the morning of the 14th, on which day I left again and reached Orizaba the same night.

A money shipment of 20,000 pesos in gold, which I had to take to Orizaba, provided me with the convenience of a continual escort of our hussars and preserved me from an encounter, which I did not at all desire, with the highwaymen, who are now more numerous than ever and, particularly between here and Veracruz, plunder the stage-coach almost every other day.

According to various rumours, my company is to be transferred to Mexico in the near future. I would be very pleasantly inclined to this, for although materially I lack nothing in Orizaba, I am nevertheless very bored, whereas in the capital, after all, one has various amusements.

Of political conditions in the country you will not learn much from me. On principle I write nothing about this, for no mortal can see clearly through this chaos and it would be over-hasty to prophesy where, for the present, not a soul can form a judgement. One always has to answer like an oracle here. It is possible that the whole business will succeed, but it could also go to pieces in a surprisingly short time through unforeseen events. But in any case the consolidation of the empire will require a long time, many wise heads, much money, much endurance and patience and very many soldiers. This is my opinion about Mexico, which, however, I only put on paper for you, since I am not anxious to get into controversy over the situation, as has already happened to some here, who conveyed their certainly exaggeratedly pessimistic views to Europe in too public a manner.

As indeed I told you before, I lack nothing in Orizaba. I have a very nice riding horse again, and my fever has left me; in a word I want nothing but company, that is female company, which in this country and particularly in Orizaba one has to renounce completely.

I do not think that we in Orizaba are likely to be troubled by the enemy for the time being, for although a Liberal detachment of 1,500 men is roving around in closest proximity, they do not yet dare to enter, while we do not have the order to take the offensive.

During my stay in Mexico I let fall a few gentle hints to Kuhacsevich about how much I would like to have some employment at court, since the conversation had happened to turn to the circumstance that it was felt that the empress really badly needed a private secretary. Although Kuhacsevich promised that he would remember me should occasion arise, I am not counting a great deal on the fulfilment of this not very modest aspiration. In November, it is said, Their Majesties will make an extended journey to Yucatán. By then the yellow fever season there will be over. Should I still be here then I will see the whole party on their way through . . .

Today, the 23rd, three sections of my company with Captain von Hedemann have again set out on an expedition to a locality twelve leguas distant, which has declared for the Republic. Such things happen here every day and are usually resolved quite peacefully by the installation of new village chiefs, the arrest or shooting of a few people and the demolition of one or two houses whose occupants have gone over to the enemy. This time I have stayed behind, which I do not at all regret, since one cannot get much peace on such enterprises, but rather faces a lot of sweat and the prospect of bearing responsibility.

Ernst continued his diary:

On the last day [in Puebla] I acted as second to First-Lieutenant von Csismadia at a duel with pistols which he fought with a Mexican colonel war prisoner, with whose wife he is supposed to have entertained somewhat too close relations. Both duellists behaved brilliantly and it was one of the finest of such affairs. On reaching the barrier, ten paces wide, each left the other to fire the first shot, almost certainly lethal, from our excellent Kuchenreiter pistols. The seconds thereupon made a proposal for an accommodation, which was not accepted, and we then agreed that on the signal 'Fire!' each of them should fire simultaneously. The Mexican's bullet went very close past Csismadia's chest and he then fired into the air. A stone fell from my heart.

At two o'clock on the morning of the 14th I left Puebla and reached Orizaba at midnight on the same day. Here I found my dear friend Hedemann and the poor, brave 2nd Company and as a result I feel decidedly better.

The amusements which one encounters in Orizaba are of course not very great and to be honest I am bored here beyond all measure. For the present I am not yet visiting any private house and as, moreover, we are only very few officers here, all living alone, by half past eight in the evening I cannot think of anything to do but go to bed. Fortunately the circus is coming in a few days and things should then become more amusing. I and Captain Latinovicz of the hussars are together a good deal, but the evening hours always lead him – he is of a somewhat amorous disposition – to one or other of his many loves. Fortunately our life is not as monotonous in every respect, for the Liberals roaming around in the very closest proximity keep us continually on the alert and I even believe that today or tomorrow they will pay us an unforeseen visit.

After some time the last days have fortunately again brought us news of successful engagements which our brave troops, although always numerically inferior, have conducted against the enemy. At several places Cavalry Captain Khevenhüller and Infantry Captain Miesel defeated the enemy with considerable losses. In the coming days we expect Bideskuty to return from his detention and then our company will increase a little.

For good measure, I will now mention my latest horse deals which,

I hope, are not unprofitable. In Puebla I bought a horse of Kurzrock's for 100 pesos and sold it the same day for 150 thaler; and here I have acquired from First-Lieutenant Codelli quite a good bay, which has only cost me 72 pesos and for which I have already been offered 120 thaler. But for the present I will wait before selling – perhaps I will get still more.

The accursed rainy season will still not end. It is already 27 September and every afternoon it pours torrentially. This hinders us a great deal in our recreational rides. In any case, one would be a little surprised in Europe to see us engaged in such rides. We are always armed with sword and revolver when we ride out of the town, for nothing is easier than to chance upon the enemy in the immediate neighbourhood at half an hour's riding distance and then it is a question of defending oneself as best one can. Nevertheless, I cannot deny that this continual insecurity and conscious proximity of danger has a stimulating effect on me and keeps my nerves, which would otherwise certainly go to sleep, in a state of agreeable tension. Were I a man in possession of respectable financial means and in a position to allow myself a comfortable existence in Europe, who knows if I might not have become the most cowardly blackguard. True, I would not avoid danger *per se*, but I would keep out of its way because I would be sorry to be no longer able to use my fine ducats for the benefit and well-being of my own carcass – should it please fate to let me hit the dust on such an occasion. And perhaps it would not be like that. Anyhow, I can never really imagine what sort of figure I would cut if, instead of a poor devil, I were a rich fellow. It seems to me that my otherwise rather lively imagination has only pursued the subject this far because it is written in the book of destiny that as long as I live I shall never achieve anything of the kind I desire. But I see that I am almost beginning to lament and argue, which I did not do at the beginning of this journal. Thank God, I only complain orally and have no need to commit to paper all my expressions of opinion on this subject.

Ernst wrote to his mother from Orizaba on 15 October:

Although I have as yet not received the hoped-for letter from you by the French mail-boat, I cannot nevertheless let the present day pass without telling you how unceasingly I think of you and how I wish you, dearest Mother, all the very best on your anniversary. It is moreover exactly a year today that I parted from you and left Vienna. Much has happened to me since that time, but fortunately I have no reason so far to regret the decision I took and the only really bitter thing about our situation in this country is the infinite barrier which separates us from the homeland and our loved ones. If God allows us life, I shall hope for an all the more happy reunion within a few years.

On the 1st of the month I marched out from here with 101 men, without having a second officer with me, with the order to clear the enemy from a place twelve to sixteen leguas distant named Huatusco. However, we got as far as Córdoba, where we learnt that the Liberals had already withdrawn from there. As it would therefore have been pointless to continue further – indeed sheer madness on roads devoid of firmness and unspeakable at the end of the rainy season – I telegraphed for further orders, which duly recalled me to Orizaba, which I reached on the 5th. The mud between Orizaba and Córdoba reaches in places to a pedestrian's armpits. Laden mules in large numbers get stuck in it and suffocate. On the route one sees at least twenty such dead animals. At times soldiers with packs had to be pulled out with ropes slung under their arms. My horse plunged several times and even once fell, burying his whole head in the mud, so that he could hardly draw breath. In a word, it is indescribable and no European can form the faintest idea of the state of our roads at this time of the year. In other respects, too, the monsoon season is very damaging. As all military operations are impeded, the guerrillas collect together everywhere in large numbers; at present they are positioned with several thousand men in close proximity to us and occupy the whole *Tierra caliente*. The war will now in any case assume very serious dimensions, for the infamous deeds of these robbers have forced the government to take energetic measures. On the 7th of this month four to five hundred of these scoundrels stopped the train on its way from Paso del Macho to Veracruz by lifting out the rails, shot the driver and several stokers, dragged all the passengers off into the mountains, where they sifted them according to nationalists and then released all of them except for the French, after they had been thoroughly robbed. But they shot the unfortunate French, seventeen in number, without regard as to whether they were military or civilian. However, according to an imperial decree* these people will from now on no longer be treated as dissidents, but only as robbers and everyone who is captured with a weapon in his hand will be shot. Although they will of course take reprisals and those of our people who may be taken prisoner will face a sad fate, nevertheless all the world is in agreement with this measure, for firstly severity will have its effect and secondly from now all our soldiers will sell their lives that much more dearly. In a month the roads may again begin to be passable and then operations on our side will also probably begin.

* See p. 57 above.

18 October

. . . Although Yucatán is remote from the world and during the monsoon, because of the yellow fever, is also not one of the most agreeable stations, you nevertheless judge it too severely, for, strictly speaking, one is still better off there than here; the people are at least more honest and they really treated us with every consideration. Now that I have been in the interior for several months I would not at all mind wandering down there again for a bit . . .

That our little expeditions are so widely reported in the Austrian newspapers pleases me particularly on your account, as in this way you also receive news of me indirectly. The passage about my behaviour in the engagement at Jonuta, of which you tell me in your letter, is taken word for word from Captain Hedemann's report of the engagement and he and I were very amused today to be able to observe this.

You also wish to be enlightened about the nature of my nourishment. I can give you the most reassuring information in this matter and for this purpose I will give you the menu of yesterday's dinner, which Lieutenant-Colonel Schaffer gave us in recognition of our courtesy to him during his stay here:

Soup
Oyster pâté
Beef with peas and mushrooms
Goose liver pâté
Château Margaux cutlets
Chicken ragoût
Turkey filled with truffles
Roast venison with salad and stewed fruit
Leg of mutton
Cake
Cheese
Tropical and European fruits
Sweets and confectionery
Black coffee
Sherry, burgundy, Rhine wine, champagne and chartreuse with the coffee

Now although our everyday dinners are not quite so lucullan, we nevertheless still eat very well and only as regards drink do we have to restrict ourselves: since the food alone costs about 70 florins a month on a subscription basis – without subscriptions as much as double that – one cannot possibly spend much more. But in the conditions existing here one peso for lunch and dinner is not at all expensive and in Austria, too, I do not believe that one could get the same for less then

2–2½ florins. All the officers of the garrison take their meals together and so we also have the amenity of constant company.

20 October

I am closing my letter today, as the mail for Europe is leaving. Since yesterday we have been on increased alert here, because were are in hourly preparedness for an attack by the united bands of dissidents from the *Tierra caliente*. But our numbers here are fairly substantial – we have some 700 men in the town, while the enemy has at the most 2,000 badly armed men, so there is really nothing to fear and one therefore only has to guard against a surprise attack.

Ernst wrote in his diary:

At present we have the Chiarini circus here, which of course we visit without exception. The company is very good and in the figure of a certain Palmira Holbossy possesses a very nice young person, who pleases us all, but particularly our friend Hedemann, very much.

Anyhow more life has developed here for the time being, since the Babarsys squadron arrived here on the 7th with four officers and Lieutenant-Colonel Schaffer is also here on account of his marriage to Miss Bringas and spends a lot of time with us. Furthermore, Captain Hobza builds barricades on all sides and appears to see ghosts everywhere. The whole world, down to the local press, laughs at this and we officers the most. For the last few days all the officers have been assembled in the Hotel Diligence for meals. Our example seems to have worked, but unfortunately we the regular customers derive small profits from it, for we have even acquired the not very popular Hobza at our table and the unfortunate man spoilt our appetite more than once with various *costumbres del país*,* which he has already adopted and performs here.

The Chiarini circus, which has been here for eight days, certainly gives us the opportunity every day of killing the evening, but this amusement costs 16 pesos a time. The company is very satisfying. A game of Preference with Lieutenant-Colonels Schaffer, Babarzy, Latinovicz and Kalumsky has also been costing me enormous sums for several days, which because of several unfortunate 'misères'† I always have to pay in the end. But for that let us hope that my enormous good fortune in love will sufficiently compensate me.

2 November

The last month passed without particular incidents for me . . . It is true

---

* Customs of the country.
† Poor cards.

that we expected an attack every day and passed our nights in a state of preparedness, but nevertheless did not come to firing a shot. On the 25th I took part as a volunteer in a double march of our 20th Hussar squadron from here to Canada. We hoped in vain to come across the enemy and came back here again on the 28th with half the Hipp battery, which we found in Canada . . .

Their Majesties are expected here in the next few days.

Today, All Souls Day, the whole of Orizaba, otherwise dead, was on its feet in order to promenade towards a small church nearby. We also watched the commotion, but at the same time were well armed, as of late one has to be careful. Only a week ago a soldier from my company was murdered in the middle of the town at half past eight in the evening, as he was walking home. Recently, too, travel has begun to be no longer among the particular pleasures. The stage-coach which left Veracruz yesterday for the interior was attacked at Potrero, one of the travellers was murdered, his wife and a second traveller wounded and all the baggage was completely plundered as well.

At last the affair of poor Bideskuty is also ended, but regrettably we are losing this good officer from the corps, as he is being transferred to the Mexican army, about which he is said to be in despair – and rightly so.

Ernst wrote to his mother from Orizaba on 16 November:

When I posted my last letter to you, Orizaba was in a state of considerable excitement, as the bands of dissidents, relying on the inaccessibility of the terrain they occupy and emboldened by the delays to the combined operations of the imperial troops brought about every year by the monsoon, had ventured right into the immediate vicinity of the town. Although of course it would have been madness for them to attack it, and this was not at all their intention, the psychological effect of these demonstrations on the ill-disposed and timorous section of the population was sufficiently noticeable for us to initiate a calming of spirits on the one hand and a suppression of all sanguine hopes of the adversary on the other by increased vigilance, permanent night patrols etc. And indeed the leader of the hostile bands, named Figueroa, had also disappeared from our neighbourhood one fine day with his whole troop, but only to fall into the arms of retribution all the sooner. On the 25th of this month the whole enemy column turned from here against Tehuacan, a small town of 2,000–3,000 inhabitants with an Austrian garrison of 300 men. About two months previously the same Figueroa had succeeded in forcing his way into the place, which was then held by forty Austrian riflemen, in capturing the garrison and in exacting 110,000 pesos from the population. Presumably he was hoping for a similar prize on this occasion. Eighty of our hussars and forty Ulans, the former under the command of Captain Count Khevenhüller, the latter led by Captain Bythel – so only 120 cavalrymen all told – attacked the 900-strong enemy in the *barranca* near Ajalpan, killed more than 200 and dispersed the whole band in all directions. Many prisoners, Figueroa's flag and private correspondence, masses of weapons, fifty horses, thirty mules, were the reward and the result of this fine day. Sadly we have to mourn the death of First-Lieutenant Ritter von Kavetsky, furthermore one hussar. Three more of our officers and five to six men were wounded: it is almost unbelievable how slight our losses are compared to those of the enemy. This disparity of numbers can only be explained if, firstly, one considers the force of a cavalry charge and, secondly, if one knows the behaviour of the enemy who, once he has been thrown into disarray, only seeks salvation in flight and allows himself to be struck down by the pursuer without resistance.

The squadron of hussars which is stationed here left on the day of the engagement in order to fetch one of our batteries in Canada, halfway between here and Puebla, and escort it here. In the hope of thus chancing upon the enemy and taking part for once in a cavalry attack I joined the squadron as a volunteer. But on the way we learnt of Khevenhüller's successful action, the destruction of the enemy and consequently of the unlikelihood of ourselves being attacked. Although we were disagreeably disappointed by this, we could not restrain our pleasure over the brilliant success of our comrades and we sent a messenger from Canada to nearby Tehuacan in order to be informed of what had happened by Khevenhüller himself. The hundred and thirty-one enemy were buried on the battlefield by the hands of our hussars alone – and the others, who had been dispersed and succumbed to their wounds, were recovered later; so not one man more than those who actually fell has been shown and the habitually doubting Europeans should know that the famous story about the dead Russian is not applicable to us.*

The same squadron of hussars, under the command of the excellent Khevenhüller, fought an equally brilliant action about a month ago and, although the latter is perhaps not calculated in its consequences to bring about a particular turn in the whole campaign, it is nevertheless perhaps the outstanding occurrence of the whole expedition. On the same day First-Lieutenant Kalumsky of the squadron stationed here in Orizaba had the remarkable luck, with fifty of his men, to attack the

* I have not been able to trace this story.

murderer of those French people who perished in the attack on the railway train of which I told you in my last letter, to defeat his far superior force and to kill him himself.

Finally, to conclude my news from the theatre of war, the army corps of the enemy general, Arteaga, was completely destroyed and Divisional Generals Arteaga and Salazar, fifty colonels, many staff and senior officers and finally 400 men were made prisoner and a great amount of booty taken. All the prisoners were shot, which is truly fortunate.* All these events have made Orizaba again the most peaceful city of the world and were it not for the fact that recently, on the 28th of this month, one of our soldiers was murdered in the open street at half past eight in the evening, one could really believe that one had been transported to an idyllic little German provincial town.

The day after tomorrow the empress will arrive, to go alone from here and tour Yucatán. The emperor is either staying in Mexico on account of state affairs or is taking the route via Jalapa and will join his wife in Veracruz.

I learnt from Wilkowski† that all our successes here quickly became known, especially in military circles, as *Kamerad*‡ is always kept informed of such matters by the volunteer corps command.

Ernst wrote to his mother from Matamoros on 28 November:

As I told you earlier [in his last letter], we were awaiting the visit of the empress, who arrived in Orizaba on the 11th and stayed there for two days before leaving for Yucatán. During her stay I was twice a guest at her table, the first time as orderly officer and then as officer of the guard. She immediately recognized me, was very pleasant and enquired particularly after Marie – her little child, as they say – and whether all were well. When I replied in the affirmative she said to me, 'I was very fond of your sister and would have been glad to take her with me. But I recognize that she must feel much happier as she is and that she was right to stay behind.'

The empress undertook various excursions by carriage or on horseback into the surrounding country. We officers of the garrison always accompanied Her Majesty at her side on horseback.

Generally the reception on the part of the inhabitants left much to be desired and the mob exhibited a shocking indifference.

---

* A shocking statement, which however has to be seen in the context of the extreme brutality of the war, Maximilian's decree of 3 October 1865 (see above, p. 57) and the standards of the age.
† A friend in Austria.
‡ Austrian army journal.

On the 12th the empress left for Córdoba and Veracruz. In the former place the reception was very much better and in Veracruz even outstanding. Yucatán will, I believe, far surpass Veracruz and the empress's disagreeable memory of Orizaba could again be erased thereby. The noble lady had to make the journey to Paso del Macho almost entirely on horseback, as the heavy travelling coaches continually got stuck in the mud. At one place on the route forty mules were harnessed in front of the empress's carriage and only after two hours' work could it be extricated from the pool of mud. You can judge from this what obstacles have to be overcome when travelling in this country.

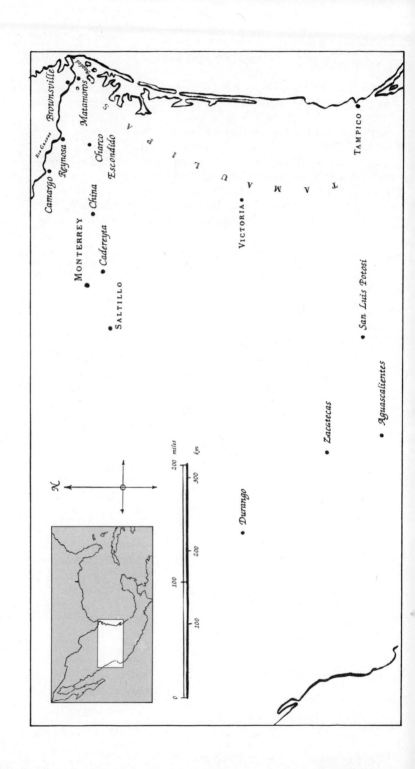

Mission to the North

Already in the last months of 1865 a noticeable deterioration in the general situation had become evident. Louis Napoleon had always counted on a victory of the Confederates in the American Civil War – or at least on the continued weakness of the United States through internal strife – to bolster his Mexican adventure. The victory of the North in April 1865 put paid to these hopes and marked the beginning of a period of increasing United States support, both political and material, for the Juárez government. Threatened also by looming perils nearer home and by French public opinion, which was becoming increasingly critical of the war, Louis Napoleon, contrary to his contractual undertakings, informed Maximilian late in the year that the French army was to be withdrawn. Meanwhile the French commander, Bazaine, had already begun to evacuate previously held positions in different parts of the country.

It was at this very moment that the Austrians were asked by Bazaine to provide a contingent to reinforce the northern stronghold of Matamoros near the United States border. A French force had recently been there, but had been withdrawn because of swamp fever among the troops, Bazaine evidently preferring that the Austrians should undertake this uncomfortable commitment even though it meant dividing the corps, already so small in numbers. The imperial troops holding the city were under the command of General Tomás Mejía, a courageous and resourceful Indian officer profoundly loyal to Maximilian. Mejía had asked for cavalry reinforcements to give him the mobility to attack the Liberal forces under General Escobedo which, with increasing assistance in men and supplies from beyond the border, were dominating the entire region; this could have enabled Mejía to break the ascendancy of the Liberals and, by getting trade moving again, to raise the revenue needed to pay his army. Bazaine, however, turned down this request, with the result that the force in Matamoros was committed to the defensive role of protecting the city against Liberal attack, but without the strength to engage in offensive operations against the enemy in the surrounding countryside. The only purpose of holding on to this outpost was to demonstrate to the world – and particularly the United States – that the power of the empire extended to its northern border, for the deployment could bring no military benefit in terms of combating and reducing the Liberal presence in the area.

The Austrian contingent sent to Matamoros consisted of two rifle companies of 280 men with eight officers, two mountain batteries complete with crews and two officers, and one doctor. The commander was Lieutenant-Colonel Kodolitsch, who had been detached from the staff for this purpose.

Meanwhile American pressure across the frontier in support of the Liberals was increasing. Infiltrations of various kinds multiplied. Recruitment for Juárez's forces was stepped up and hand-bills circulated on the Mexican side offered generous inducements to residents as well as members of the imperial army to volunteer. This led to a number of desertions from the Austrian force.

Further evidence of American designs manifested itself when a force of irregulars crossed the Rio Bravo del Norte river and occupied the town of Bagdad at the mouth of the river early in January 1866. A reconnaissance party from an Austrian gunboat was attacked, one man being killed and two taken prisoner. The attackers rampaged through the town, causing widespread destruction, and on their withdrawal the Liberals took over, being joined for a time by regular American troops. The two Austrian prisoners were taken to Brownsville, but after resisting strenuous pressure to volunteer for service under Juárez, were handed over to Kodolitsch. The Liberals, however, were unable to hold Bagdad, which was soon reoccupied by the Austrians.

Ernst's letter to his mother continued:

On the afternoon of the 12th a telegram from Mexico arrived in Orizaba ordering the immediate departure of the whole disposable garrison there to Matamoros. The dissidents had encircled that town, which lies on the furthest North American frontier and at the mouth of the Río Bravo del Norte, and rapid reinforcement had become necessary. Early on the morning of the 13th the column was already on the march.

Ernst noted in his diary:

On the evening of the same day we received marching orders to proceed to Matamoros. For this purpose the 15th Company, which had just arrived in Orizaba, was disbanded to provide reinforcement for the 2nd and 5th and I lost the command of the 2nd Company I had held for two days, which was taken over by Captain Ludovici. I should mention that I am now the only remnant of that formerly excellent company. My friend Hedemann has become assistant chief of staff at corps headquarters and as a result of the addition of so many unknown people the rank and file is no longer the same in its composition as it used to be . . .

In Paso del Macho Lieutenant-Colonel Kodolitsch arrived to take over command.

Ernst continued the letter to his mother:

On the same day I was also promoted to First-Lieutenant and this pleased me considerably, as I was already finding my previous commission somewhat tedious.

In Córdoba we again met the empress, who had stopped there for one day. The place was teeming with troops, who were to clear the road between there and Paso del Macho of guerrillas. On the 16th we reached Veracruz and immediately embarked in the French transport *Allier*, which after three days' sailing, during which we had rather stormy weather, brought us to Bagdad. This place lies close to the mouth of the Río Bravo in the Gulf of Mexico and is only in process of coming into existence. Although on Mexican soil, the town is nevertheless almost completely American and furthermore is inhabited by foreigners of all nations. The houses are all transportable and built on piles. Whenever there is a north wind all the streets are transformed into canals, like Venice, and nowhere are so many rats to be found as there.

Ernst adds in his diary:

The place built there is called Bagdad and has the true character of the towns brought into being – often in a fabulously short time – by our present neighbours, the Yankees. Everything of wood, everything provisional, everything practical, everything contrived for profit, nothing for solidity; no consideration whatever for health, cleanliness etc. and a medley of people from all over the world, but particularly Americans, Spaniards, Italians, French, Germans, Greeks and, really least of all, Mexicans.

Ernst continued in his letter:

After stopping for twenty-four hours, we proceeded to Matamoros, which lies some sixty English miles inland, on three raft-steamers, which looked like floating bungalows. The vessels were protected all round with bales of hay, sandbags etc. and armed with several guns, as we expected an attack during the journey. We had strict orders in no circumstances to fire at the United States side, whether we were attacked from over there or not. Also no kind of provocative language was to be used. With these directions we covered the whole distance without incident and arrived in Matamoros on the 23rd.

Ernst wrote in his diary:

We were very well received. There are very many of our German fellow-countrymen here, who welcomed us in the kindest way, and we are all very well situated – First-Lieutenant Kalmucky and I best of all, since we are superbly lodged and fed in the house of the Prussian consul of the firm of Dröge, Ötling & Company, and, in a word, are splendidly accommodated in all and every respect.

So far one dinner has succeeded another and I do not believe that in my whole life altogether I have enjoyed so much champagne, Rhine wine, claret and all sorts of delicacies as in the five weeks of my stay here.

A ball which we gave the town of Matamoros in return, together with the Mexican officer corps, cost us some 5,000 thaler. On the other hand the town gave the garrison here a banquet such as I never saw before in such a magnificent form: 3,000 elegantly served places at table in the open in the great square. Every man with his bottle of claret, masses of English beer and champagne, furthermore stewed fruit and roasts and pies and ham, in a word everything imaginable.

We at home can have no idea of the immense cost of such entertainments, but expensive as all things are here there is also an enormous amount of money in Matamoros, where there are people who during the war of the Union against the Southern states easily made hundreds of thousands of dollars in the cotton trade alone. At present, however, trade is pretty much at a low ebb, as all communication with Monterey is interrupted.

Although the dissidents are beaten back everywhere, we with our small numbers must nevertheless confine ourselves to holding the positions in the country with whose defence we have been charged and cannot engage in any pursuit of the enemy, who is at least equally strong, as otherwise we would lay the town bare to attack. Moreover, this is in any case almost impossible for the very reason that in view of the very suspicious and perfidious attitude of the northern states the enemy simply crosses the bank and is then on American soil where, reorganized and with new recruits, he is provided with munitions, weapons and money before the eyes of the American government. Altogether the closeness of the frontier and the ease with which the river can be crossed, in particular, provide us with much opportunity for serious reflection and hours of discomfort.

Six men of my company, either seduced by emissaries or suborned by the tempting assurance that they would make a lot of money, deserted to the other side in breach of their oath and without any other reason. On 24 December Lieutenant-Colonel Kodolitsch made a strong speech to the troops, drawing their attention to the shameful nature of the behaviour of their deserting comrades and at the same time reminding the company of the severe measures which had been taken to discourage desertion. In spite of this two more men absconded the same evening, but were overtaken by fate. One of them drowned in the river; the other was caught while swimming down it and on the following day, Christmas Day, was shot in accordance with regulations. Let us hope that this will not fail in its effect as a warning example.

We spent Christmas Eve in our house and had a splendid Christmas tree, which we decorated with various presents for our kind host.

Yesterday, the 27th, there was again a great dinner at Dr Schwesinger's; at the same time news is again received that the dissidents are beginning to move against Matamoros. We shall try to receive them as well as possible.

At the same time Ernst wrote to his mother from Matamoros:

We were extremely well received, as our arrival was very opportune. The town had recently been in a situation of severe danger and particularly the many Germans living here welcomed our appearance most warmly. We have so far been fêted in a way which I have not yet experienced either here or in Europe. I board and lodge permanently with the Prussian consul and enjoy an absurd degree of comfort. The most splendid thing is that excellent riding horses, carriages etc. are at my disposal at any hour. An abundant library in the German language was calculated to entertain us for a considerable time if the continual banquets which they give us and at which they practically drown us in champagne, Rhine wine, port and pale ale did not impede any further thought and action on our part . . .

Yesterday I was in the American town of Brownsville on the other side. It is a very odd sight over there. One meets people with all kinds of features, innumerable officers of the dissident army, Yankees and Confederates as well as representatives of all the peoples of Europe. Of course we had to appear in civilian dress over there as otherwise one could easily have been insulted in a most disagreeable manner and perhaps, as an imperial officer, could even have been beaten up by the Republican gentlemen. Altogether the relationship between the imperial Government and the northern states is extremely strained and the latter are trying in many ways to provoke a conflict. I am very interested to see the solution of this whole question. At present the outlook in this part of the country is not so happy, as the enemy is not only numerically strengthened by the accession of all sorts of riff-raff from the United States, but also receives weapons, provender and moral encouragement in abundance. As we are very weak, we must confine ourselves to the occupation of Matamoros and cannot hold all the less important places in the interior, of which the enemy naturally takes advantage and robs and steals assiduously. If at some time we were to march deeper into the interior towards Monterey, Durango and Chihuahua etc., it would be extremely interesting in one respect, but on the other hand I am very depressed at the prospect of then seeing our correspondence interrupted in such a way that one can hardly foresee when and where I am to receive news from you again. Of course it will always be less difficult for me to find a way of sending my letters, but how yours will reach me God only knows. Anyhow just continue to address your letters to Frau von Kuhacsevich. Let us hope that she has already heard that I am no longer in Orizaba. We left so suddenly that I hardly had time to write to tell her this . . .

I have just remembered, as I was at table, that on 1 December it was a year since I left Trieste and Europe and I can say with satisfaction that even though I have certainly at times been in difficult and sad situations, I do not for a moment regret having come here and if there is anything here that noticeably detracts from my contentment it is solely the consciousness of the great distance which separates me from you, dearest mother, and the difficulty of our correspondence.

Ernst wrote to his mother from Matamoros on 19 December:

Here in Matamoros we are much worse off as regards postal arrangements than in Yucatán. For there is no permanent communication at
all with Veracruz by sea and the mail is only carried by naval steamers
which happen to be sailing and that can often not be the case for two
months. On the other hand, there is no possibility whatsoever either
of travelling or of sending letters by land. Thus, for instance, Monterey
is some fifty miles away from here and in earlier times was in constant
communication with Matamoros, being the next town. Mail-carts and
stage-coaches travelled every day and brought news from one place to
the other in three days. Today we do not even know the result of an
engagement between imperials and dissidents which took place at
Monterey on the 23rd of last month and although nearly a month has
elapsed since then it is impossible to obtain official news of it.

Apart from these small inconveniences we enjoy a good life here.
There has still been no end to the banquets and feasts. One follows
another . . . A great ball on the 16th of this month . . . cost us some
10,000 florins altogether and tears a fair-sized hole of 50–60 florins in
the pocket of each one of us. Altogether one can hardly form an idea
in Europe of the ridiculous expense and the poor value of money in
this part of the country. Everyone here wants to get rich overnight and
no tradesman is satisfied with a moderate gain, but wants to make a
great profit immediately or would otherwise rather not start. Thus for
instance the decorator of the hall on the occasion of our last ball
presented such a horrifying bill that our hair could only stand on end.
For every sofa we paid 10 florins and for the chandelier, which was of
a very primitive kind, 100 piaster or 208 florins silver; and this only for
the hire of these objects for one night. The total bill of this scoundrel
amounts to 5,000 florins. The officers who are not as fortunate as I and
have to pay for their meals spend 108 florins monthly for breakfast and
dinner and yet eat pretty poorly for it.

Ernst wrote to his mother from Matamoros on 8 January 1866:

For several days we have been in constant battle readiness and we
spend the night with the troops, for the political horizon has clouded
over considerably and relations with the United states have taken a
rather serious turn. We here in Matamoros were of course the first to
be affected by this. Unfortunately for the time being no honest war
according to our European conceptions seems to want to develop and
the perfidious Yankees act in every possible way to unsettle the position
of the handful of imperial troops on their frontier.

In Bagdad we had a garrison of 180 Mexican troops. These were attacked from across the American bank on the night of 4–5 January and taken prisoner. For this purpose 600 men of the negro troops of the United States, in full uniform and led by their officers, crossed the river and after the attack (in which, moreover, treachery was presumably involved) had succeeded, began to plunder and massacre, in a way that perhaps commonly occurred at the time of the vandals, throughout the town. Having completed their work, the rabble returned to the other bank with their plunder and in their place so-called Liberals occupied the area in the name of the Republic. The licence to plunder and a payment of 15 thaler to every negro was the price at which these patriots allowed a town of their country to be captured.

Lying at anchor in the roads there is at present only one French paddlesteamer, which does not have enough crew to undertake a landing and therefore only tosses grenades and hollow shells into the town – a situation which is said to be particularly agreeable for the present occupants.

We here in Matamoros, with a strength of 1,700 men, of course cannot afford to be without a single soldier, as we have to hold this much more important place. The fortifications alone extend for two-thirds of a German mile; you can therefore imagine that there are not too many of us, if it is a question of keeping not only the real enemy, but also the troops of a power which is supposed to be neutral, away from such a tempting morsel as wealthy Matamoros. It is true that the American general named Weitzel, who is commander-in-chief of the troops in Texas, has expressed his regret over the events that have taken place and declared that they occurred without his knowledge and against his will, but no one any longer believes the excuses of this crafty and knavish scoundrel in a general's uniform. And this is altogether typical of the American officer – coarse, mean, devoid of honour and character, completely mercenary and only brave where there is something to steal.

Because of the events, as I have already said, we are constantly on the alert. Within a few days significant shipments of troops must arrive at the mouth of the river as a result of the occurrences which have been reported to Mexico and it is more than likely that in the meantime the rabble, encouraged by their success in Bagdad, will make another attempt on Matamoros, which, let us hope, will go badly for them.

When the attack on Bagdad took place one of our river steamers (which we had armed with two cannon and provided with a crew of fifty men from my company, with the captain and one lieutenant) happened also to be there. By chance I had remained in Matamoros with the other company. This steamer, which assures transport between here and the river mouth, was always a thorn in the dissidents' flesh, and the negro troops hired by them did everything possible to capture it. Although the assault on the town took place so quietly one knew nothing about it on the steamer two hours afterwards and the ship, with no steam up, lay close to the shore, a threefold charge was victoriously repulsed by our men and during this time they were able to get up steam and sail off. It was high time that they did so, for the negroes were firing their cannon from a distance of a few paces at the very thinly protected vessel, which might well not have been able to withstand it for long. On this occasion they employed a curious method in order to be able to fire on us without danger when only a few paces from our soldiers. They drew the cannon behind one of the wooden houses nearby, placed the barrel roughly in the direction of our ship and then shot through the wooden walls of the house – in doing so they were several times quite successful with their shots. Unfortunately we lost in this encounter a very nice young man from my company, Cadet Leading-Rifleman Seuchter, who received a rifle shot through the head, and also a French non-commissioned officer, who received an identical fatal shot.

Recording the same incident, Ernst continued in his diary:

The enemy is believed to have lost some twenty dead and wounded. Also two men of our company were cut off and taken prisoner.

Within a few days, however, we expect the arrival of the French warships and the short period of rejoicing will then have reached its end for the bandit gentlemen. But since the Rubicon has nevertheless been crossed in this way and the Americans have violated neutrality in such a blatant manner, nothing is more on the cards than a sudden attempt by them to seize the large and much wealthier town of Matamoros. This very general assumption has also brought it about that since that day we stand in constant battle readiness and that our duty is very arduous, particularly at night. All we officers sleep with the men, who for their part have been quartered in the new and spacious theatre. Everyone remains dressed, horses and mules stand saddled and the guns are in readiness. Our patrols go along the fortifications so as to keep the Mexican sentries, who are not otherwise very wide awake, on the alert. In addition, the rain god has once again sent us weather which transforms all the streets, paths and tracks into unbelievable seas of mud. To wade around in them for hours in the dark is also not particularly enjoyable.

Ernst continued in his letter to his mother:

> Altogether the corps has lost very many officers recently: the last
> victorious engagement at Tlapacoyan alone, in which that place was
> taken with the bayonet, has cost us seven officers of whom three died
> on the spot and four are seriously wounded. My poor friend First-
> Lieutenant Auersberg, one of our bravest and most brilliant officers –
> the same one with whom I spent my leave in Teschen two years ago –
> met a hero's death there, most deeply mourned by all the officers of
> the corps.
>
> But we console ourselves in this with the proverb 'on ne fait pas
> d'omelette sans casser des œufs'. For the rest, I am very well here and
> our main inconvenience is simply the infrequent arrival of letters from
> home.

Ernst wrote in his diary:

> We long for reinforcements, which surely were never more necessary
> than now. But unfortunately, although these were announced months
> ago, they have still failed to arrive. However, we hope that, if the
> Americans over there do not provide the dissidents with too many
> freebooters, we will finish the job ourselves.
>
> In Brownsville there is a special recruiting office against the imperial
> government. And in any case it is interesting to look at this place,
> separated from Matamoros only by a shallow river fifty paces wide,
> and to observe the different physiognomies. Apart from a mass of
> American military, the headquarters of the dissident leaders are also
> almost permanently there. From there they are provided with men,
> with money, with water and munitions, and also with intelligence.
> They wander around everywhere openly and ostentatiously, fraternize
> with the Yankees, regularly insult all those of imperial sympathies and
> people going there from Matamoros – in short, they behave more or
> less as if they were the lords of creation and threaten twenty times a
> day to make a meal of us here . . .
>
> 17 January 1866
> The day before yesterday it was one year since I arrived in Veracruz in
> the *Brasilian* and I can say with satisfaction that despite the many
> sneering prophecies about the life to be expected here – the inevitable
> depression, the longing for blessed Austria – which were made to me
> and to many of my comrades, these have not been fulfilled; and that in
> spite of hardships and privations occurring occasionally I would not
> only much rather be here, but would maintain that, from a material
> point of view, I live a far better and more carefree life. Nevertheless I

would be very happy to see my good mother and my dear Austria for a short time and even though it is only likely to remain a castle in the air, I would like to go to Europe for a few months in the spring of 1867. In forming this wish I am also motivated, in particular, by the not exactly flourishing social conditions in this country and the monotony of everyday life and terrible boredom generated thereby, which would drive one to despair if the conditions of war did not absorb one's most complete attention at every moment and introduce tension and excitement into the general apathy. So, for instance, we have been expecting an attack on the town every night for twelve days – we do not get out of our clothes, we build entrenchments and make patrols, and in this way we while away the time reasonably well.

At night, to pass the time, a little game of *chemin de fer* is often arranged, and in this I have once again had stunning bad luck. But it does not at all distress me in so far as, in consequence, I cannot possibly lack an abundance of fortune in love. Moreover, I have fortunately not inconvenienced myself particularly as a result; but I am sorry that a dearly held wish, namely, to make my mother and the little child of my sister Marie a present of 100 thaler each, cannot be fulfilled for the present.

Since today I have just finished bringing my diary up to date, I am taking this opportunity of appending the address of my mother, to whom, in the event of something human befalling me today or tomorrow, these lines as well as the proceeds of my other belongings are to be sent, together with my warmest kisses. I do not write this in at all a pessimistic mood, but the circumstances at least allow the possibility of a sudden crossing into a better beyond:

Madame Thérèse de Pitner,
née de Sommer-Sonnenschild,
Vienna, Austria, in town no. 6 Riemerstrasse, 3rd floor.

Matamoros, 17 January 1866
On perusing these lines I ought to reproach myself with ingratitude for having so completely forgotten in my notes on Orizaba to mention my three amiable home-helps, Guadalupe, Sancha and Nicacia. They were always particularly friendly to me and to Nicacia especially, I am indebted for many an innocent bit of fun. I was so contemptible as not to visit them again at all before my rapid departure, whereas it would surely have been my duty to spare at least a few minutes of my time, limited though it certainly was, for this purpose.

Among other things, I have also not yet mentioned the sale of my good chestnut [horse] to the treasury for 100 piaster.

Unfortunately I have also allowed myself to be persuaded to part
with my dear little Monkey. Latinovicz has this on his conscience and
now I miss the dog very much.

21 January, 11 p.m.
This evening we at last received the long-awaited order to set out for
Bagdad and to recapture it. A company of ours drawn from the 2nd and
5th with Captain Ludovici, First-Lieutenant Krauss, your humble
servant and Second-Lieutenant Adam, half the Hipp battery, 100
Mexicans on foot and 300 cavalry will leave for there tomorrow. It is very
likely that the enemy will make off before our arrival, so it may be assumed that the expedition will pass off without much blood being spilt
– which, however, could also possibly not be the case. Lieutenant-
Colonel Kodolitsch is commanding the enterprise and with this alarming
news I shall go to bed, resolving to commit to paper afterwards the result
of our operation, provided a bullet does not prevent me from doing so.

12 March 1866
After a four-hour journey downstream, which was full of the most
desperate incidents affecting our vessel and during which we constantly
ran aground, broke the rudder twice and had partly to march on foot,
we reached Bagdad at 8 o'clock in the evening of the 23rd to find the
place completely empty and pillaged, abandoned both by the enemy as
well as by all its inhabitants. The next few days, however, saw the
return of the majority of these poor fugitives, most of whom had lost
all their possessions, and the work of reorganization, installing the
imperial administration, recording what had happened, construction of
entrenchments etc. began.

26 March
On 28 January the French gunboat *Lutin*, under the command of
Lieutenant de Saihsait, arrived in the roads followed on 29 January by
the gunboat *Adonis*.

I presented a protest by Lieutenant-Colonel Kodolitsch regarding
the war material stolen and transported to the Texas side to the
commander of the negro troops in Clarksville and was particularly
gratified by its success since, after reference to Washington, the
material was restored to us in full.

On 19 February, I had an exchange of words of no importance with
Kalumsky, but which he took very seriously and resulted in a duel
whose outcome was somewhat unfortunate. I was severely wounded in
the armpit. The nerve was severed and today after almost six weeks
the wound is still partly open and I have to carry my arm in a sling.
These are my first attempts to write. Kalumsky received a blow on the
head.

Otherwise hardly anything new has happened here. Our Leading-Rifleman Hollasta – a very depraved individual as it turned out later – shot a rural guardsman while under the influence of drink and, for fear of the punishment, and after having found time to steal 170 thaler from Captain Ludovici, deserted to the United States.

We have built a splendid little redoubt here, which was christened Fort Carlotta and at whose inauguration a big target shoot with wine and delicacies was held, followed by presents for the men . . .

Since the middle of February I have very solemnly given up gambling and have even pledged my word for the year 1866, as in the past weeks I had lost nearly . . . piaster. Hipp was the champion. He won incalculable amounts. In spite of all this poor luck I still sent 100 thaler to Vienna this month so that my mother could give herself a treat with it.

We hear little news of the war zone in the interior. The Sierra is finally pacified. Sadly we still have to deplore the death of poor Susani, who was shot through the head at Papantla as he led his squadron to blow up an enemy fortification. It was learnt from his will that the poor man was secretly married and has left behind in Austria a young wife, with a child, who in consequence – and because the marriage cannot be recognized by the government – remains completely without support. A collection for her among the officer corps would, it would seem, raise at least 6,000 florins and one hopes that His Majesty will also add something to it.

Ernst wrote to his half-brother Franz from Bagdad on 3 February 1866:

Dearest Brother,

Yesterday I received your letter of 20 November in one from mother and I hope that you know me too well for me to have to begin by assuring you how infinitely pleased I was to see that at such a great distance and with so many preoccupations you remember me so warmly. That our mutually promised correspondence has hitherto proceeded so feebly is not to be held against either of us, for I still hope that my detailed letter to you from Campeche of June last year will in spite of everything still reach you, while you have been waiting in vain for its arrival, announced for so long. The description of your own circumstances at the present time has distressed me very much but, like you, I confidently foresee a lucky star and – if there is such a thing – a just dispensation of providence, which cannot – and never could – abandon a person of your character and capabilities. I will now repeat fully what I wrote in the aforementioned missing letter about the prospects which would present themselves to you in this country.

There is perhaps no country in the world which can offer such a prosperous life even to people with less outstanding abilities than yours and particularly with less talent for making themselves indispensable everywhere as quickly as you are able to do. One can earn as much money here, in whatever capacity, as is possible at home only for the highest office holders and unusually long-lived and tough people; on the other hand, however, there is the considerable disadvantage that one cannot envisage a permanent and solid position because conditions in the country are as yet insufficiently stabilized to make this possible. In a perfectly correct appreciation of these circumstances you have therefore already recognized that such a post is only to be found in the immediate proximity of Their Majesties. Since, however, to arrive there is not among the easiest things to do it would not be advisable for a person in your position to leave home without firm assurances in this connection.

Without doubt – and indeed with complete assurance – I could certainly give you the guarantee that even without being employed at court and solely by utilizing your linguistic accomplishments you are in a position to earn 300 piaster a month; but you will use 150 of this monthly, thus being able to save the other half, which would amount in two years to 7,200 florins in silver – too small a sum to enable you, should you no longer wish to remain here, to pay for the journey home and live on the rest in Europe, where meanwhile everyone had forgotten your name.

In a word, there are only three possibilities, namely the position at court; or, secondly, to leave Europe completely and to content oneself here with an income that is entirely sufficient and can be earned everywhere until the time when through sufficient savings or other contingencies one is in a position to say goodbye to the country again; or then, thirdly, to carry out your proposal, which seems very reasonable to me, and, summoning all one's energy, to strive for that particular permanent appointment in the Bourbon family, which indeed cannot and will not elude you if you seriously desire it.

As far as I am concerned, I can say with satisfaction after being here for more than a year that I have not so far regretted for one moment my decision to say goodbye to my home country. My needs and habits are quite different from yours. I have only sought to have an active military life, full of changing sights and continuing interest, together with income sufficient for one's material existence and I have been not only satisfied, but surpassed in my expectations. Within a year's span I have come to know a large part of this vast country from south to north and at present we are separated by the fifty-paces-wide Río Bravo del

Norte from the United States, on whose territory I have also set foot repeatedly in Brownsville and Clarksville.

Last year, a Lieutenant Second Class, I have for the last few months been a First-Lieutenant and, if the Lord grants me life (which has to be added to every statement one makes here), I expect to be a Captain in a year at the latest.

Finally, I am very well paid: the day before yesterday for example, I received 201 pesos or 418 florins silver in monthly pay. It is true that until now I have not yet thought of saving, since we here risk our hide in the true sense of the word from one day to the next and also because, with the high cost of living here, if one does not deny oneself anything at all – as I do not – one doesn't have much left over. But as soon as conditions assume a somewhat less warlike and perilous form and, in a word, as soon as there begins to be a prospect of enjoying some of one's savings, I shall think of this seriously. For the present I am only thinking of giving our dear mother a helping hand with 200 florins. I shall send you this money shortly through the good offices of the corps command and of Colonel Leiser in Vienna and I beg you then to find out from mother at once what she really needs, then buy it, give her 100 florins in cash and send approximately 50 florins to Trieste for our little niece, for Marie to make use of as she thinks fit. I will take the necessary steps for this straight away, but should warn you that a good three months will pass before the money reaches Vienna, as I must first deposit the appropriate sum here in the pay office and this will then be reported to the corps command in Puebla by the next mail, that is on the 20th of this month; from there the instruction is then sent by one of the next steamers to Colonel Leiser to pay such and such a sum to such and such a person in Vienna – a procedure that always absorbs a considerable amount of time.

You will know from my last letter to mother, in which I also enclosed a photograph of me for you, that we were then in a somewhat critical situation in Matamoros. But since then it has developed quite favourably and I will briefly tell you the details of the events which have occurred here recently. After the town of Bagdad, situated at the mouth of the Río Grande, had, as I wrote to you recently, been attacked at night by North American negro troops and totally ransacked, there was a danger that the imperial garrison of around 1,600 men in Matamoros would be similarly attacked by the negro troops of some 10,000 men lying on the far shore. We believed that the American government was secretly protecting these undertakings in order to create a *casus belli*, which they desired. Since the dissidents were also provided with every kind of support from the other side in the most flagrant manner – in a word, the required neutrality was violated in every way – the aforementioned viewpoint was fairly tenable. We therefore confined ourselves simply to putting Matamoros in the best state of defence and left Bagdad, expecting that the French fleet would retake the place. Since, however, this did not happen for a whole fortnight and we had pretty well assured ourselves through personal discussions with the American general Weitzel, in command on the other side, that the negroes would be prevented with all energy from crossing the river a second time, our commander, Lieutenant-Colonel Kodolitsch, persuaded General Mejía, the commander in Matamoros, that an expeditionary column of Austrians should reoccupy Bagdad. To this end we set out from Matamoros on the 22nd and occupied Bagdad without firing a shot on the night of the 25th. At our approach, the dissidents stole and took to the further shore everything that the negroes had left, down to the last chair, before evacuating the town. Only eye-witnesses can form an idea of the state the place was in. In the town, which before the events had had about 7,000–8,000 inhabitants, there was perhaps six or eight people. All the rest had fled; the houses were completely empty and everything portable had been stolen. Since we have been here at least half the inhabitants have returned and with a speed characteristic of this land the impression of the events, which reduced thousands almost to beggary, after they had perhaps acquired a fortune in a few months for which a lifetime is needed at home, is beginning to fade. 'Easy come, easy go,' one says to oneself and everyone is now trying to repair the damage. And indeed all the shops are again full of wares and, materially speaking, it is a fact that we lacked comfortable dinners etc. for hardly a few hours. With all that, Bagdad unfortunately remains a dreadful hole and I would dearly love to be in Matamoros again, where I enjoy all the amenities of horse, carriage and free dinners and breakfast in the house of my host.

One of the main advantages of the occupation of Bagdad was that we received our mail, which we had been longingly awaiting for a month and in which I found your letter, as well as two from mother. Judging from the latter, the European newspapers appear once again to be able to find no better material than all sorts of lies about Mexico. I can assure you that all that is empty chatter and that from day to day the situation is slowly but surely improving. We occasionally have sight of such newspaper articles and one would really have to laugh, if it were not so sad, that there are so many people who for a few florins or in pursuit of goodness knows what interests not only seek to bring a government into disrepute, but also constantly inject fear and fright into a thousand relatives of their compatriots here. I beg you to urge mother on my behalf not to believe these journalistic *canards*, as I am quite sufficiently acquainted with conditions to be able to let her have reliable news . . .

Imagine, my naval career in Austria has had a repercussion here. Yesterday I was appointed commander of our river gunboat, as the French naval officer commanding her until now has joined his proper ship, together with his sailors. Fortunately I have a river pilot on board and do not therefore have to bother much about the steering, but only the shooting, with which I am much more familiar.

Ernst wrote to his mother from Bagdad on 5 March 1866:

Dearest Mother,
First I beg you not to take fright at the sight of this unfamiliar handwriting, for I am completely well and only an insignificant accident – a fall of my horse and a dislocation of my arm which was its consequence – prevent me for the time being from using it.* I would gladly have spared you this little shock and waited until I was completely recovered to send you my next letter, but since I know that a prolonged absence of news only worries you more, and the post is just leaving today, I have decided to avail myself of the kindness of one of my comrades and let you have news of me in this way.

From my letter of the 3rd of last month to brother Franz you may have learnt of the occupation of Bagdad by our small expeditionary column and it only remains for me to tell you that since that time we have remained stationed here and, as can be imagined in such circumstances, are dreadfully bored. Conditions on the whole northern frontier are becoming most alarmingly peaceful, important reinforcements are expected in Matamoros daily; of the enemy there is no trace anywhere; yes, they have even got so far as to restore the stage-coach connection between here and Bagdad, which has been interrupted since last year, and to start replacing the telegraph, which has lain destroyed for so long.

From all this you can see how peaceful it looks here and I almost believe that our role here, where we appeared as much-needed saviours, could soon be played to an end. It is probable that we will then return to the district of Puebla, only I would wish that, if we are not to remain in agreeable Matamoros, our return journey would not be by the familiar sea route, but if possible on land via Monterey, San Luis Potosí etc.† In the latter case our correspondence would of

---

* The real reason, of course, was the injury he sustained in the duel referred to in the entry in his diary dated 26 March (see p. 110).
† It is ironic that Ernst should have hoped for a route which was to prove so disastrous.

course suffer a considerable interruption, but in any event I will inform
you before our departure – and indeed then by my own hand – of ways
and means of continuing our correspondence as best we can.

In the middle of May, according to my calculation, a small remittance
should arrive from me, which I have sent to Franz with instructions
that the sum of 50 florins should be used for my little niece Louise and
sent to Marie for this purpose, but the remainder of about 170 florins
should be placed at your disposal so that you, dearest mother, may
treat yourself to a present of your choice in my name. It would have
given me infinite pleasure to send more, but you know how we soldiers
live from hand to mouth and I, in particular, was unfortunately not
accustomed to make large savings.

Ernst wrote to his mother from Bagdad on 27 March:

Dearest Mother,
Today I am again more or less able to use my own hand to give you
news of our latest experiences. Unfortunately, thanks to the complete
standstill of all political events in this region, I have hardly any material
for the task. Just as two months ago, we are still sitting in this miserable
Bagdad, where we are heartily bored, but spend an appalling amount
of money owing to the prohibitive cost of living. The long-announced
arrival of the French in Matamoros has still not taken place and only
when it does is it likely that we shall be relieved from here. Until then
we must remain patient.

The irregularity of the mail particularly is one of the things which
causes me the most annoyance. It very often happens that the mail-
steamer which comes only once a month appears in the roads, but the
weather is so bad and the sea and the bar rise so frightfully that no
communication is possible with the longed-for ship and, since it can
only stay twenty-four hours, it calmly goes off again with our letters
until the next month. Such a moment is always one of the most awful.
One curses heaven, wind and water, together with all steamers in the
world.

Unfortunately your letters are also often very short. The last, marked
no. 25, followed no. 24 after only one month and was just four octavo
pages long. Understandably you do not have a great deal of new
material if you write to me only about our closest relations and
acquaintances, but everything interests me here and I beg you earnestly
to inform me about all possible other things which might interest me.
You could also exhort Franz, Marie etc. occasionally to write to me.

In order to widen my correspondence I have also written to Max and
Mathilde in a cover for the next mail – to the latter a six-page letter in

Spanish. If my time still permits I will write to Marie and Ludwig as well, though I fear that all these letters will have an alarming resemblance, since the material available here is too meagre to be able to fill four to five letters all at once.

31 March

Today I received permission from the doctor to withdraw from his treatment and to go to Matamoros for my complete recovery and the strengthening of my arm, which is still somewhat stiff and weak. I am extremely pleased about this, particularly for financial reasons, for whereas my food alone here costs 200 florins a month, there I can live for nothing.

You are no doubt shocked by these enormous sums, but it is nevertheless so. Breakfast and dinner together cost 3 piaster a day or 90 dollars – i.e. 200 florins – a month. To give you an idea of the cost of living here I attach a bill which we had to pay to an innkeeper for provisions supplied on the occasion of our march from Matamoros to Bagdad. We were charged 5 florins for a chicken and 10 florins for a turkey. A keg of beer costs 24 dollars or 55 florins etc.

On the other hand, a simple day labourer or porter can earn up to 12 florins a day and in Bagdad's heyday, i.e., during the last two years, such a fellow earned up to one gold coin – that is, 38 florins – daily. It is a fact that in this country no one who has two healthy arms and wants to work will not only not perish, but can make a small fortune in a very short time . . .

On the 23rd we had a tropical storm such as I have never seen. It began at half past six in the evening and lasted until two hours after midnight and was accompanied by a south-east hurricane and continuing cloud bursts. Flashes of lightning and claps of thunder followed one another for seven hours. Our large, two-storey-high wooden barracks, fortunately with no one billeted in it and only guarded by a detachment of ten men, collapsed completely and buried the men in such a curiously fortunate manner that only one man had a few light abrasions, while the rest were completely unharmed except for the fright. The whole building was overturned by the hurricane and lay on the ground entirely demolished.

Yesterday, for a change, we had a splendid lunar eclipse.

Ernst wrote to his mother from Matamoros on 2 May:

As I already indicated to you in my last letter, on 1 April I had gone from Bagdad to Matamoros, where I again lodged with my old host in similarly agreeable conditions.

A few days later our column also followed, but went away again two days later with 100 men from the garrison to undertake an expedition towards Monterey. I myself, as a convalescent case, remained behind with about thirty men – marauders, detainees, those unfit to march and similar riff-raff – in the town, which was almost completely denuded of troops and I count those three days which I spent here until the return of the garrison among the less agreeable of my stay in Mexico, as the most alarming rumours made it appear that the town was threatened every moment. However, it fortunately did not occur to our enemies to take advantage of the situation and a few days later our trusty men were again in our midst and with them a substantial reinforcement,* which had meanwhile arrived and which enables us, without exposing the town, to clear the neighbourhood of the bandits, who roam around under the name of Liberals, in a radius of more than thirty leguas.

In the last ten days the band of the notorious General Cortina was twice completely defeated by the Mexican troops of the garrison, whereby nearly 200 prisoners, as many saddled horses, one rifled cannon and many rifles and munitions fell into the hands of our men. Furthermore some sixty of the enemy were killed on the spot, while only a few unimportant wounds were sustained on our side. Through these successes the cause of the Liberals in the state of Tama Ulipas may well have suffered a significant blow and concurrently the rebellion in the other parts of the country, which is only nurtured from here and is only saved from extinction by the hope of an intervention by the United States in Juárez's favour, could also have been brought to an end. Recently, however, the demeanour of North America has become such that the expectations of our Republicans have been considerably reduced. At present neutrality – at least so far as one can see – is practised in a fairly impartial manner and the government on the other side has had General Weitzel, who was commanding the sector of the Río Grande at the time of the attack on Bagdad, relieved and brought before a court martial. It seems that neither France nor the United States seriously contemplate the possibility of a war between them. Consequently, also, no one here believes in a serious confrontation between the two powers, just as there is also no doubt that the French are far from being near the end of their sojourn here.

I am now completely recovered again and feel no consequences whatever from the little misadventure with my arm.

At the same time as the last mail, which also brought me your letter no. 26, we received news of our posting to the interior and although

* Ernst does not say what this reinforcement consisted of, but he appears to have overestimated its importance.

we are materially better off here than anywhere, everyone is satisfied with the order, for our position here is in many respects disagreeable by reason of the fact that, exceptionally, we in Matamoros are placed under a Mexican general. General Mejía is perhaps still one of the best and most honest citizens of this country. None the less he is still too much of a Mexican – in other words too far enmeshed in the old system of corruption which, nourished by the fifty years of civil war, is so far rooted in the army that generations must pass before one can impart to the native officer corps those concepts of honour which are current with us. Everyone here regards state property as a milch cow: all the world steals as much as it can, the horses, for example, being fed with only half the proper forage measure, which, given the astronomic forage prices amounts to enormous sums every month. We know for certain that at auctions and at other opportunities the senior officers buy up horses, oats and hay in large quantities at bargain prices to resell them to the public purse thereafter at three to four times the price. All this seems to the people quite natural – so natural, that it never occurs to the commanding officer to intervene, perhaps because on close examination he would find he could no longer rely on his men. In our position it is impossible to do anything about it and we shall be glad to be in the midst of our corps and among decent people once more, since at times it requires a very special self-denial to keep within the bounds of required courtesy in dealing with such notorious rogues and scoundrels (who, moreover, carry the insignia of senior staff officers) and to observe the consideration due to their position in a diplomatic manner.

On the occasion of our impending departure we organized a picnic in our house the day before yesterday, at which our host, Lieutenant-Colonel Kodolitsch, I and a few officers and single young gentlemen of our acquaintance took part as paying guests and to which the cream of local society was invited. The affair turned out very nicely – though the expense of this modest little house ball of fourteen couples and with an attendance of forty people at the most amounted to approximately 1,200 florins in local money – a sum for which one could certainly have produced something pretty grand at home. Unfortunately one always comes increasingly to realize on every such occasion here that with these people every penny spent on their entertainment is really to be regretted. The girls are almost without exception so incredibly dumb it is frightening. Moreover, they exhibit on all public occasions – *I say only on public occasions* – such ridiculous prudery, that in the end one is quite nauseated by it. Thus for instance on this occasion at the cotillon they spoilt all the fun for us. We had arranged several very pretty figures, spent a lot of money on them, and when the dance began and after the gentlemen had gifted the ladies with bouquets and the latter were to decorate the dancers in the same manner with medals and bows, not a single one got up, as it seemed to them unbecoming and compromising to select a dancer for themselves and so single him out for distinction. Lieutenant-Colonel Kodolitsch, who arranged the cotillon, was so angered by this stupidity that he expressed himself in a pretty sarcastic manner against the ladies and particularly his partner and he signalled to the band to stop the cotillon. Such behaviour, however, appears ludicrous in the extreme if, as already mentioned, one has learnt to judge these ladies in their more intimate relationships . . .

Ernst wrote to his mother from Matamoros on 26 May 1866:

Dearest Mother,
As you can see . . . we are still in Matamoros without knowing for certain what the immediate future will bring us. It is true that we were informed by the last mail that the transfer of our column, which was then intended, had merely been postponed to the end of May or the beginning of June, but in the conditions obtaining here one can only say, contrary to the proverb, 'postponed is cancelled' and patiently reconcile oneself to waiting. I for my part, incidentally, would not much mind staying here longer, had not an order also arrived by the last mail that Lieutenant-Colonel Kodolitsch was to proceed alone to Puebla, without awaiting the departure of the column here. I am very sorry that we are losing this commander with whom, in particular, I am on the best and most intimate terms and of whom, in the difficult conditions here, our troops would have continued to have very urgent need . . . To meet your wish regarding a description of the appearance of Matamoros and its inhabitants I am also sending you a few photographs and will supplement with my pen what is not explained by them. Matamoros is above all what is called a hole with us. It has about 20,000 inhabitants, of whom however thirty or forty families at the most can be counted as respectable people, if indeed one is sufficiently indulgent to concede the existence of such a class of people in this country. The town lies on a bend of the Río Bravo del Norte and is therefore only separated from the United States by a strip of water 120 paces wide. It is laid out in straight lines and, with the exception of a few houses on the plaza with an upper floor, consists almost entirely of rather miserable ground-level buildings with flat roofs, on which one could on occasion relax of an evening, were one so minded. But unfortunately the people here want nothing whatsoever other than to stay at home. Speaking of course always only of those of the female sex, I cannot but be scandalized by this life of idle luxury of

the women and girls, which is equally rooted in all circles here. They never go for walks. Only acquaintances among individual families, reduced to a minimum in any case, are cultivated; otherwise no one penetrates into these fortunately immeasurably boring circles.

One and a half years ago, when the American war had not yet come to an end, Matamoros is said to have been incomparably more amusing. At that time it numbered more than 40,000 inhabitants, of whom more than half consisted of American families, merchants, etc. But since all is peaceful again over there – while, on the other hand, the outlook here is all the more warlike – and the cotton trade, which in those days was conducted from here with the utmost energy, no longer exists, this whole company has departed again. At the time poor beggars became millionaires in one to two years. The money came flowing towards one without one wanting it – hence too the luxury and the cost of living were fabulous.

But today things are admittedly no longer so promising. Many have feathered their own nest, many others have gone bust; business is mostly stagnant. And at this moment several love-lorn cats are howling in front of my window – it is eleven o'clock at night – so woefully that I am completely confused. Besides which I am surrounded by innumerable mosquitoes.

I have just fled from the theatre, where they were showing a frightful play, 'La Pastora de las Alpas', in which an Alpine scene was represented with an abundant snowfall, for which shredded cotton wool was caused to fall from the sky in the most extravagant manner. I am convinced that the good Mexicans, who for the most part have never seen snow in their lives, will now believe that in our country the snow falls, as in the theatre, in snowballs of four to five pounds. Incidentally, the building was, to please a benefactress, so crowded that in the prevailing heat, which even outside registered 28 degrees, I could not endure it for more than an hour and am now conversing with you instead.

As regards describing Matamoros, I had almost forgotten to tell you the most amusing thing about the whole town. For to the right and left of the houses there are pavements, but pavements raised high above the level of the streets. These streets, however, because of the lack of stones and the carelessness of the town council, are entirely unpaved and therefore form standing canals and pot-holes with miasmic exhalations in which carriages sink up to their shafts and horses up to their chests – yes, in which even during my presence in Matamoros three mules or horses have drowned. The pathways dry quickly, but by the same token are quickly bottomless again and, as it now rains almost every day, women can hardly venture on to the street at all and men only in high boots. Moreover, not only immediately outside the town, but often also in the streets themselves there lie the rotting carcasses of dead horses and mules, whose smell of course is not very pleasant. Altogether in no town in Mexico have I yet seen as much dirt as here and it is particularly telling proof of the otherwise healthy nature of the climate here that with such uncleanness we do not have plague, cholera and yellow fever permanently here.

30 May

A few days ago Kodolitsch received two pieces of music from Vienna, namely a march 'Dedicated to the Austrian Volunteer Corps in Mexico' and a waltz entitled 'Viennese Dialect', composed by Heinrich Wallner. Please inform him of the safe arrival of these pieces with many greetings from me.

In a few days one of my fellow-officers, Artillery Captain Hipp, who has just resigned, retaining officer status, will leave Matamoros and travel to Vienna via New Orleans, New York, Southampton, London and Paris, etc., etc. He is an exceptionally capable and deserving officer, with nice decorations, but has already grown tired of staying here and so – since he is moreover well off – is returning home. He has promised me that he will visit you and will tell you a lot of interesting things. But since he is stopping everywhere on his journey, he is hardly likely to arrive in Vienna before the middle of August. Since he has the weakness of finding everything bad that does not please him personally, you need not view everything that he happens to tell you about the situation of the empire exactly as he does.

The warlike reports which made their way across the ocean to us and the possibility of a conflict between Prussia and Austria were awaited by us here recently with particular interest. But, unfortunately or fortunately, the two sides seem yet again to have had no desire to pick up the gauntlet which each had thrown down to the other and so a long cherished wish – and some advancement – eludes the poor Austrian army. Instead, perhaps, we may expect setbacks since, as the newspapers reported, Italy on its side also seemed to be joining in to help make our position very precarious. It seems to me that Austria has only the great politician on the Seine to thank for peace, and the Mexican enterprise – Austria's willingness to send more volunteers* and Napoleon's future plans for Austria, both of which could have a bearing on the enterprise – contributed not a little to France's moral intervention in the Austro-Prussian conflict. But I notice that I am so imprudent as to enter – here, at a distance of 2,000 miles – into a discussion about European politics. I must stop this immediately, as

---

* Austria went back on her promise under pressure from Washington.

this would be the best way of making a complete fool of oneself. One speaks here of peace being preserved, while three battles may perhaps already have been fought there or else something quite different may have happened . . .

For myself, I can tell you that I live here in extremely comfortable, yes even luxurious circumstances . . . The furnishing of our house is new throughout and really sumptuous. I have such an elegant living-room as I shall hardly see again here in Mexico, let alone occupy. A splendid tester-bed with feather mattress etc., sofas, armchairs, tables, chests of drawers and washstands, a bathroom with shower and full-length bath, in a word everything. Moreover, we are completely undisturbed, as only three to four young single gentlemen occupy the rest of the house. Furthermore we also enjoy the particular amenity of superb food – in short, from a material point of view we have nothing to complain of here. This is all the more fortunate since otherwise it is really extremely expensive here and in other circumstances one would have had to limit oneself a great deal in order to get by. Recently we have organized some very agreeable picnic evenings here in the house, at which the gentlemen of the house as well as Kodolitsch, his adjutant, I and some of our officers were present as paying participants and organizers. The cream of local female society was invited and a married lady of our acquaintance acted as hostess in this bachelor establishment. The less agreeable part of such entertainments is the moment of paying the bill, for although the supper and other arrangements were very simple, the cost nevertheless came to 800 florins silver. Poor Kodolitsch and the master of the house, as the richest, each paid 200 florins, while the rest of us squeezed by with 40 florins or 20 dollars . . .

Of the four pictures I am sending you one shows the big corner house on the square, the second the cathedral, the third a water-carrier and the fourth an Indian family eating *maistortillas*.

Disaster

Months passed after the Bagdad incident without much happening. The Liberals made occasional forays on the outskirts of the town, but undertook no major operation. Neither did the imperial troops, being incapable of doing so. Their enforced inactivity, however, as well as their feeling of isolation, played on the nerves of the garrison, especially the Austrians, and the number of desertions and other breaches of discipline increased.

General Thun had repeatedly urged Bazaine to withdraw the Austrian contingent from Matamoros. The main body of the corps, its number severely depleted, was badly in need of reinforcement and when the rains set in the Austrians would be exposed to the same seasonal sickness which had already decimated the French. Bazaine finally agreed but, instead of allowing the contingent to return by sea to Veracruz, decided that it should proceed by land via Monterey, with a detachment of Mexican troops of General Mejía's army, to escort an important convoy leaving for the South. Thun protested against this proposal, pointing out that to move so large a force over a distance of 1,000 kilometres through hostile territory in the monsoon season would be courting disaster. Bazaine, however, stuck to his decision.

The 300 Austrians and 1,400 Mexicans set out from Matamoros on 7 June. The force was under the command of a Mexican general who was to prove both cowardly and incompetent. Progress was slow and difficult because of the heat, the hazards of the terrain and the heavy transport vehicles. On 16 June, on the plain of San Gertrudis close to Camargo, the convoy encountered and was attacked by a large Liberal force, which had been awaiting its arrival from prepared positions. In the fierce fighting which followed most of the Mexican troops went over to the other side (their general fled) and the small Austrian contingent was overwhelmed: 130 men killed or wounded, 126 taken prisoner. A French force not far away had failed to come to their assistance.

In a message to his victorious troops the Liberal commander, General Escobedo, said: 'You have fought against Austrians and traitors. The former at least had the courage to risk their lives and to die for their cause on the battlefield. The latter are not even ashamed not to have had this courage.'

With his garrison reduced to only 600 men by the defeat near Camargo, Mejía was forced to conclude that Matamoros was no longer tenable. By agreement with the Liberals he was able to withdraw his troops without further fighting on 23 June. The loss of Matamoros, however, by its psychological impact rather than any immediate military consequences, was the first of a succession of setbacks foreshadowing the overthrow of the empire a year later. The disaster at Camargo was also one of the worst that befell the Austrian volunteer corps during the fighting in Mexico.

Elsewhere the corps was having other difficulties to contend with. Fed by mounting support from the north, the tide of Liberal operations was gathering momentum. As it did so, the character of the war began to change: from being a dispute between two Mexican parties, it increasingly became a war against the foreigner. Having suffered substantial losses, the corps could only continue to play an effective role if it received reinforcements: Franz Josef had undertaken to send 4,000 men, with a further 2,000 annually for the next four years, but at the last moment, when the first contingent was already prepared for departure from Trieste, he cancelled the project under pressure from the United States. Meanwhile the imperial government found itself unable to continue to pay for the corps, and Maximilian was forced to accept an offer from Bazaine to assume this responsibility as a temporary measure if the corps was placed under French command. As a result of this rearrangement the Austrian and Belgian corps ceased to be independent units directly under the emperor and became the 2nd Brigade – the French Foreign Legion formed the 1st Brigade – in a new Division Auxiliaire Étrangère commanded by the French general Neigre. This unit was intended as the nucleus of the new Mexican army, which would have to be formed after the French left in the autumn of 1866. Being thus deprived of his contractual appointment and because of the ill-feeling already existing for some time between him and Bazaine, General Thun thereupon resigned his command, handing over to Lieutenant-Colonel Bertrand, and left Mexico in September. The change caused intense dissatisfaction among the Austrians, not only because of the unsatisfactory command arrangements, but more immediately because of the loss of pay suffered as a result. French pay was less than that of the Austrians and was paid in arrears, whereas the Austrians were paid in advance. So the Austrians were left without pay for a month. Maximilian promised to make good the difference in monthly pay from his own funds, but the promised supplement was not received after July. The Austrians' Mexican auxiliaries were not paid at all. Inevitably this situation led to growing ill-feeling between the Austrians and the French, leading to a near-mutinous confrontation in Puebla in the autumn and to increasing disaffection among the auxiliaries.

Ernst wrote in his diary:

> I begin the second part of my diary in a situation which perhaps belongs to the saddest of my life, and since, moreover, I lack neither time nor opportunity, I can at least report as fully as possible everything that has recently happened to me.
>
> Perhaps I would never again have taken up my pen to keep a diary if a veritable nod of destiny had not invited me to do so. For when I lost all my worldly possessions in the unhappy engagement at Camargo and, severely wounded, fell into enemy captivity, I expressed to one of the officers visiting us my particular distress that, among other things, my large and so greatly prized collection of photographs had disappeared. He promised to make enquiries about it but only succeeded in finding a few letters of my mother, my paybook and the first part of my diary, which things he duly passed to me. As only a few pages were written in the second part of my diary I changed my decision 'not to write anything more' and I will fill in the little that is missing and try to continue my little work.
>
> On the 1 April, I left Bagdad and travelled to Matamoros by the river steamer *Ulamo*. On arriving there I again lodged in the house of my previous friendly host.
>
> A few days later our whole column also returned to Matamoros from Bagdad, but a few days later they undertook a small expedition to

Charco Escondido, where our troops met those of General Jean-ningres, and Mejía, as well as the former general, discussed the further operations to be undertaken and then marched back again in their respective directions.

On the day when our expeditionary column returned to Matamoros it was attacked on the way by a detachment of dissidents under Canales, or was fired on from the bush, and as a result we lost one officer killed and five or six wounded. During the five-day absence of this expeditionary column I remained as a convalescent case in Matamoros and those five days were certainly not among the most agreeable of my stay there, as we constantly expected an attack on the town, which had been denuded of almost its entire garrison. Fortunately nothing of the sort occurred and we passed the months of April and May in the quietest and most agreeable manner. Admittedly the theatre which was present at the time was a bit of a disappointment, but at least it provided an opportunity to see the fine world and to form or continue acquaintanceships. Altogether our pressure latterly had succeeded in bringing some activity into social life. Two balls, in the form of picnics, held in our house, to which we each contributed between 20 and 40 thaler, then a ball in the house of Dr MacManus on the occasion of his daughter's marriage to Mr Gervason, a French *sous-intendant*, each time brought together the whole of elegant female society in Matamoros and we performed impossible feats on the dance-floor . . .

With the mail of 17 May we received, besides letters and corps orders, the disagreeable news of being placed under the command of the French General Neigre, incorporation in the Division Étrangère, pay reductions etc., etc., etc. At the same time we heard of the unhappy engagement of Czillich, the deaths of Sebastian and Ehmik, the wounding of Krickl and Tavecchia etc., etc. Finally there came the order that we were to rejoin the corps at Puebla and that a French transport vessel would arrive at the end of May or early June for this purpose. Lieutenant-Colonel Kodolitsch was instructed to join the corps as quickly as possible at the first opportunity. I do not know how it was, but from this moment I had a vague sombre premonition that we were approaching hard events and situations.

Latterly our relations with the Mexican officers of the garrison had changed in the most disturbing manner. The meanest deceits, practised with shameless effrontery by the most senior officers, the defective administration, the insufficient energy of what was perhaps otherwise the only decent Mexican general, Mejía – all this may have aroused a certain feeling of unease and uncertainty in us, which at least in my own case was considerably heightened by the departure of the influential, energetic and skilful Kodolitsch, who, in my opinion, was one of our mainstays. On 4 June, Krause and I provided our lieutenant-colonel with a final escort to Bagdad and, although the early arrival of a transport ship was then in prospect, it was nevertheless with a heavy heart that I parted from this commander, with whom I had lived in the friendliest relations for six months and whom during this time I had learnt to respect and esteem.

The embarkation on the *Sonora* took place in particularly stormy conditions. The sea was running unusually high, the bar was very bad and on our return we sailed on to the bar in the little steamer *Pomec of Wales* in the most hazardous manner, were soaked through and through and were altogether most uncomfortable. The whole company, with the exception of Kodolitsch, Gómez and myself, were most outrageously seasick and I have never seen so many slippery signs of that sickness squandered on deck as that day.

Next morning, after a most miserable night, I went to the beach at three o'clock for an early bathe. Krause slept peacefully for another two hours despite mosquitoes and other animals and as a due reward for his endurance it was granted to him by destiny to see, through a crack in our highly deficient wooden partition, a young American married couple in the purest state of nature enjoying the pleasures of love. Although Krause later calmly denied this, I think I can maintain almost with certainty that that sight cost him 5 heavy thaler, for on the very same morning he rushed to visit one of his former lady friends, probably in order to give vent to his oppressed heart.

At eight o'clock on the morning of 6 June we set out on the return to Matamoros, using for this purpose the stage-coach which runs on the Texan side of the border. One of our acquaintances, Mr Gresse from Bagdad, travelled with us. After a miserably boring journey of five hours we arrived in Brownsville, crossed the river immediately and, hardly had we reached the other side, when we learnt to our great surprise that during our two-day absence an order had arrived from Marshal Bazaine that the Austrian column stationed in Matamoros was to march to Mexico by land via Monterey and that, should a convoy be leaving Matamoros, it should at the same time act as escort as well. Since it so happened that the departure of a convoy was just being arranged and, moreover, news was received that the French had to come as far as Mier to meet us, the departure of this convoy was immediately decided and put into effect. I had hardly time to pack my bags and to put my few belongings in order, for already on the evening of 6 June we marched out of the town and camped, in order to be able to begin the march at daybreak on the morning of the 7th.

Lieutenant Kalumsky had remained in Matamoros and had not left

with Lieutenant-Colonel Kodolitsch, as the latter had asked him firstly
to continue the management of the column's affairs and, secondly, to
take into his charge his five new, expensive American horses. Kalumsky himself had three fine horses of his own and we others had almost
all recently provided ourselves with fine, big horses and new saddlery,
hoping to be able to do excellent business with it in the interior.

Very little time was left to us all to say goodbye. The order had
come so suddenly that we did not have sufficient time for our most
necessary final arrangements. The convoy which we had to escort
consisted of more than 200 large goods wagons, each harnessed with
ten mules, and had a value of 6 million thaler apart from the material
of the wagons and the team of 2,000 mules. The distance over which,
on the average, the whole train stretched amounted to over two leguas,
if the wagons – which was rarely the case – were all in motion, but
otherwise much more. The troops escorting the convoy were:

Austrians: 2 Rifle Company	240	
11 Batallón Sierra Gorda	350	
Batallón Cazadores de Querétaro	300	
1 Company Zapadores	60	
Regiment Cavallerie S Louis	80	mounted
Squadron Lanceros S Louis	60	mounted
Contra Guerrilla Gesard	120	mounted
Rurales Captain Gómez	70	mounted
Rurales of Matamoros nr. II	30	mounted
six field batteries	80	men
two Austrian mountain batteries	50	men
	1,440	men

Comprising   950 men infantry
             360 men cavalry
             130 men artillery with eight guns
Total: 1,440 men

The march we undertook was surely among the most difficult which
can be undertaken. The main trouble on the whole route is the
continual lack of water and the stages had to be arranged solely
according to the water-holes to be found at certain quite unequal
distances. Added to this is the disagreeable circumstance that the track
constantly leads into the thickest chaparral, from where one can at any
time fall into the prettiest ambushes; moreover, this very circumstance
means that one has always to set out in broad daylight and consequently, because of the slowness and immovability of the convoy, to
march throughout the day in the most searing heat of the sun. What
one suffers during such a day is beyond anyone's imagining. The march

continually comes to a halt; the sun mounts ever higher above the horizon and its glowing rays are almost unbearable. To that is added the lack of shade and water, the dust and the stiffness arising from the frequent stopping and the increased tiredness: in a word, it was one of the most awful marches.

On the 7th we marched to Santa Rosalía, some eight leguas distant from Matamoros, and on this march five men among us Austrians died of sunstroke. On the 8th we came to Lagunita, a further five leguas, and on this march too three men died of sunstroke. On the 9th we went to Gancho, four leguas further, on the 10th to Artesitas, another three leguas, on the 11th to Jacalitos, five leguas on, and on the 12th we arrived at an uninhabited *rancho* after a march of six leguas. On the way our people ate many of the so-called *tunas* or cactus figs because of lack of water and at the halt some sixty men fell sick with violent diarrhoea, vomiting etc. But on the following morning everyone was more or less on his feet again. Dr Fuchs and Keczkemety had also fallen ill. On the 13th we came to an uninhabited *rancho* after a march of about five leguas where there was very little and very bad water. The Mexican troops and the transport camped about a quarter of an hour further back. When darkness fell we were ordered to withdraw from there because of the exposed position of the *rancho* and to retire to the camp of the other troops. As we left at nine o'clock at night we were fired on quite vigorously from the undergrowth. Our cooks, who had still had work to do in the *rancho* building and had stayed back alone, had to abandon our cooking utensils and clear out, as the bullets were penetrating into the illuminated residence (which was only constructed of wattle) in the most alarming manner. However, we had no wounded.

On the 14th, after a march of three leguas, we again came to an abandoned *rancho*, where there were only a few stinking pools, half dried up and already covered with green slime. On this day too the marching column was fired on both in the morning and in the afternoon and the Mexican troops had one dead and five wounded. A few rounds of grape-shot into the undergrowth sufficed that day to keep these small, single bands, composed largely of *rancheros*, off our necks.

On the 15th we set off with the intention of reaching the Río San Juan in order to obtain water there for men and animals. But the route was very bad and twice the Mexican engineer company and our soldiers had to fill in deep *arroyos** to make them passable for the wagons, thus causing halts of several hours. On this day the column was repeatedly fired on during the march. Finally, towards five o'clock in

* Ravines.

the evening, our column reached a plateau called Mesa de San
Gertrudis and we were still about two leguas from the water. There,
however, the advance guard was seriously attacked and as it was learnt
from a captured prisoner that the entire enemy fighting force was
facing us we stopped despite the lack of water and food, since it was
already too late that day to give battle. However, we undertook a
reconnaissance of about an hour to the front, assisted by half-battery
and also by the Batallón Cazadores and the cavalry. At about six
o'clock the cavalry of the rural guard encountered the enemy outposts,
a few shots were exchanged and one of our men was killed. As night
fell we marched back into the camp. Hardly had we arrived there when
we were greeted with a veritable volley from the shrubberies running
alongside the camp in closest proximity which, although fired as I say
at very close range, caused only quite insignificant damage and brought
with it the advantage that during that night security duty was at least
carried out somewhat better. Hungry and, what was much worse,
terribly thirsty, we lay down to rest that night. The wine, which was
supposed to replace the water for us, only made us still more thirsty
and, to be honest, I went to sleep that evening with fairly gloomy
thoughts.

Shortly before, I spoke with the Mexican captain, Alvárez, a rare
exemplar of his compatriots – very decent, very clever and completely
aware of the many faults and weaknesses of his fellow-countrymen,
and recognized himself as a brave officer. He confirmed me fully in my
bleak premonitions. He told me that he had little confidence in the
outcome of the next day's engagement – firstly because General Olvera
was an idiot, secondly because his officers were uniformly worthless,
and especially because the cavalry (Alvárez's own weapon) which was
so necessary here, was unusable. He merely said that the two Mexican
infantry battalions were composed of reliable and decent soldiers. 'You
will see,' he said to me, 'tomorrow there will be confusion the like of
which one will not often witness and I advise you to fight on horseback,
since I fear that you may need those four feet only too greatly. The
enemy is superior to us in numbers and his existence depends on the
success of this coup. He will fight therefore with the utmost exertion
and with the courage of desperation.' I replied that I could not follow
his advice about the horse for two reasons: firstly because I am an
infantry officer and therefore have to fight on foot in all circumstances;
and secondly because it is against our habits and customs to think of a
retreat on the eve of an engagement or in any case before its outcome.

Poor First-Lieutenant Radoczay, who came to us shortly before we
went to sleep and at that time saw everything in the rosiest light, was
furious that we did not press on to the Río at once that evening and

thought that the enemy could be dispersed to the four winds with a few bursts of shrapnel.

Otherwise the night passed quite peacefully. Regardless of hunger and thirst – and despite the certainty of a bloody morrow – we all slept splendidly on the sandy ground.

At four o'clock on the morning of 16 June the men took up their arms and half an hour later all the troops moved off, the wagons driving in fours in the middle.

The 2nd and 5th Austrian Rifle Companies moved forward as advance guard and, on arriving at a certain distance from the enemy line, formed themselves into two independent columns with sections. The half-battery marched in the middle between us. Presently one section was released into the cordon by each of the two companies. In 2 Company I happened to be in the first section.

Quite soon afterwards we had sight of the enemy and firing began in the cordon, but without particularly heavy return fire from the enemy. To begin with, we only saw single riders appearing on the crest of the row of hills opposite, while the main forces seemed to be lodged in concealed positions as yet invisible to us.

On both our flanks, to the front, Gómez's horsemen patrolled the bush in order to be able to warn us in good time of any unexpected lateral attacks. The two Mexican infantry battalions marched at a fairly considerable distance on both sides behind us to provide cover for the transport column. Immediately behind us there followed only the Mexican Zapadores Company, sixty men strong. The Contraguerrillas were used as a rearguard, while the rest of the cavalry, out of our sight at that time, were roughly in the middle of the whole column.

In this way we advanced for about half or three-quarters of an hour, halting occasionally and making room for the artillery in our midst, which thereupon always fired a few shots against the enemy line, trying to achieve a disclosure of the enemy position. Two Mexican guns also took part in this, but caused more noise than damage, since it was clear to us from the point of departure of their shells that their aim was just not of the highest order. Our artillery, on the other hand, fired splendidly, for although there was no real target for them, our shrapnel shots always burst so close to the single groups of horsemen who appeared that the latter always rapidly withdrew.

At last we arrived on the crest of the row of hills behind which we originally supposed the enemy to be. In quick time our cordon occupied the upper edge and at once we saw the enemy, who broke out of a woodland and in close order advanced offensively towards us. I reported this to Captain Ludovici, who was still below with the company behind the hill and moved up immediately and also occupied the crest. At the same moment we saw the Gómez horsemen rebounding at full tilt because of the advance of the enemy cavalry on our left flank. We saw our remaining cavalry attempting an apparent attack against the enemy but, having arrived at a certain distance from them, turning round and chasing away hell for leather pursued by the enemy.

At the same time a violent exchange of fire had developed between us and the enemy infantry column some 300 paces opposite us. My section had rejoined the company, we had marched forward in line and exchanged volley with the infantry battalion which outnumbered us by at least two to one. It was a moment of the most frightful small-arms fire and the men in their ranks fell down dead in droves. Finally, after rank fire had been repeated three or four times, the bayonet was fixed, the signal to charge was given and, to continuous cries of 'Hurrah!', we ran across the space separating us from the enemy until we found ourselves about fifty paces distant from them. At this moment another hostile infantry column materialized on our right flank, also showering us with the fiercest fire, and furthermore the same enemy cavalry, which had repulsed our own cavalry shortly before, appeared in our rear.

Already half the company lay dead or wounded on the ground; there was only one possible salvation and that was to try to reach the refuge of the wagons. Our 5 Company, which had come to a position somewhat behind us, took us in temporarily, and we tried as best we could to gather together the remains of our poor soldiery and continued to move back towards the wagons in a storm of bullets. Captain Ludovici had already received a severe glancing shot to the head and I saw him pass close to me, covered in blood. Lieutenant Keczkemety had already fallen and all the ground was covered with dead and wounded.

Having arrived near the wagons, I suddenly found myself surrounded by the enemy cavalry. One of the men pointed at me with his sword, indicating that I was an officer. I saw only one means of escape. With one leap I threw myself into the midst of the riders and, with the revolver in my right hand and the sword in my left, I tried to clear a path to the wagons for myself. I shot one officer, who attacked me, from his horse; another jumped down from his horse, seized hold of me and aimed a sword stroke at my head, which I parried with my left arm and at the same time shot him in the stomach with my revolver. But at the same instant I felt a stab and acute pain in my throat. I felt as if I was lifted and hurled forward and indeed I fell to the ground right next to the mules of a team of one of those big goods wagons. With quick resolve, however, and seeing my escape only in so doing, I crawled away under the animals and thus arrived between the wagons;

and although I was fired after and pursued I nevertheless succeeded in remaining hidden from my pursuers among the wagons. As I was covered in blood all over and in particular was losing much blood from the mouth I feared for a moment that the big artery in my neck had been pierced. Later, however, I realized that fortunately – and remarkably – it had remained intact, though my throat had been pierced in two places and that the food and drink canals – in a word the gullet – had also been severed internally. Summoning all my strength, I succeeded in scaling one of those high goods wagons to creep under its canvas top and remained lying there completely exhausted and battered. For company I found two Mexican soldiers from the Mejía division there, who were unwounded but said they were ill. But I think that the fellows were only hiding there.

From then on I saw nothing more of the battle. I heard only bullets whistling all around, shooting, cries of 'Viva la libertad' – in a word, an infernal din. I learnt only later of the behaviour of the remaining troops. In fact, after our poor 280 Austrians had joined battle alone and been attacked from all sides the two Mexican battalions deemed it preferable not to become involved in the affair. The 2 Battalion Sierra Garda stuck the points of their bayonets into the ground and laid down their arms with the cry 'Viva la libertad'. The Cazadores de Querétaro would perhaps have fought, but were likewise surrounded on all sides and also surrendered. I have already mentioned earlier that the cavalry opted out from the start and in conseqence we enjoyed the support solely of the sixty-strong Zapadores Company who, resting against us to the left, bore themselves quite well, with the result that almost all their men also fell. In sum, therefore, 340 men fought without cavalry in what was almost exclusively cavalry terrain against an enemy of 2,000, among whom there were at least 600 horsemen, very well armed and led. And the result also reflected these circumstances. Captain Hobza, First Lieutenant Radoczay, Lieutenant Keczkemety and Dr Fuchs fell – the latter had his head split by a passing cavalryman just as he was bandaging a wounded man. Captain Ludovici, Lieutenant Adam and I are wounded, the last two of us quite dangerously so. The rest of the officers, consisting of First-Lieutenant Krause, Lieutenant Faber and Lieutenant Kalumsky in the event came through unscathed, but were also taken prisoner. Of the men about 120 died on the battleground, around 115 to 120 were captured unwounded, 42 were wounded cases here in the hospital and perhaps 5 or 6 may have escaped. The great disparity between dead and wounded is to be explained by the fact that the enemy killed all the severely wounded and indeed all who fell into their hands during the fighting. Many of the people here were eye-witnesses to such actions.

Some time after I had got into the wagon it began to move, together with the others. I had no certain knowledge of the outcome of the battle, for although I had to assume that it was more than likely that we had been beaten, I had nevertheless not been able to learn anything definite. I did not know whether the wagons were still in our possession or whether they now belonged to the enemy. In this not exactly comforting situation we jolted on along a miserable track. My throat burnt like fire because of the wound, my mouth kept filling with blood and I had the most searing thirst imaginable. Imploringly, I repeatedly asked for a drop of water, but no one had any or was willing to give it. Finally, when it was already afternoon, a vessel with water was handed to me. I seized it greedily, but hardly had I a drop in my mouth than I felt such an appalling, piercing pain in my swollen throat, that I had to stop immediately and watch the two Mexicans in the wagon with me drink it all themselves.

At about 10 a.m. I saw part of the Cazadores battalion marching past close to our wagon. I did not know that they were being led past as prisoners and imprudently leant out of the wagon a little. Immediately a single rider came up to me, put his carbine to my head and demanded my rings which, argus-eyed, he had seen as he rode past. I of course gave them to him, whereupon he also took my money as well, and my revolver and thereupon took his leave.

It was only then that I saw that I was a prisoner and my train of thought as a result was not very jolly. The mere prospect of being dragged around for months as a prisoner among such people is not comforting and there was the great probability that they would shoot the officers. Fortunately, however, after great exertions and physical suffering one is so apathetic and indifferent to everything apparently still rising up against us that really I did not worry too much about the future.

At four o'clock in the afternoon the wagons halted in an open field about three-quarters of an hour from Camargo. After they had originally refused to let me step down from the wagon, I was nevertheless eventually allowed, on my plea, to come down. I lay on the ground and a shower of rain falling soon after refreshed me in a beneficent manner. Finally an officer appeared. He allowed me to travel to Camargo in a four-seated vehicle with three other wounded persons to the hospital to have my first dressing applied. I had been wounded for nine hours.

On arriving I found two to three hundred wounded all in one house and all lying on the bare stone or mud floor; most were not bandaged and friend and enemy were all mixed up. The head doctor of the Mejía division, Dr Ealo, who had also been taken prisoner, gave me a makeshift dressing. Of the wounded officers I found Lieutenant Adam there with a very dangerous shot in his right foot. The bullet had entered behind the toes and come out again at the back near the heel.

This first night was really awful. A place to lie down was nowhere to be found. Finally I discovered a spot in a corner that was still empty, in which I lay down; but it was full of fine particles of glass and every sort of muck. The following morning I had to pull many splinters of glass out of my thigh. The next morning my resting place was at the side of a dead Indian – which did not, however, prevent me from sleeping for two hours in his company. My condition otherwise was lamentable enough. My throat and neck were very swollen. I could only swallow water and soup with the greatest pain and infinite effort and today after sixteen days I have still taken nothing but liquid for nourishment – milk, soup with egg, pap etc., liquids which, as a bonus, run out of the hole in my neck while I am drinking them.

My clothing was truly pitiable. I had thrown my tunic away after being wounded in order not to be recognized immediately as an officer. My hat had got lost during the *mêlée* and during the journey I had continually torn strips from my drill trousers to quench my blood. Moreoever, I was covered in blood and, apart from my boots, had only a woollen shirt and my torn trousers on my body.

In the hospital some of the enemy wounded and later also a Mexican officer of the hospital guard wanted to take my boots away, but fortunately I succeeded in keeping them. My gold English anchor watch I had stowed in a very original place, namely in my suspensory and thus hidden from everyone's sight, but the repeated attempts on my boots made me anxious and I was imprudent enough to ask the enemy head doctor, who seemed to me to be a fairly decent person, to take charge of the watch, sell it and let me have the proceeds, as I was completely without means. He promised to do this and gave me two thaler on account; but then I did not see him again for several days, not until he finally came with the news that he had sold the watch, which was worth 120 thaler, for 45 thaler at the Rancho Davis across the river. He asked if we needed the money and, on being given an affirmative answer, gave us another 20 thaler on account, but has not since made any further mention of the matter.

In the night after the battle Captain Ludovici also came to the hospital. His clothing was roughly as mine had been only, after cleaning him out completely, they had also stripped him of his boots as well and the poor man had to walk a considerable distance in bare feet, driven on with rifle-butts from behind.

On the 17th I saw General Díaz de León in the hospital. I

approached him directly, introducing myself as an Austrian officer and asking for better treatment if possible. He was extraordinarily friendly and obliging, immediately procured a separate and airy room for us in another hospital, gave us mattresses, gave the strictest orders for us to be well treated and finally gave each of us a gold coin – in a word, he behaved in the most charming and chivalrous manner. Visiting us several times every day, he also enquired after our wishes; and since his intervention on our behalf, my existence has become very much more bearable. We were provided with beds, a table and two chairs, we were given permission, on our word of honour, to go out freely and altogether we cannot complain. Even the food is reasonably good. So now the three of us – Ludovici, Adam and I – lie here moping and waiting for whatever lies ahead . . .

A comic incident occurred a few days ago when Ludovici and I went to Colonel Canales, a robust *ranchero* here, and asked permission to go to Matamoros by steamer. After a lengthy discussion he told us that he could not give us the permission for this as we were General Escobedo's prisoners, not his, and when we told him that we understood this and therefore wanted to approach Escobedo in writing, and apologized for the trouble we were causing, he suddenly seized a gold coin lying on the table and pressed it into my hand as though it were a charitable donation. When Ludovici and I observed this our faces fell and my first thought – a very foolish one – was to reject the money. Fortunately this idea was only of the very shortest duration and with the politest smile imaginable and some mumbled words of thanks I speedily let the coin disappear into my pocket, remembering the practices which are customary in this country and our sad situation, in which my proud impulse would really be ridiculous.

Of the three of our captured officers who remained unwounded I only saw Kalumsky, who was the particular prisoner of Canales; he spent a few days here in Camargo and during this time was able to visit us every day under escort of one of Canales's officers. But a few days ago he was taken away to Matamoros. It so happened that his pockets had not been searched, as a result of which he saved his money bag with five gold coins. He was so good as to make over two of these to us.

I must also not forget to mention the frequent visits of the American officers and their rather strange behaviour. The day before yesterday a general, a colonel and another such fellow were here. Their first word was to discuss politics, to ask us how it could occur to us to serve such an unjust cause – Maximilian was only a usurper, had no business in the country and since the United States had ordered him to pack his bags he *must* leave without further ado. 'No doubt you also know,' he said, 'that Seward* has let the Austrian emperor know that he is not permitting any further shipments of volunteers and, as I have already said, where the United States has given an order, it has to be obeyed.'

The fellow continued to talk in this stupidly arrogant manner until I eventually made him understand that every person has their own opinion, whereupon he became more polite and finally took his leave with many clumsy compliments. I had the impression that before his promotion to general the man had been a cobbler somewhere.

Two days ago we received by chance the news of a war having broken out between Prussia and Italy on one side against Austria, which left us in a state of the greatest agitation. We thirst after news and take the very liveliest and warmest interest in the fate of our brothers in arms across the ocean. May they be fortunate in all their battles and engagements and may they be spared such sad experiences as have befallen us here.

I had almost forgotten to mention the doctors here and their manner of treatment. Of all the four or five persons availing themselves of this title, not a single one is a real doctor. All in fact are nothing but quacks and are, moreover, possessed of a fabulous indolence with regard to their patients. In our case, for instance, it is true that during the seventeen days of our presence here the doctor came to visit several times, enquiring in a general way about our state of health; however, it did not occur to him to look at the wound of any of the three of us or himself to put on a dressing. This would not have occurred to him in his wildest dreams, but my Josef, who is our factotum here, rinses the wound of each of us with water twice a day and puts a plaster and a bandage on it; and now we must see to it that it heals, for certainly no one other than those affected will bother any more about it. Woe to a severely wounded person, who really needs careful medical treatment. The poor man is certainly lost, just like our poor Rauch, who had a bullet lodged in his shoulder blade and who, in spite of repeatedly asking, could not get the doctor to extract it, probably because the latter did not know how or dare to undertake the operation, or was too lazy to do it. Whatever the reason, he consoled the poor man by promising him that he would be well within a month, but on the sixth day, in our presence and in full consciousness, the poor devil expired in the most terrible agony. Rauch was a former officer, had only come to Mexico from Europe in November and was a very decent and lovable person, about whom we were all very sorry.

The riflemen, first class, of 2 Company are also remarkable in their misfortune. Since I have been with the company five of them, all

---

* United States secretary of state.

equally solid, decent people, have perished. Pesch and Randhartinger died in Campeche of yellow fever, Seuchter fell at Bagdad; and in the last affair both the riflemen, first class – that is Cadet Fränkl and Prekop – were casualties. They were two outstanding men, the former one of the most excellent officer cadets. In addition, Senior Rifleman Lukaczy, Rifleman Prehnal, Rifleman Macher, Corporal Grerato and the number of other people already mentioned also fell.

It now still remains for me to mention a few facts concerning the behaviour of General Olvera in the engagement. Above all, it was his conspicuous lack of eagerness which became apparent after battle was joined. Olvera appeared once before the bayonet charge for a moment in our vicinity and I then heard him shout, 'A la bayoneta, a la bayoneta'. Immediately after this we made the charge, whereupon I lost sight of him, but he is said to have ridden to 5 Company, to which he at once shouted, 'Atrás, atrás,'* thereby creating disorder among the men and causing the officers the greatest difficulty in restoring calm and order again. Immediately thereafter he again cried 'A la bayoneta' and while 5 Company then advanced he made himself scarce with the remains of his cavalry.

Two days after we were taken prisoner we heard the funeral bell sound in the morning and at the same time saw from our window a closed carriage drive out of the town under cavalry escort. Inside were Lieutenant-Colonel Iglesias, commander of the battalion Cazadores de Querétaro, one of the best officers, I may say, of the Mejía divison, also his adjutant Captain Gómez, a Spaniard who had only been in imperial service a few months, then Lieutenant-Colonel Alcantara and finally another *licenciado*, whose name I no longer remember. All four were shot – Lieutenant-Colonel Iglesias because he was reputed as commander of Bagdad to have had several Liberal prisoners shot, Captain Gómez because he was his adjutant, Alcantara because he had previously belonged to the Liberal party and the *licenciado* for reasons unknown to me. The other Captain Gómez, commander of the rural guard, was also captured and at Trevino's demand shot while still on the battlefield.

The individual enemy military commanders who were assembled on the day of the battle were: Escobedo, Trevino, Espinosa, Baranjo, Canales and General Díaz de León, who, however, had no independent command but was chief of the general staff. According to recent information, the enemy troops in action that day numbered 3,000 in all.

On 26 June, the news, which affected us very disagreeably, was

* Back.

received here of the evacuation of Matamoros and the entry of the Republican general de la Garza. Mejía is understood to have withdrawn with approximately a thousand men, partly troops, partly compromised inhabitants, with military honours by the way, in three river steamers to the *boca*,* there to have embarked in several merchant ships and, escorted by the French naval steamer *Adonis*, to have proceeded either to Veracruz or Tampico. We have no other specific news, but it is said that at the moment among the many leaders of the opposition party present in Matamoros there are a multitude of candidates for governorship and that in consequence there is a considerable amount of strife and discord among them. I would add that the evacuation of Matamoros by the imperial troops was to be foreseen after the battle of Camargo, since after the departure of the 1,500 men escorting the convoy the garrison of the former town was no longer strong enough to come within measurable distance of occupying the extended positions of the town, let alone of defending them . . .

In order to have a rough idea of the loss I have suffered through the affair of the 16th in respect of baggage, horse etc., I will enter here an inventory of all the things, to the best of my recollection, together with valuations . . . [There follows an itemized list of all his lost possessions.]

Ernst gave the news of what had befallen him to his mother in a letter from Camargo dated 2 July 1866:

I hope that these lines will arrive in Vienna in time to relieve you of groundless fear for my person. Since my last letter from Matamoros dated the end of May this year many important, though unfortunately very disagreeable and sad things, have happened. The main thing, however, for you as for me, is that I have once more squeezed through – and this time perhaps from the most critical situation of my life – if not with my skin intact, then at least with the prospect of having it so in a little time. By comparison, all other concomitant misfortunes hardly deserve any consideration, even if in themselves they are anything but particularly consoling.

After describing the advance of the convoy from Matamoros until contact was made with the enemy, Ernst continued:

The following morning we set out at four o'clock and at five the battle was joined. I will not enter into a description of it and will only say

* River mouth.

that our whole Mexican cavalry rode away right at the beginning, that the two Mexican infantry battalions laid down their arms without resistance and only we 250 Austrians, together with a Mexican engineer company sixty strong, so altogether 310 men, faced an enemy of 3,000 among whom, to say no more, there were 600 well-armed cavalrymen.

In consequence the outcome reflected these circumstances. Of our ten officers four were dead, three were wounded and only three remained unscathed but nevertheless, like the three wounded, among whom I find myself, came into enemy captivity. Of our column numbering, with the men who stayed with the baggage, 285 all told, about 120 were dead, fifty were wounded and about 150 unwounded persons were taken prisoner, and perhaps ten escaped.

Of his own experiences on arriving at Camargo after the battle, Ernst wrote:

I was brought to the hospital half naked, covered in blood and, in particular, bleeding severely from my mouth. Although I was almost dead from thirst, I could hardly swallow a single drop through my swollen throat and what went down caused me terrible pain and also in part came out again behind through the external wound on the neck. For sixteen days I could take only liquids such as milk and soup and all this, as I say, came out again in part through the opening of the wound behind. But now my condition is again quite reasonable. I am completely out of danger: the wounds are closing and I can already take bread and meat finely cut.

He ended on a hopeful note:

At the beginning we thought that the enemy would have us shot, but this, fortunately, did not happen; on the contrary, we are very well treated, are free on parole and hope shortly to be exchanged. Under the circumstances, therefore, we are in fair trim.

Unfortunately all our possessions have fallen into the enemy's hands. My valuable horse complete with riding equipment, my weapons, watch, rings, money, trunks with all my belongings have gone to the devil and the loss I have suffered as a result is at least 1,300 pesos – about 3,000 florins – so that at present, as it were, I am not much richer than a beggar. Let us hope we receive some compensation and with this sum and my full pay I intend after our exchange to take a spell of leave for the recovery of my health and go to Europe for six months. Since in any case my company no longer exists and, in view of the present war with Prussia and Italy, reinforcements from Austria could hardly reach us now, I hope that no objection will be made to my request . . .

I cannot express myself more fully now, as our letters have to be shown to the authorities before despatch, but I will give you details in due course. For the present let it suffice, dearest Mother, that I am already almost completely well physically and that this misfortune which has befallen me may perhaps enable me soon to embrace you in person. I beseech you not to be upset, for I am relatively very well-situated, am in excellent spirits and regard what has happened to me merely as one of the vicissitudes of a soldier's life.

Continue to send your letters to Puebla as before, I will surely receive them from there in due course.

Kiss my brothers and sisters and relations, remember me to our acquaintances and be embraced a thousand times by your grateful son,

Ernst

Captivity

Despite the hopes of early release expressed in the last letter, Ernst was to spend nearly eight months as a prisoner. During this time a general deterioration in the situation foreshadowed the end of Maximilian's empire. Louis Napoleon had maintained his resolve to extricate himself from the Mexican débâcle and had given notice that all French forces would be withdrawn by February 1867. The United States as well as the Austrian governments were unwilling to intervene to resolve the conflict or to assist Maximilian in his predicament. On the military front the French, knowing that they were soon to leave the country, withdrew from successive positions without firing a shot and abandoned large stocks of arms and provisions to the Liberals in the process. The whole of the north, including the west coast ports, was thus evacuated and finally in August the important Gulf port of Tampico was handed over (the prefect, a man highly regarded in the community, was publicly hanged two days later). As the tide of war began to tilt in favour of the Liberals the population everywhere increasingly supported their cause and became hostile to the empire and particularly its foreign supporters. In the Sierra an upsurge of guerrilla activity brought the Austrians, desperately short of men and supplies, under growing pressure. Unable to hold out in their isolated positions, the Austrians withdrew in a series of fierce engagements until finally, in November, the last stronghold of Jalapa was evacuated by its garrison under a negotiated truce, with the surrender of their arms. Further south the corps was less fortunate: in the same month an Austrian force was sent to the relief of Oaxaca, the last remaining stronghold in the south,

but was repulsed at Carbonera by the troops of General Porfirio
Díaz with the loss of more than 400 killed or captured. Shortly
afterwards Oaxaca itself, with a garrison of Austrians and French
under French command, surrendered to the Liberals. Apart from
the capital, only San Luis Potosí (soon to fall to the Liberals),
Querétaro, Puebla, Orizaba and Veracruz, of the major cities,
now remained in the hands of the imperial government.

In these desperate circumstances and deeply afflicted by the
news that the Empress Charlotte, who had gone to Europe in a
vain attempt to drum up support for the empire, had suffered a
mental breakdown (which proved to be irreversible), Maximilian
resolved to abdicate and leave the country. With this intention in
mind he left the capital at the end of October to proceed to
Orizaba, a pleasant hill station on the way to Veracruz, where an
Austrian corvette was waiting. In Orizaba, however, Maximilian
allowed himself to be persuaded by the monarchists, whose
interests were linked to the continuance of the empire, and by
some Austrian officers (one was Count Khevenhüller, who
reproached himself for this afterwards) to stay on. Despair over
the news about his wife and the thought, encouraged by reports
of the unhelpful attitude shown in Vienna towards the possibility
of his returning, that there was no future for him in Europe could
have contributed to this decision; so could a continuing sense of
responsibility towards his adopted country. Maximilian was also
encouraged by his military advisers to believe that, even without
the French (whose departure, together with the Austro-Belgian
volunteer corps, would rid him of the taint of foreign support), an
effective national army could be created. He also had hopes of
arriving at a peaceful solution of the constitutional problem by
convoking a national congress to decide on the country's future.
So he returned to Mexico City.

With the impending departure of the French and the imperial
government's chronic lack of money there could now be no future
for the volunteer corps. A decree issued on 6 December accordingly announced its dissolution. Those members of the corps who
wished to return home would be provided with a free passage to
the place from which they had come. Those who wished to remain
were offered transfer to the national army at one grade above
their existing rank.

Maximilian naturally hoped that many in the corps would accept his offer of enrolment in the Mexican army, but the proposal gave rise to an unseemly controversy, the Austrian minister Baron Lago, in particular, maintaining that Austrians in the corps should be advised to accept the offer of a free passage home. This involved him in acrimonious exchanges with senior Austrian officers who had elected to remain and were close to Maximilian. The French too, who until recently had supported the formation of a national army, now did everything to dissuade their nationals from joining it. In the event only some 800 Austrians opted for Mexican service. The remainder, numbering about 3,600, chose to be repatriated with the French and left in February. Of the 7,100 Austrians who had come to Mexico with the corps two years previously, some 1,500 had been killed or had died: about 1,000 were prisoners or had chosen to remain in Mexico.

The new national army was formed into three army corps commanded by the generals whom Maximilian considered the ablest and most loyal – Miramón, Márquez and Mejía. The backbone of the army, however, was provided by three units under Austrian command. Count Khevenhüller raised and led a cavalry regiment which came to be known as the 'Red Hussars' their uniforms were entirely red – the only available material left by the French. Baron Hammerstein, who had distinguished himself in the recent fighting in the Sierra, commanded an infantry regiment and Count Wyckenburg the constabulary. Other Austrian officers held posts in the government and Colonel Kodolitsch served as *aide-de-camp* to the emperor.

At this stage Maximilian can have entertained no illusions about winning the war. He may, however, have hoped that if the new army proved able to contain the Liberal offensive – and knowing that popular sentiment could quickly change – it might still be possible to arrive at a negotiated settlement of some kind.

Ernst wrote in his diary on 16 July:

> Today one month of our captivity has passed. Nothing essentially new has happened during this time. Despite the lack of all and every medical care our wounds remarkably – and thanks to the care we ourselves have given to them – are well on the way to being healed.
>
> For the rest, we know absolutely nothing of what is in store for us. Kalumsky alone is in Matamoros. Krause and Faber with the greater

part of the prisoners are said to be in Reynose and it is said that they are expected soon to arrive here. Vague rumours are also circulating, which we do not find very pleasant. We ourselves have already noticed how systematically the enemy seeks to disperse and distribute our captured men. Many were employed as servants for the enemy's officers; others moved here and others there. But yesterday, after General Trevino had arrived with about 300 horsemen, in a new development three of our wounded, who had already more or less recovered, were taken out of the hospital and without further ado were forcibly merged with the rest of the cavalry. Simultaneously we heard that it is intended to do the same with the rest of our compatriots. Should this really happen it would be another misfortune for us, as we would then have to bear the shame of knowing that our own compatriots were in the ranks of the enemy and of having to endure the many sneering remarks and false constructions to be expected in this context.

The behaviour of the prisoner Dr Ealo, who is entrusted with the administration of the hospital here, is also beginning to be very peculiar. Leaving aside his indifference towards the wounded, to which I have already referred, he gives himself all kinds of airs, punishes our men according to his whim, promises others to procure favours for them and tells them that they will not have to return to the corps – in a word, none of us gives a farthing for his loyalty any more, believing, rather, that the good fellow is nurturing quite extraordinary ideas and plans, characteristic, be it said, of his race, and is probably already negotiating with the other side about going over to them. God grant that he is accepted there, for in truth it would be a gain for our side to be rid of such a fellow.

Mr Hermann* came here a few days ago from Matamoros and visited us. He had always been a Republican and therefore does not seem to be particularly displeased by the turn of events. He also left us two gold coins.

In Matamoros Carbajal rules at present with Cortina and Canales. According to all reports one of those habitual fights is again brewing between the aforementioned three gentlemen which could shortly break out and end in the fall and departure of one or other of them.

Escobedo and Díaz are expected here within days. We will try to secure from them permission to go to Matamoros.

The day before yesterday another officer of his staff,† Enking by name, arrived, and also a Prussian named Alvensleben‡ who had come down in the world. Both were formerly Yankee officers. Enking,

---

* He is not otherwise identified.
† Presumably Escobedo's.
‡ Baron Max von Alvensleben. In his book *With Maximilian in Mexico* Alvensleben claims to have fought for the empire at Camargo and, like Ernst, to have been wounded and taken prisoner.

an American by birth of Danish parents, is a dedicated Republican but otherwise, so far as is possible in the circumstances, a decent person. Alvensleben was once an aristocrat, but all he has retained of his caste is a hatred for everything that is not noble; for the rest he has, as he himself admits, pretty well ceased to cultivate the aristocracy's good qualities after four years of association with the Yankee riff-raff.

He offered us the residue of his purse, consisting of four reals, in comradely fashion. We naturally declined and also took care not to let our available cash, consisting of 40 thaler, be seen in his presence, since otherwise the situation could easily change and the magnanimous donor become a cadger. Incidentally we are up to now – touch wood! – more or less well provided and a certain Relsey here continually offers us loans . . .

On 10 July, the rainy season began here and from that day on it has rained almost without stopping, which is all the more disagreeable for us since the ceiling in our room is not at all watertight, but on the contrary drips from all sides.

It is already the 19th and we still have no news either as regards our own situation or concerning the war between Austria and Prussia, which causes us all such great anxiety.

On the 9th we tried by letter through the local merchant Deker to obtain a credit from Dröge, Ötling & Company and therefore await the return of the said businessman with considerable curiosity.

Three days ago I received through one of the Liberal officers a parcel with clothes and underwear presumably sent to me by Schumacher, but without a line. As a result I am now again equipped in most luxurious fashion and am only afraid that here in this company it might on some occasion again be taken away from me.

A few days ago we received a very polite letter from Colonel Naranjo in reply to a letter of ours in which, on the advice of Dr Argnindegui, we thanked him for his exertion on our behalf etc., etc.

The day before yesterday Generals Escobedo and Díaz arrived here and today we received orders to leave for the interior. God knows where we are being dragged off to and how much longer our captivity will be stretched out. Fortunately we are at least tolerably well provided with linen, clothing and money and so are covered for at least six weeks.

We are to set out at 12 noon tomorrow the 23rd.

Ernst wrote to his mother from Camargo on 22 July:

Dearest Mother,
Only in haste and with few lines am I able to give you news of myself today. Thanks to my robust constitution I have entirely recovered from

my three wounds and am now physically completely well. Our treatment is also pretty good and we are again more or less provided with clothes and also with some money. The latter we owe in part to the favour of the firm of Dröge & Ötling in Matamoros, as also to the kindness of the Republican commander here, General Escobedo, who supplied us with the necessary.

Tomorrow, however, we must leave here and march to the interior, whereby our exchange, which hopefully is already in train, could well be somewhat delayed, as well as my correspondence with you, dearest Mother, being interrupted for some considerable time. Our future destination is not known to us, but whatever happens I will write to you from there too when it is possible.

I beseech you again, dear Mother, not to take their misfortune which has befallen us too much to heart, as this is only an accident of war, which has already happened to so many people. I am not in a position to tell you more as I still have a great deal to do today, also our letters have to be delivered open.

Kiss and greet all our relatives, especially the brothers and sisters, and continue as before to write to me at Puebla. The letters will probably remain lying there for the time being, but sooner or later will come into my hands and will then give me infinite pleasure.

Remember me to all our acquaintances, particularly the Schmerling family, most warmly.

Be embraced once more a thousand times by your grateful son,

Ernst

Ernst continued in his diary:

At six o'clock on the morning of the 23rd we drove off from Camargo and were transported in a carriage intended for General Díaz and in the company of that general. On the afternoon of the same day we arrived in Quemada, about seven and a half leguas from Camargo. On the 24th we arrived at Paso del Zacate after a journey of ten leguas. At another three leguas from there our carriage broke down and we had to continue the way on foot. On the 25th, after a ride of four leguas on miserable horses we arrived in El Torro. There General Díaz, our protector hitherto, left us and we were ordered to await General Escobedo in El Torro in order to learn from him in what manner we were to be taken on.

We stayed there until the 28th. On the 27th our other prisoners of war with Krause and Faber arrived there and left from there again on the morning of the 28th. On the same day, Escobedo also arrived and with him the order to go to a place called China, three leguas distant.

Riding on a mule without a bridle and having therefore to exert myself considerably we – that is Ludovici, Adam and myself, they mounted on beasts no better than mine – arrived in China and here we receied orders to remain for the time being. The place is wretched, but we have a tolerable house to live in and together lead a tranquil rural life. The French prisoner Lieutenant Montier runs the mess.

                                                        12 August
Today I am spending my twenty-eighth birthday in rather sad circum-stances. Apart from the congratulations of my companions in misfor-tune it is not granted to me to receive the good wishes of my dear mother, who is certainly continually thinking of me. Although on this day last year in Campeche we also found ourselves under the influence of somewhat critical conditions, our situation then was nevertheless a relatively excellent one compared with today, where only an immeas-urably long vista of privations and worries presents itself to our vision. God grant that it may not be so and that we may soon be delivered from our captivity.

Ernst wrote to his mother from Monterey on 17 August:

Dearest Mother,
I am happy that it has been granted to me so far to be able to let you have news of me from time to time. Although on the other hand there is not the slightest guarantee that all these letters will reach your hands, I nevertheless at least console myself with the hope that not all will get lost and that you therefore do not live in too great anxiety on my account. The time of my captivity is a hard moral test, despite the fact that I am physically completely well and not suffering any material deprivation: indeed, I am astonishingly well treated in the circum-stances, allowed free movement on my word of honour, etc., etc. On the other hand, so many shattering reports which affect us closely are circulating here that a good dose of composure is needed to bear all this with peace of mind. Reports of great lost battles against Prussia, the cession of Venice, armistice etc., etc., are circulating here, and even though they are not completely confirmed, there is a fair likelihood that they are correct. Here I feel for the first time what a good Austrian I am, for I assure you that the said reports went more to my heart than my own captivity and that I gladly wished to be able to purchase with my life, if possible, the victory of Austria in this just war, which is so popular in the army.

Equally with regard to the situation of the Mexican empire the most fabulous rumours are circulating here, according to which one is to believe that the whole affair must be over in two months at the most. Fortunately one need give all these reports no more credence than they deserve, for, firstly, since the evacuation of Monterey by the French that city has gone over body and soul to the party of the Republic and, secondly, all routes to the interior are completely blocked and only now and then do reports, mostly of a strongly partisan complexion, reach the Republican camp through individual travellers. But for all that there can be no doubt that the imperial cause has recently become precarious. Through the battle of Santa Gertrudis* the evacuation of Matamoros, Monterey and Saltillo, in fact the whole northern frontier of Mexico, was brought about. The menacing attitude of North America seems equally to have affected the French government, for there is increasing talk of a withdrawal of the French. The forces of the Republic multiply daily and are supplied with first-class weapons, money and men by the great neighbouring republic. Finally, lack of money in the imperial coffers also seems to have reached its limit; they say that the Empress Charlotte has already travelled to Europe and that the Emperor Maximilian has completely fallen out with Marshal Bazaine. Now whether these things accord with the truth or are exaggerated, there must surely be something in them and that something is big enough to aggravate our situation here and prolong the time of our captivity. Meanwhile I ask you to keep these reports to yourself, as I would not wish to be known as their disseminator.

As I mentioned in my last letter, we were despatched from Camargo to the interior on the 23rd of this month. We were left for a few days in various small intermediate places and finally we received the news, already mentioned, of the evacuation of Monterey by the French, whereupon the Republican headquarters were immediately transferred there and we prisoners of war were also brought to Monterey. The latter town has about 40,000 inhabitants, is charmingly situated and in other circumstances would be a very agreeable quarter for me. We have here all possible amenities and, as I have already mentioned, we are as yet still well placed as regards money.

The last three wounds I received are completely healed and without any subsequent pain. Now that I am at it I can also inform you that in February this year at Bagdad I sustained two further wounds – one of them very dangerous – and did not fall with my horse, as I wrote to you.† Thanks to my exceptional constitution all this bloodletting has not only done me no harm but, to my great dismay, even now in captivity and in spite of wounds, worries and tribulations, I am getting fatter every day.

---

* Camargo.
† The wounds were the result of the duel in Bagdad, see above p. 110.

I spent my birthday in a very lonely and boring manner and for the first time the thought came into my mind that I too am beginning to come to an age when one is sorry not to have filled the years with anything more sensible than allowing oneself to be caught in Mexico. This time next year I shall already be entering my thirtieth year and soon after that I shall have passed the first little divide . . .

Ernst's diary continues:

Monterey, 19 August 1866

On 6 August, we received orders to set out for Monterey. An enormous freight wagon drawn by four mules was assigned to us for our transportation and we left the next morning. During the journey Lieutenant Adam's condition worsened in a disquieting manner. In addition to the wound in his foot he had a gastric fever, which in Cadereyta developed into typhus. He had, in fact, to stay behind in that place, where we commended him to the care of an American doctor resident there, by name Santiago Bellenay.

Cadereyta itself is a very nice little town and we took lodging there at moderate prices in the Hotel de la Trinidad, took a rest-day there and only left for Las Lermas on the second day. On the way, at an *arroyo*, we came across a hanged man, whom the Liberals had strung up on a tree because, or so I believe, he had letters from General Mejía on him.

On the 13th we finally reached Monterey. The column halted before the town, formed up and, after everyone had fallen in, the customary procession and display of the prisoners was immediately begun. We officers were fortunately released from this since, having freedom of movement, we kept as far away as possible from the performance from the very start.

I record the stages between China and Monterey:

7   River crossing with the convoy towards Los Angeles: half a legua
8   march to Levano: nine and a half leguas
9   march to Hacienda Dolores: eight leguas
10 march to Cadereyta: seven leguas
11 march to Las Lermas: seven leguas
12 march to Monterey: three leguas

Monterey is a very pretty and particularly well-situated town of about 40,000 inhabitants who, however, like those of Cadereyta, are throughout of Republican persuasion and do not regard us in at all a friendly way.

6 September 1866

In regard to our situation, everything is as before. Continually bad news about the position of the empire. We are constantly subjected to harassment regarding our accommodation by a certain Colonel Gómez.

Ernst wrote to his mother from Monterey on 7 September:

Dearest Mother,

Although for more than a whole half year now I have no longer had the joy of receiving news from you, I am nevertheless continuing tirelessly to let you hear something from me, as often as an opportunity of doing so presents itself, and this so limited conversation is nevertheless consoling and cheering in my present sad situation. In my own and my comrades' fate nothing has changed up to this moment. We have been prisoners of war here for nearly three months and although we are not particularly lacking in anything materially and are well treated nevertheless our morale worsens from day to day.

The situation of the empire seems to be assuming an increasingly critical appearance. Were one to lend credence to the highly partisan reports circulating here, it would only be a question of a few more months. But quite apart from these Job-like reports, there are reports from Europe that suggest that the empress's mission to the French court has failed and that it is certain that she will not return. Added to this is the fact that so far no steps of any kind for the purpose of an exchange have been made by our corps – yes, not even a sign of life intended for us alone has arrived here. Finally the sad and disheartening news from Austria – only slightly alleviated by the unrewarded successes of our brave army and navy in the south* – has brought our frame of mind to the zenith of melancholy and dejection. That said, however, our hopes for an early release from our disagreeable situation have not disappeared in so far as, according to rational analysis, there are only two possibilities, both of which must lead to the same result: either the empire remains and we are exchanged or it does not remain, the emperor abdicates and, before the withdrawal of the foreign troops from the country, an agreement is reached with the future government for the release of prisoners on both sides. In the first eventuality I am minded to take a spell of leave and to spend six months with you, dearest Mother, always assuming that the situation of the empire forbids a still longer duration. In the second eventuality, we would see each other anyhow.

---

* The Austrians had won resounding victories over Piedemontese troops at Custozzo and over the Italian navy at the battle of Lissa.

I have no idea whether the lady Kuhacsevich accompanied the empress to Europe.* In the event that Her Majesty does not return this would be very disagreeable for me, as through representation to the former I had placed high hope on the compensation of the severe financial losses I had suffered in the last engagement. According to the itemized list I have prepared these amount to about 1,200 thaler at their present estimated value or, according to the present exchange rate for the paper money in Austria, around 3,000 gulden, a fairly respectable sum for a poor first-lieutenant.

I send you herewith a poor photograph of me and my companions in misfortune, the residue of our officers who were in Matamoros. The three of us who are seated were severely wounded, the clean-shaven first-lieutenant on the left at the back was lightly wounded and only the lieutenant standing at the back to the right came through unscathed. The others are dead. If you look carefully you can see my wounds in the picture. There are two gashes running down my cheek from the left ear along the cheek-bone and a scar to the left at the back of the neck. I also have a light sword wound on my arm. I have felt no pain from all these for a long time now and – touch wood! – am healthier than ever.

Of my poor comrades from the army in Austria I will no doubt not find many left; nor from the brave navy, whose triumph† makes me very proud.

Let us hope that nothing has happened to any of my cousins. I can well imagine the anxiety of uncle, aunt, Mathilde and the others. Poor Irene, too, must have endured a great deal. I hope that nothing has happened to her husband either. Anyhow I presume that he was not serving in Bohemia but in Italy, where at least effort was rewarded with success.

I would so much have liked to ask you about other things, only the depressing consciousness of not being in a position to receive the answers from you stops my tongue and forces me to postpone all this to a more opportune time.

I do not have much else to tell you at present, dearest Mother. Monterey is boring, particularly for us. Those who perhaps favour the empire are actually afraid to talk with us, in order at all costs not to compromise themselves. We live in a charming house quite outside the town, are at home almost all day and only go for walks in the evening, in order to enjoy the delightful position and view, which offer themselves to the eye on every side. Monterey is perhaps, in truth, one

* She did and, with other members of the suite, had to witness the distressing scenes when Charlotte lost her reason in Rome.
† Over the Italians at the battle of Lissa.

of the most beautiful places in the world. A pity that different kinds of people don't live here. In all the spare time I have I make many castles in Spain. If, after all my experiences, I now return to Europe I shall for some time be prone to all kinds of bourgeois projects and ideas. Propose to me, on my return, a pretty, young and intelligent woman; should she be a widow, as well, with a little wealth, I'll not leave Europe again. But if this has not come about after a few years, then I shall go back to America, never to tread the ground of Europe again. Try therefore to make this modest wish possible for me and I will, once again, be a new acquisition for the Austrian army . . .

Ernst wrote again to his mother from Monterey on 9 October:

Dearest Mother,
Again a month has gone by since I last wrote to you and still I cannot report any change in our situation to you. June, July, August, September and part of October have already passed without our having been advised by a single line on the part of the corps command what we can hope for and expect. Equally, as I wrote to you recently, all news from Europe is lacking and it is terrible for me to learn nothing about you and the well-being of all my loved ones for so long. It is nearly three-quarters of a year since you wrote me the letter which last came into my hands and you see now how much pleasanter it is with correspondence if one is in Vienna, instead of the interior of Mexico. Besides, the former is also – so as not to be unjust to the town of my birth – pleasanter in many other respects. It is particularly difficult for me in my present situation to fill a letter of even four pages, as our life here is of a monotony that can hardly be imagined.

As all communication with the part of the country occupied by the imperial side is interrupted, we learn little more than nothing from the interior. The many rumours circulating in the town in terms partly to the advantage, partly to the disadvantage, of one or the other party deserve as little attention here as elsewhere. But I believe that this much is clear: a serious campaign by the imperial side in these areas is in preparation. God grant that we are exchanged before the start of the hostilities, since otherwise we will be faced with the prospect of a variety of future difficulties. The most likely in that case is that we shall be dragged off to God knows what corner of the land so that the happy day when we are liberated by the imperial troops may never come.

We have become acquainted with a number of German businessmen here, who with few exceptions have received us in a friendly manner though they are extremely reticent, as they do not want to spoil their relations with any party, least of all with the one at present in control, and are continually afraid of compromising themselves.

In my view it is almost certain that the empire is only capable of continuing in existence for a very short time longer. As it seems, Napoleon wants to be rid at all costs of this whole enterprise, which is now becoming an impediment for him in many different directions – yes, even liable to compromise France's political ascendancy hitherto – and I believe that nothing would be more agreeable to the Emperor Napoleon than Maximilian's abdication, so that he could then extricate himself from the affair with a modicum of propriety. On the other hand, the Emperor Maximilian is only too well aware of the unpleasantness of his future position as ex-emperor and from his point of view is quite right only to yield when the French, contrary to their original obligations, give way to the pressure of the United States and of their own opposition party in France and, in the face of the threatening events brewing in Europe, have finally withdrawn from here. I really regret this probable outcome of the drama which has been enacted here, for without doubt a further succession of bitter trials will take place for the unfortunate population here up to the moment when the greedy North Americans will take possession of the fat morsel being presented to them.

I will not enter into a description of the conditions here, because I would not wish to compromise myself either here through a possible disclosure of these lines or there, where by the way I ask you to keep secret these outspoken views.

15 October – understandably a day holding
a multitude of memories for me

It is two years since I left you and how much has happened meanwhile, how variously have the vicissitudes of the war already acted for me! Even the medallion with the kindly inscription, which you gave me to take with me in memory of that day, passed into the hands of goodness knows what fellows in the last engagement. But even if I do not possess the visible evidence of your motherly blessing any more, I know all the same that I am not without it at any hour. Receive, dearest Mother, the most heartfelt wishes of happiness and blessing for this day from your son so far distant, and be assured that my thoughts were with you from my very awakening. If God wills, I will spend your next saint's day with you in Vienna. Be reassured and consoled about my destiny which, if in itself at present disagreeable, boring and even depressing, is nevertheless not of such a kind as not to be looked forward to with complete confidence as to the future. Other people have certainly been in much worse situations and nevertheless are quite well today . . .

Ernst wrote again to his mother from Monterey on 11 November:

> Dearest Mother,
> Although another month has again gone by since my last letter to you,
> I can nevertheless still not give you any completely satisfactory news
> of our situation. That notwithstanding, I will not allow the time limit
> of our – or rather my – regular correspondence to pass without
> informing you of the little that has happened recently.
> After we had been completely without any news of the corps and
> from the interior of the country for almost five months a German
> gentleman, with whom I am on friendly terms, arrived here from the
> capital on the 8th of this month and brought me a detailed letter from
> a comrade with the assurance that the matter of our exchange was
> being zealously pursued and would shortly come to fulfilment. At the
> same time I was also informed by the Republican general Escobedo
> here that he too had been advised of the impending arrival of an
> imperial commissioner, sent here in the matter of our exchange, and
> that he was expecting him to appear from day to day. You can imagine
> that we are awaiting this man like the Messiah.
> The empire, as you people in Europe surely know, is at an end. The
> poor empress gone mad, a victim of Napoleonic deceit; the emperor,
> as we hear today, gone to Europe by the English steamer on the 29th
> of last month. In a short time we will follow, intending – unless a trick
> of some kind is to be played on us – to reoccupy the places in the
> Austrian army which we left.
> Except for a second decoration which, according to that officer's
> letter, I have received for the last engagement, I shall probably return
> home only a few scars better off. As for the losses I have suffered,
> amounting to 2,400 florins, I shall no doubt have to whistle for these –
> just as the same fate awaits my other companions in misfortune.
> Nevertheless I shall certainly not, once I have returned home, regret
> having taken part in the Mexican expedition. We have seen and learnt
> a great deal and the memory of that will be priceless.
> And so my fantasy of being in Vienna again in the year 1867 could
> in a strange way be realized. In Austria, too, I shall not find many an
> old comrade any more and have to hear many sad details about things
> past and present.
> The most disagreeable aspect of our present situation still remains
> the uncertainty, particularly in the matter of finance. To provide for
> our maintenance here we had to borrow money against our arrears of
> pay and it would be embarrassing for us to have to be owing this should
> we not be paid. The state of our outfits is also pretty dicey and once
> we are freed we shall need many additions.

As for you, dearest Mother, I have now been without any kind of news from you for three-quarters of a year. This is really terrible – to have no idea at all how things are with you and all my other loved ones. You must admit that in our mutual relationship your position is enviable compared to mine.

I believe that Colonel Kodolitsch accompanied the emperor to Europe. As I am on very good terms with him and he can give information about me, do not fail to send any officer of our acquaintance – for example Moritz Asten – to him, so that in this way you may also learn something.

General Thun, with a few officers of his staff, has already previously, as you will know, said goodbye to the corps.

Kuhacsevich, together with his wife, is probably also in Europe again. I ask you to be so good as to approach her on my behalf and say to her that my gold Guadalupe order was stolen from me in the fighting and that I beg her, as Chancellor of the Order, to reserve one for me if there are still some left, so that, if I arrive in Europe too late, I am not perhaps given the name of the goldsmith, with the friendly advice to buy one for myself for 60 florins. The latter would be quite possible, for it is said here that the expedition has cost Their Majesties much of their private fortune.

I take this opportunity of repeating the plea I have already made several times not to make my letters very public, on account of the remarks occurring in them here and there – however innocent they may be – as I would be very loath to cause damage to myself thereby. After, as I hope, my early return I shall be willing to tell all that is possible, but I do not like to set it down on paper . . .

I kiss you many thousand times and confidently hope to be with you in a quarter of a year.

Your faithful son,
Ernst

Ernst wrote again to his mother from Monterey on 6 December:

Dearest Mother,
I would have liked to postpone the despatch of this letter until the moment when I would be in a position to inform you of our release and return to Europe. However, the final resolution of the political situation here, which is in a state of decisive crisis, is dragging on and being delayed in a most disagreeable manner. The emperor, who according to a report published by the official Republican newspaper here, as I wrote to you in my last letter, was supposed to have left for Europe on 29 October, is, according to more recent reports, still here

– although it is said that he no longer handles government business. He has also taken up residence in Orizaba and seems to be awaiting the departure of the French there. The latter, however, seem to want the Emperor to abdicate first, in order then to be able to shift the blame for the failure of the undertaking from their shoulders to those of Maximilian. A German who arrived here a few days ago from Mexico and who had frequent contact with the court chaplain Fischer* and also with officers of our corps told me hair-raising things about the perfidy of the French. The latter have for a long time not been mounting expeditions but, evidently intentionally, allowing the reinforcement and concentration of the enemy to continue. They move only in large columns, which enables them always to return unmolested to their bases. They cause their flanks and generally all exposed positions to be occupied by small isolated detachments of the Austrian and Belgian corps, as a result of which these two forces have recently – given the six- to tenfold superiority of the enemy prevailing everywhere – suffered immeasurably. According to reports received, the fortress of Oaxaca had to capitulate because a column of 400 Austrians sent for its relief was attacked by 4,000 men under Porfirio Díaz and destroyed. Jalapa, with a garrison of 600 Austrians, had already been surrounded by 4,000 Republican troops for several weeks and although Colonel Dupin with a considerable force of French troops was twelve leguas away nothing was done for them, so that, after the town had been completely starved out, the garrison had to surrender unconditionally. The same sort of thing occurred at many other places as well and in fact quite systematically. It seems that the French government has already involved itself so far in negotiations with the United States or perhaps even with Juárez that it would be highly inconvenient for them if the emperor tried to stay on in the country after their departure and so Marshal Bazaine has hit on the praiseworthy idea first and foremost to liquidate and destroy the Belgian/Austrian Legion in the manner described, as being the main support of the emperor after the departure of the French, so that nothing is left for the emperor but to abdicate and go home as well. You can imagine how indignant we all are at this infamy. It is on a par with the many other villainies committed by the 'grande nation'. Let us hope that we have another opportunity of repaying them with interest.

Otherwise there is not much news from here. The cholera has been our guest for about two weeks, but – touch wood! – has so far manifested itself in a fairly mild form.

In Matamoros there is turmoil, as has always happened under the

---

* A disreputable cleric, who wormed his way into Maximilian's confidence and exerted a baneful influence over him.

Republican regime in Mexico. The Republican governor there, Canales, rebelled against Juárez, who for his part despatched General Escobedo with a military force to chastise the former. The two are fighting each other there now, while the Americans, in order to put an end to all quarelling, crossed the river a few days ago and occupied Matamoros by armed force in the name of the United States. No one knows how the affair will end and how order will be restored out of this chaos.

In the last few weeks we received a remittance of money from the corps, which enabled us to provide ourselves with clothes and other necessary things – unfortunately everything at horrendous prices. I had to pay nearly 100 florins for a pair of trousers, waistcoat and a simple thin autumn coat.

Generally, and as far as our material situation is concerned, we are well off: we are as free and unrestricted as possible and in the last few weeks, at the invitation of our German compatriots here, we have taken part in two country excursions with splendid dinners several leguas outside the town without any questions being asked. The one really miserable thing for me is the lack of news from you and the other relations and friends. Had I dreamt that we would remain here so long, I could quite easily have arranged a correspondence between us, as the German trading firms here receive their European letters with the greatest regularity and their correspondents in Europe would be very glad to send our letters along as well. However, it is now no longer worth the effort, for I am sure that we shall be free in one to two months. So this short time more has to be endured with patience. Within a few months I hope to hold you in my arms. Until then I kiss you ten thousand times and ask you to convey my warmest greetings to brothers and sisters, relations and friends from your faithful son,

Ernst

Ernst wrote again from Monterey on 31 December:

Dearest Mother,
Although alas I can still not provide you – apart from my heartfelt good wishes for the New Year – with any joyful tidings having regard, in particular, to a change in my situation, it is nevertheless not possible for me to end this year of 1866, which has been so fateful for me, without at the same time remembering you in writing, since no doubt you at this time – and surely with thoughts similar to mine – are casting your thoughts back over the past twelve months and all the good and bad that they brought you. Even though I had to endure the realities

and you only their description, I nevertheless know how greatly you must have suffered from them and my ardent wish would be soon to be able to compensate you again with a really agreeable announcement for the worries you have had. As I mentioned at the beginning, however, nothing has so far changed in our situation.

The imperial government continues to exist *de facto*, even if in a fairly restricted part of the country, and takes no steps of any kind to have us exchanged, in consequence of which the Republican party, which holds us prisoner, also seems for the time being to have no wish to let us go. In the various further discussions which I had on this subject with the commanding general, Escobedo, this gentleman always answered me in the diplomatically sufficient manner peculiar to the true Mexican. One always receives vague assurances, never definite undertakings, never a 'yes' or 'no', never a 'today', but always 'Quién sabe?' or 'Mañana' in reply. I asked this gentleman to permit me to travel to Mexico – always as his prisoner and in a word binding myself to return – in order then to pursue the matter of our exchange from there and to be able to support our financial demands forcibly in person. He apparently assented, but I was put off from one day to the next; finally, however, my request was not flatly turned down, but circumvented by the general leaving with his whole crew without giving my request a further thought. Now we are back in the old position – in other words, we have to wait indefinitely and comfort ourselves with the hope of better days, which with the high cost of living here, and the fact that five officers cannot manage as easily as one, does not exactly present a very comforting prospect.

In the last few days two of the largest towns in Mexico, San Luis Potosí and Guadalajara, were again occupied by the Liberals and so the circle is drawn ever more closely round the capital and the poor emperor, betrayed by both French and Mexicans. It is an open secret that the last reverses of the imperial forces were deliberately brought about by Marshal Bazaine simply to compel the emperor to leave the country before the departure of the French, whereas the former, as it seems, wants to take note of the way in which his ally is deserting him.

Ernst wrote again to his mother from Monterey on 8 January:

It will soon be a year since you wrote the last letter which has come into my hands. How much can have changed at home in that time without my having an inkling of it. It cannot be denied that this is the one feature of my present lot which I find most unbearable. One thought alone comforts me and that is the firm conviction that the year of 1867 will see me in Vienna again and with you, when I shall forthwith seek plentiful compensation for the many months in which I have been deprived of news from you.

No doubt you will this time have spent the recent holidays at the Herzigs' and therefore have felt less lonely than otherwise. I too did not lack a Christmas tree, although I have for some time been accustomed to not seeing one. I was invited for this occasion to three German families and spent some time with each of them. Altogether we cannot complain of the social conditions. The local Germans, mostly rich merchants and cultured people, have received us in their homes in a very friendly way, we are on almost intimate terms with all of them, are welcome in their houses and, as is the custom here, are always entertained in the most lavish manner. We have even danced twice in the last two days and thoroughly enjoyed it. All this would be very fine if the psychological situation was not so oppressive.

The cholera, which was quite strongly prevalent here for two months, has died away again . . .

There is much more I could ask, but since unfortunately I know the impossibility of receiving an answer I will refrain from doing so and confine myself to embracing you a thousand times and asking you often to think of your grateful son,

Ernst

Ernst wrote in his diary:

Today, on 15 January, after two years have passed since my arrival in Veracruz, I am beginning the third booklet of my experiences in Mexico and at the same time express the sincere wish that it may be the last.

Turning over the pages of the notes I have recently written during my captivity, which are expressed in very laconic terms, what has chiefly struck me is that I forgot to mention the impression which the accounts of the unhappy war of Austria against Prussia aroused both in me and in my comrades who are here. The victories won against Italy on land and at sea afforded us comparatively only slight consolation for this, since nevertheless they did not protect us from the cession of Venice, which the Prussians demanded. Here for the first time I came to realize how fond I am of my dear Austria, for since that time I know no more ardent wish than that it may be granted to me as soon as possible to be able, in the ranks of the Austrian army, to score a spectacular revenge against the despicable Prussians. The naval battle at Lissa in particular gave me special pleasure and I duly remembered with pride the two years when I also belonged to our navy.

Continuing the description of the political situation in the north of

Mexico and particularly the state of Tama Ulipas, which I already
began in November last year, I must mention that General Tapia, who
was sent to Matamoros to overthrow the rebellious Colonel Canales,
succumbed to cholera in camp before the town. In him the Liberals
lost one of their most esteemed generals and soon thereafter, as I also
indicated in the previous booklet, General Escobedo from here
marched off in order – as the official newspaper in Monterey ceremo-
niously announced – to put an end to the scandalous occurrences in
Matamoros and at least to have their originator, Cadrón Canales,
spitted and roasted or, failing that, at least to have him hanged.
Significant troop arrivals strengthened the investing force already
encamped before Matamoros and everything was put in train to storm
the recalcitrant city. On 25 November 500 Americans from Brownsville
even went to Matamoros, but without using force against Colonel
Canales. On the contrary, they contributed a further delightful addition
to the general ambiguity of their intentions. Although President
Johnston recognized the Mexican Republic under Juárez and ordered
that it should be supported in every way, it never occurred to the
American commander in Brownsville, General Sedgwick, to take sides
in favour of Juárez's superior general, Escobedo, against the rebel
Canales; on the contrary, as already mentioned, he occupied the
interior of the town of Matamoros and thereby allowed Colonel
Canales to use all his forces for the defence of the fortifications. On 27
November, Escobedo really attacked and got an awful beating, losing
more than 900 men. His dispositions are said to have been appallingly
stupid and the whole world – above all his officers – complain of the
senselessness of the attack. Bolstered by his success, Canales thereupon
began new negotiations, which resulted in Escobedo entering the town
on 1 December and installing a new governor there. Cortina and
Canales (who never relinquished his command of troops) were supposed to march to the interior after this agreement with Escobedo and
in this way the two disturbers of the peace were to be manœuvred out
of the state of Tama Ulipas. But Escobedo had again made a worthless
calculation. No sooner were Canales and Cortina outside the city than
they declared a new allegiance, this time in favour of General J.
Gonzales Oriega and struck sideways into the bush in the direction of
Victoria. Still mindful of the beating he received before Matamoros,
Escobedo is glad to have come through like this and is certainly not
going to allow himself a second time to have the idea of wanting to
chastise the rebels and indeed he came straight back here quite quietly
with his own troops. In consequence nothing has changed in the
situation of the unfortunate inhabitants of Matamoros and they expect
from day to day to fall into the hands of Cortina and Canales again, as

the weak garrison cannot possibly withstand an attack from one of these brigands.

Since the imperial commissioner, whom we have been longingly awaiting for so long, failed to appear, I again tried to persuade General Escobedo to allow me to travel to Mexico in person, so that I could myself pursue there the matter of an exchange for all of us. The general did, indeed, promise me at least twenty times that he would grant my request, but finally nevertheless departed from here on the 7th of this month to place himself at the head of the pack of warriors who are to operate towards the interior, without having finally decided on my application. He in fact gave the French officer, Lieutenant Moutier, who had approached him with the same request, a passport, which however did not extend as far as Mexico, but only to his future headquarters, probably San Luis. But since Moutier has no money to pay for the stage-coach as far as that he will probably also stay here.

We spent the recent holidays passably pleasantly and visited several houses of our German compatriots, where Christmas Eve was celebrated in the traditional manner with a Christmas tree. Otherwise there was also a great deal of boozing and carousing and even dancing on two occasions, when a very nice little American lady enjoyed my particular approval.

The change of temperature observable here in the last few days was quite remarkable. In the first days of January we had half a foot of snow, which was still partly visible after two days, and three degrees of frost. On the other hand, yesterday we had heat of 33 degrees Réaumur in the shade at one o'clock in the afternoon. How easily one can catch a cold in such conditions is very clear.

In the last few days I came to know the well-known Colonel Carl von Gagern here. After having been a prisoner of war for some considerable time in France, having travelled in Germany and done some writing in the United States, he came back here again to place himself at the disposal of the Republic (for whom things were now going more favourably) and perhaps also to make an endeavour, at a favourable opportunity, to cash in on his reputed claims for arrears of pay amounting to 27,000 thaler. He was not received in a very welcoming manner by Escobedo and so he went with his adjutant, a certain Herr von Glümer (a former Prussian cadet then in the Foreign Legion, subsequently a deserter and now Sub-Lieutenant in Mexican service), to the president in Durango to support his claims there in a suitable manner. Gagern is a very intelligent man – only a little highly-strung and by now too Mexicanized in a certain sense. However, the latter may perhaps only be pretence. 'Every man sings the song of him whose bread he eats – or wishes to eat'.* His greatest fault is obviously his disreputable adjutant.

Practically nothing is now left of our prisoners. Most of them are dispersed in all corners of the earth and only a small number – and they the biggest rascals – are still here. Almost every day one or the other fellow is put under arrest, drunk as a pig. With our servants we also have trouble; however well we pay the brutes they are still impertinent, obstinate and often drunk. Recently one of these gentlemen stole my entire wherewithal – 25 thaler – out of my trunk. The thief and his loot were never seen again, which in our situation is not exactly pleasurable.

Otherwise our way of life is monotonous in the highest degree. We mess at home, go into town in the evening and visit our German acquaintances there, then go from there to the inn for a few glasses of beer, sleep till 10.30 in the morning, play innumerable games of piquet in the intervening moments and then start again from the beginning. Our general irritation and ill humour makes it almost impossible to occupy oneself with anything sensible. Everything is loathsome; for letter-writing I have neither desire nor material; I confine myself to a very laconically worded letter to my mother every month. How I keep my supposed diary can best be seen if one compares the intervals between the different dates.

Recently I have again had to renew my whole wardrobe, which had gone to the dogs, and the resulting expense is giving me a severe headache.

There has been much unhappiness of late in the family of the Goldschmidts, who live here and are very friendly to us. Two brothers of the head of the family are lying severely ill and yesterday morning his three-month-old child, his youngest, died.

It is impossible to make any kind of judgement on how the political situation in the interior is developing. So much is certain: that everything is in a state of complete chaos, and no one can make head or tail of it. The departure of the French seems to be definite – at least they have withdrawn from all parts of the country towards Orizaba, Puebla and Mexico. The Liberals have followed them and as a result have gained possession of the biggest and richest towns of the country, such as, for example, Guadalajara and San Luis, without blood being spilt. Of the emperor, on the other hand, it is learnt that despite everything he does not want to leave the country. He has announced this solemnly in a proclamation on 1 December. One hears also that the clergy and landowners have persuaded him to do this and have

---

* A similar English saying might be: 'he who pays the piper calls the tune'.

offered sufficient finance for the creation of a national army. Nevertheless one hears nothing at all of this national army and the circle drawn
round the capital, Mexico, contracts ever more. Already the Liberal
forces are threatening Querétaro and Toluca; Oaxaca and Jalapa they
hold already; and except for Veracruz the whole coast belongs to them.

Ponder as one will, then, one cannot deduce from all this what the
future may bring. Hardly something pleasing for us. It is, then, not to
be wondered at if we are gradually filled with deep disgust over all
these circumstances. We sit here in a corner of Mexico, forsaken by all
the world, with the prospect of perhaps being set free one fine day
after the fall of the empire and of having then to beg our way home.

My fixed idea of being in Vienna on 1 June 1867, where my friend
Thoren invited me to breakfast and where I have also arranged a
second meeting with our amiable compatriot Lohmann, can surely
hardly be fulfilled within that time limit and I will simply have to
apologize to these two gentlemen and ask for a postponement of our
agreed meeting.

But now I think I have written diligently enough for this time and
will postpone to next month the continuation of this booklet, so
worthily initiated.

San Luis Potosí, 29 January 1867

Man reflects and fortune directs. Two weeks ago today I was still
counting on remaining in Monterey and instead, after four days, I am
already 160 leguas away from there. Lieutenant Moutier, of whose
departure I was recently still doubtful, got going nevertheless and went
with the stage-coach to San Luis on the 16th of the month. A few days
later the official newspaper of Monterey brought the news of the
dissolution of the Austrian volunteer corps, which had come about by
virtue of His Majesty's decree of 6 December last year. Of course this
news caused not a little excitement among us: I immediately went to
the governor and obtained permission also to be allowed to go to San
Luis. On the 21st I left Monterey with bag and baggage and I have
been here since the 25th. The journey was not very agreeable, as I
found myself in the most frightful company. Eleven Mexicans of the
stupidest and coarsest kind were crammed into the box and combined
with the dreariness of the route to make the whole journey thoroughly
disagreeable.

Except for a few towns and *ranchos*, whose immediate neighbourhood is somewhat cultivated, the whole terrain between here and
Monterey is not much better than desert. Sand, dust and masses of
prickly pears and cactus are the only variation which presents itself to
the eye. The lack of water is particularly evident, for it is undeniable
that if this element were present in sufficient quantity those immense

unpopulated wastes could be transformed into the most fertile and populated territories.

Near the hacienda del incarnación we saw many of those rat-like prairie dogs, who live in thousands in subterranean holes immediately round the hacienda. We also killed a jackal, who in broad daylight and without allowing himself to be disturbed by the stage-coach clattering along was gnawing at the remains of a dead mule.

Almost all the haciendas which we encountered on our way bore the traces of battles which had taken place there recently or at least within the last two years. Everything is arranged for defence: crenellated walls, embrasures, redoubts on all sides. But unfortunately, on the other hand, despite the apparent splendour of the buildings, the multitude of cattle etc., the food is so miserable one is hardly able to believe it. Travellers on their journeys, usually covering thirty to forty leguas a day, are often unable to obtain even the slightest bit of food at those intermediate points where mules are generally changed. Recently the route had again become insecure through frequent attacks and the country between here and Querétaro, in particular, is traversed by bands of 25–200 men to such an extent that the same stage-coach is usually attacked and pillaged three times on its journey. Naturally the first band does not leave much over for their successors and the latter seek to avenge themselves by giving the passengers a sound thrashing . . .

Already at one of the last stops before San Luis we learnt that the imperial General Miramón with two to three thousand men was marching from Aguas Calientes towards Zacatecas, while another imperial general named Bastille was advancing along the road from Querétaro towards San Luis. The Liberal forces immediately moved towards Zacatecas in order to confront General Miramón who had already taken that town. General Miramón immediately withdrew at the approach of the greatly superior enemy, but was overtaken and completely defeated at San Jacinto. Next day 131 foreigners, mostly French and German, who had been taken prisoner on this occasion, were shot on the orders of President Juárez. On the following day the same happened to General Joaquín Miramón, brother of the commander-in-chief, who after being wounded had also fallen into the hands of the enemy.

Ernst wrote to his mother from San Luis Potosí on 4 February:

Dearest Mother,
Since I last gave you news of myself I have been diverted some 160 leguas further towards the interior of Mexico and have every reason to

be extremely satisfied with this exchange. As I informed you, Escobedo promised me that he would let me go to Mexico as negotiator for the other prisoners. However he left Monterey without fulfilling his promise and all of us were completely resigned and convinced that we would have to remain in that town for several months more. Then one day the local official newspaper brought the news of the disbandment of the Austro-Belgian volunteer corps by virtue of an imperial decree of 6 December last year, whereby, as it appears, Emperor Maximilian closes the period in which he relied on foreign help and throws himself completely into the arms of the Conservative Mexican party. As a result our positon was suddenly completely changed. The emperor himself discharges us. In consequence we are private individuals without any obligation to the empire, the more so since the latter itself abandoned us, and moreover a valueless burden for the Republican party, since under present conditions an exchange, as already mentioned, is all the less to be thought of since we no longer belong to any force in imperial service. I asked the governor of Monterey for permission, in the prevailing conditions, to proceed to General Escobedo's headquarters in San Luis and received it. On 21 January, I left with the stage-coach and arrived here after an uninterrupted journey of five days.

Thanks to several letters of introduction I received the friendliest reception in the house of Herr Bahnsen, the consul-general of Hamburg. I lodge and live completely with him and enjoy a degree of comfort such as I have not seen for a long time. Herr Bahnsen is a young man of thirty-two years, very rich and still unmarried. Two of his sisters – one because of her health, the other as her companion – are also here and are really as amiable as they are cultured and it is a real relief for me to be in such company again after such a long time. I travel around a good deal with the ladies, also ride often, as there are ten horses which are very seldom used, and always spend the evenings in the house.

General Escobedo received me in a very friendly manner, the more so as Herr Bahnsen supported me most effectively by himself accompanying me there. Escobedo promised me on his word that he only wanted to await the arrival here of President Juárez, which was to take place within a few days, in order then to set us all free. Of his own accord he promised me most honourable attestations by the Republican government both as to our conduct in battle as also in the long period of our captivity and he also told me that his government certainly wished to give us the means for our journey home.

But all these fair prospects seemed not to want to be translated into reality, for suddenly news reached us that the imperial general Miramón, who is as brave as he is reckless, was advancing in association with General Castillo with a total strength of six to seven thousand men. And General Miramón did indeed occupy the town of Zacatecas, which only had a weak garrison, and the president, who was there just then, had to flee. Immediately the whole Liberal army set out from here to confront Miramón and on the 1st of this month the latter was totally defeated, losing artillery, transport, baggage, in a word everything, and is reported to have joined General Castillo with only forty men. With this the imperial cause could well have received its *coup de grace*, for the circle round the capital is being drawn ever closer and the superiority of the Republican party is already such that further resistance would now be completely useless and would expose the poor emperor to the calamitous risk of being captured.

The French take no part in anything any more. They have assembled between Puebla and Veracruz and play the part of calm observers of the drama nearing its end.

I cannot tell you what conflicting emotions I felt on hearing of Miramón's defet. Sympathy for the poor emperor and the desire for an indirect revenge for Santa Gertrudis conflict with the egoistic thought that early freedom is only in prospect for me like this. For if the imperials had won, our present masters would assuredly not have released us so soon.

Juárez is due to arrive here within a few days and our fate will then be decided. If we are released I will first go to Mexico in order to extract there as much as is still possible of our claims for arrears of pay, compensation for losses etc. I fear, however, that by then I shall not find the emperor there any more or else that everything will already be in a state of utter confusion and disintegration. In either case I shall consequently fail in my demands and, if I do not get justice in Europe, shall arrive home a rather poor beggar.

Depending on the state of my finances I shall either make the return journey via the United States, England and France or, if my finances are poor, directly via France. I shall then immediately rejoin the army, where I must surely be classified as the senior second-lieutenant and immediately become first-lieutenant at the first vacancy. In the conditions of our transfer [to the volunteer force for Mexico] we assumed the obligation to serve the empire for six years in order to have the right to return to the Austrian army. Naturally, since it is not we, but the empire, which departs first and discharges us, we must now be readmitted again after only two years' absence, the more so since I for my part no doubt carry the best certificates for my conduct. Warlike prospects must then make their contribution to my advancement. In any case I shall retain from the Mexican expedition two or three decorations and a pleasant and interesting recollection for later times. By the middle of May I shall hope to be in Vienna again and there, provided Austria has not by then again become involved in a war, to spend several months recovering from the trials I have experienced.

Till then I embrace you, dearest Mother, many thousand times. Give warmest greetings to brothers and sisters, relations and friends and tell Marie that on her birthday, the day before yesterday, I thought much of her and drank her health. Again goodbye.

Your faithful son,
Ernst

PS Do not publicize my reports too much, for that could cause me unpleasantness.

Prelude to Tragedy

When Maximilian returned to the capital in early January 1867, the seriousness of the situation was becoming increasingly evident. Liberal forces were advancing everywhere and before the month was out Miramón, as recorded by Ernst, had suffered a crushing defeat as San Jacinto at the hands of General Escobedo, losing more than three thousand of his troops (of whom more than a hundred European officers, mostly French, were murdered in cold blood by the victors). Defections to the Liberal cause were multiplying and monarchists and members of the church – the twin bastions of the imperial regime – were leaving the country in droves.

Profoundly disillusioned by the behaviour of his erstwhile supporters and exasperated by the intrigue and deceit displayed all around him, Maximilian decided on a step in keeping with his romantic nature: he would assume personal command of his troops and lead them into battle against the Liberals. Accordingly, on 13 February, with a force of 1,600 Mexican troops, he set out for Querétaro, a town a hundred miles north of Mexico City. Querétaro was a poor choice for a military base; it lay in a plain surrounded by hills, from which a hostile force could easily threaten the city. It was, however, a stronghold of monarchist and clerical feeling and its inhabitants were profoundly loyal to the empire. It was no doubt largely for this reason that Márquez and Mejía – as well as Miramón, with what remained of his army after the disaster of San Jacinto – had chosen to converge there and that Maximilian had elected to join them.

Despite the pleas of Kodolitsch and Khevenhüller, who had

stayed on in Mexico solely out of devotion to the emperor, Maximilian refused to allow any foreigners to accompany him on the march to Querétaro, since he wished it to be seen that he was truly Mexican and not dependent on foreign support. He promised the Austrians that he would send for them on reaching Querétaro (and did so, but the message never reached them, being suppressed perhaps by Márquez or, as Basch thinks,* by the Conservatives in Mexico City). A foreigner who did, however, contrive to join the expedition was Prince Felix Salm-Salm, one of the most colourful personalities in the Mexican episode, who was to figure prominently in what remained of Maximilian's life. An aristocrat, who had served with distinction in the Prussian army, Salm left Europe to get away from his creditors and found service with the forces of the Union in the American Civil War, rising to the rank of general. Here he met and married an equally remarkable lady, of whose early life little is known except that she was once a circus rider. Deprived of the excitement they so relished after the end of the war in the United States, the Salms responded to the call of adventure across the border, the princess accompanied by her pet dog, Jimmy, who went with her everywhere. Although initially cold-shouldered by the Austrians who, so soon after Königgrätz, were not then very fond of Prussians, Prince Felix eventually succeeded in meeting Maximilian, only to be told, like the Austrians, that he could not go to Querétaro with the emperor. The prince, however, overcame this obstacle and a remarkable friendship then developed between the two men. Salm was to be Maximilian's closest and most trusted companion during the last months of the emperor's life.

Regrettably, a gap now appears in Ernst's account of his experiences. What is left of the diary only consists of a few brief notes on events in Querétaro and Ernst's next letter to his mother is dated 28 May – after the fall of Querétaro. However, we know in general what happened to Ernst during this intervening period from the writings of Prince Salm† and also, in less detail, from those of Basch,‡ who was Maximilian's doctor. Salm tells us that Ernst was released from captivity just as Maximilian was on his

---

* Basch, *Erinnerungen aus Mexiko*, Leipzig (1883).
† Felix Salm-Salm, *My Diary in Mexico*, (London, 1868).
‡ Basch, *Erinnerungen*.

way to Querétaro and that the Liberal General Escobedo gave him a pass to Veracruz on the understanding that he would leave from there for Europe. But when, on arriving at Querétaro, Ernst saw that the emperor had so few European officers to support him, he again offered his services (of course now as a member of the Mexican army). Salm further records: 'Márquez treated the captain, who arrived in citizen's dress, very roughly and had him even imprisoned as a suspicious foreigner, but when the misunderstanding was cleared up he took him on as a major on his staff.' Soon afterwards, Salm relates: 'On my recommendation the emperor gave the command of the Cazadores [the elite light infantry regiment whose command Salm had just relinquished on promotion to brigadier] to Major Ernst Pitner.'

Liberal troops from different areas now began to converge on Querétaro, where they eventually assembled some 40,000 men against an imperial force of about 12,000. This disparity need not of itself have proved decisive, given good generalship on the imperial side, Unfortunately disunity and indecision among Maximilian's Mexican commanders inhibited effective use of the forces at their disposal. Thus three of the generals proposed that the Liberal army advancing from the west should be engaged before it could join forces with General Escobedo's northern army – a course of action which could have been profitable. But the plan was vetoed by General Márquez, who had recently become a favourite of Maximilian and could dominate military decisions. Márquez was known as the 'Tiger of Tacubaya' because of his reputation for sadistic cruelty. The emperor was a poor judge of character almost ubiquitously ill-served by his *protégés*, and the trust he so ill-advisedly placed in Márquez contributed to Maximilian's undoing. (Basch believes that Márquez's obstruction of military planning in Querétaro may have been deliberately so intended.) Already in February, as already noted, the foreign (especially the Austrian) troops in the capital had been ordered to reinforce Querétaro, but the message had not reached them. It was then decided that Márquez should proceed to Mexico City and return from there with troops, provisions and money. Márquez left on 23 March with a force of 1,100 cavalry, but instead of returning immediately with the expected reinforcements, as he was instructed to do, he embarked on an unauthorized campaign to the south against the forces of General Porfirio Díaz. However, largely through his own irresolution and cowardice, he suffered a disastrous defeat and only the skill of the Austrian commanders enabled what remained of his original army to make its way back to the capital. Here Márquez, still making no attempt to go to the emperor's assistance and exploiting the appointment of 'lugarten-iente' (regent) conferred on him by Maximilian, established himself as a petty despot, isolating the capital from all communication with Querétaro.

Meanwhile in that city the first military encounters had been by no means unfavourable to the imperial cause. On 14 March a full-scale attack on the city was beaten off with heavy losses to the Liberals. Prince Salm-Salm wanted to pursue the enemy – a course of action which, amid the confusion and demoralization prevailing on the Liberal side, could have been productive and possibly have changed the whole military situation. But once again, on Már-quez's advice, his recommendation was not followed. The Liberals recovered from their discomfiture and continued to strengthen their occupation of the city's perimeter.

Nevertheless, in the following weeks the imperial forces made a number of successful sorties in heavy fighting, in which Prince Salm-Salm and Ernst continued to distinguish themselves by their courage and leadership. On 22 March the Cazadores, with Salm and Ernst at their head, attacked and took the village of Juanico. On 1 April Ernst was wounded in an attack on the hill of San Gregorio. Salm records the incident (revealing incidentally that Ernst had a weight problem!):

Without creating an alarm, we came through houses and gardens to the place before the church of San Sebastián and I formed there as silently as possible my troops for the attack. The Cazadores and the fifty men of Celaya were at the head of the column under Major Pitner and I followed with the municipal guard.

Scarcely had we finished forming before we were discovered at last . . . We commenced running up the hill. The Liberal company placed near the chapel San Trinidad fled in dismay and the two guns which they were placed there to guard had not even time to fire. Major Pitner himself was at once at one and Captain Maier of the first Company, a Tyrolean, at the other. We captured, with the guns, their ammunition and horses and some baggage besides. I sent all that directly to the rear and granted my soldiers a few minutes' rest, as they were out of breath from the hard run up the hill.

Our attack, so far behind the front line of the enemy, came quite unexpectedly upon them, especially to General Adrillón, commanding there and quartered in the chapel together with Colonel Villanueva of Escobedo's staff. Both these officers were in bed and had to run for their lives through the prickly cactus plants, barefooted and in their shirts . . .

After a short but necessary delay, we stormed San Gregorio. Major Pitner was in advance with one company of Cazadores but, arriving on the crest of the hill, he was checked in his rush by a greeting of canister and the fire of two battalions, placed there in readiness for our reception. The major himself escaped with a deep fleshwound in the fleshy part of the arm and the loss of a waistcoat-button, torn off by a bullet: but his men suffered much more from this heavy fire. They had to give way and, pushed towards the right by an overwhelming number, they were separated from me.

Under these circumstances Major Pitner thought it best to retreat down the hill, in which he succeeded after a great deal of trouble. The major, a rather stout young man, regretted very much that his horse had not come also, for this running up and down the hill was too much for his fat constitution. He was utterly exhausted and would have fallen into the hands of the enemy had not his good luck led to his finding a Liberal mule, which saved him. Without any other impediment he reached, with the rest of his company, the river, which he forded.

On 10 April Ernst was awarded the highest decoration for valour, the emperor's bronze medal (the bronze being reserved for officers, gold and silver for NCOs and privates). The next day, however, he was again wounded while leading his men in a badly planned operation against heavy opposition on the Garita de Mexico. Salm gives a vivid description of the events:

While occupied in this manner we suddenly received very heavy fire from the *azotea* of the *garita* and the other buildings. The Cazadores, who saw nothing but stone walls before them and who were not in their usual high spirits*, pressed themselves close against the wall and Major Pitner in vain tried his eloquence to bring them from the spot. I therefore requested Colonel Cevallos to advance with his first company to my right and seeing that it was done the Cazadores followed abreast with them. The fire by which they were received was however so severe that they soon came to a halt. Under these circumstances Colonel Cevallos, Major Pitner and myself jumped before the line to encourage

* Because they lacked confidence in the operation.

our men, but we were followed only by the Lieutenants . . . and about eight or ten men, partly Cazadores, partly from the 1st battalion of the line.

Our little party advanced until we came to a turret at the corner of the *hacienda* building, which was connected with the loopholed wall. Here Major Pitner fell right before my feet, his blood bespattering my boots; he was shot in his head, but though stunned for a time he was not fatally wounded.

On 17 April Salm was despatched by Maximilian with a detachment of cavalry to try to break through to Márquez in Mexico City, but the attempt failed, possibly because of betrayal by López.

By the beginning of April conditions in Querétaro were fast deteriorating, with increasing shortages of food and munitions. Horses and mules were slaughtered to feed the troops and the only bread at the emperor's table was provided by the nuns at the convent from flour reserved for the Host. Many of the commanders, particularly Salm and Ernst, had felt for some time that the only solution was to break out from Querétaro and Maximilian was now urged to adopt this course. Once in the Sierra Gorda, a wild mountain area only a few miles north-east of the city, whose Indian population was solidly loyal to Mejía, he would have had security and freedom for further action. Accordingly, a sortie was planned for 27 April in which Ernst, now presumably recovered from his wounds, again played a prominent part. As Salm records:

The first line of the enemy and a battery were taken on the first assault by Major Pitner. The attack was made with such impetuosity that a panic seized the Liberals, who fled almost without making any stand . . .

After our troops were once in the enemy's line it was easy work to roll it up, as they were flanked and fired in the back. The Liberals fled like a panic-struck flock of sheep. Fifteen guns, seven stands of colours and five hundred and forty-seven prisoners, including twenty-one officers, a great quantity of ammunition and arms, officers' baggage and provisions, were the result of this short engagement . . .

We had scarcely sustained any loss and the purpose of our attack was fulfilled most gloriously and beyond any expectation. Nothing prevented us from leaving the city, as some hours must necessarily pass

before Escobedo could send fresh troops from the opposite lines
around the city. Whoever knows Mexican warfare knows also that any
return or collecting of beaten troops was not to be apprehended.

Liberal officers told me later that their army lost on that day not less
than ten thousand men by desertion and cavalry was sent after them
into the country to bring back at least some of them. The defeat was
so complete, and appeared so decisive, that some of the Liberal
generals proposed to raise the siege, and all admitted that it must have
been done if Miramón had at once assisted Castillo and the Garita de
Mexico been taken.

Had the imperial forces followed up their success, as Salm
suggests, things might have gone very differently; but, once again,
they failed to do so (the main cause being over-confidence on the
part of General Miramón, whose advice Maximilian now blindly
followed) and the Liberals were able to regroup their forces.
Meanwhile the state of the garrison got steadily worse, as Salm
records:

> Our troops had been very much thinned by their many engagements:
> to such a degree had this reached that the infantry was no longer
> sufficient to man the trenches. Those between the Garita de Celaya
> and the Cerro de las Campanas were therefore occupied by the 4th
> regiment of cavalry, whose horses had mostly died by starvation. It
> was wonderful that the Liberals did not attack this position.
>
> The scarcity of maize was not felt less than that of money. Some
> cavalry regiments and the artillery teams did not receive any rations at
> all and had to feed their horses with leaves and chopped brushwood.
> The soldiers received only half-pay and the officers scarcely any.

Dissension continued among Maximilian's commanders: many
hoped that the emperor would throw off the influence of the over-
optimistic Miramón, who believed that the siege could be raised
at any time, while Maximilian continued to hope that Miramón
could somehow resolve the situation. 'Thus,' as Salm records,
'between mutual hopes, never to be fulfilled, time passed away
without anything decisive being done, and our position became
from day to day more untenable.'

Meanwhile, largely on Salm's insistence, Ernst was promoted.
As Salm recalls the occasion:

On May 7th several officers were promoted on the recommendation of Miramón. I was very much astonished not to see amongst them Major Pitner, who distinguished himself so much at the various actions, whilst much less deserving and younger majors were promoted. I spoke to the emperor about this injustice and had the satisfaction to find that Major Pitner was made lieutenant-colonel on the same day.

Conditions in the city continued to get worse. Salm writes:

On 11th May provisions for man and beast were nearly exhausted. Horses and mules did not get any rations at all and had to be satisfied with what they found on the *plazas* of the city. The regiment of the empress and the bodyguard still receive quarter rations. The horses of the emperor were kept alive by provisions which López had got somewhere and I bought for mine old straw beds, of which the contents were chopped.

A further plan to leave Querétaro was now agreed among the commanders. According to Salm:

It was resolved to break through the lines of the enemy with the whole of our little army, *which was still possible at any point we chose*. It is true that the enemy had encircled us closely with his lines, but his whole army was employed occupying them, without keeping any reserve at his disposal.

The break-out was planned for the night of 13 May, but at the last moment was postponed by one day at General Mejía's request; and it was later again postponed by one more day at the request of General Méndez. On the night of the 14th, however, the Liberals were able to occupy key positions in the city thanks to the treachery of Colonel Miguel López, a Mexican officer to whom Maximilian had shown special favour. In the initial confusion escape might still have been possible for Maximilian, and Mejía, Salm and Ernst, who had his troops in readiness, urged him to make the attempt; but Maximilian hesitated, precious time was lost and all were eventually taken prisoner. Ernst was among the small group of officers who were at the emperor's side when he was captured

Ernst wrote to his mother from Querétaro on 28 May:

Dearest Mother,

When I closed my letter of the 14th of this month I did indeed have a premonition that we were on the eve of one of those great catastrophes, which remain recorded in world history as of permanent significance. The attack which we had planned for the morning of the 15th did not take place, because several preparations for it were still considered necessary. Instead, a certain Colonel Miguel López, who had always been particularly favoured by the emperor, whose child His Majesty held at baptism and who in the course of the last years had been given two houses by the emperor, entered into negotiation with the enemy with a view to betrayal and allowed the enemy to penetrate into the city through the sector entrusted to his defence at five o'clock on the morning of the 15th without a shot being fired, receiving 7,000 thaler as reward for this honourable action.

The poor unfortunate emperor was almost surprised while still in bed; nevertheless he still succeeded in getting through the town, already largely occupied by the enemy, in great haste and in establishing a firm footing once more in the so-called Cerro de las Campanas. Standing there with some 300 cavalrymen, we were encircled by the entire enemy and bombarded from ten guns until, as any rescue or break-out was impossible, we surrendered. At the emperor's side at that memorable moment there stood the generals Mejía and Castillo, Colonel Salm, Major Malburg* and Count Pachta,† and finally myself. As to what then happened let me be silent for the moment, for the mere recollection of it is so painful and distressing that I wish some time to elapse after it before I discuss those sad events again. In any case the whole of Europe will soon be fully informed about it from another quarter.

It remains my pride that it was at least granted to me at this supreme moment to have stood at the side of my sovereign, whose brilliant qualities we really only came to know in the last period.

The whole garrison was captured. About 600 officers and 7,000 men with some eighty guns and above all the person of the emperor had been traded in for 7,000 thaler from our adversaries.

At present His Majesty, together with the two generals Mejía and Miramón, stands accused of high treason and filibustering before a court martial composed of six Mexican captains with one lieutenant-colonel presiding, with a term of sixty-two hours for defence, examination and sentence. You can imagine what we are suffering in the

---

* Major Ernst Malburg, formerly of the volunteer corps, cavalry officer (hussars), captured at Querétaro and deported before Maximilian's trial.
† Major Count Gotthard Pachta, imperial cavalry, captured and deported like Malburg.

awareness of the menacing danger hovering over the head of the emperor.

Our own fate remains completely secondary for the present, we are in any case prepared proudly to share our emperor's fate, although it is more than likely that they will not proceed to a mass shooting among us.

In this respect I personally am in an incomparably worse position than my comrades, since I only recently escaped from the hands of the same adversaries and moreover am the highest in rank of all the foreign officers present here.*

Nevertheless I look to the future for myself with the greatest tranquillity of mind. I am quite calm in the consciousness of having always done my duty and acted as a man of honour.

The only worry of myself and my comrades is anxiety for the emperor's life.

We are all locked in a convent, with sentries on all sides. That, as always in such cases, all our possessions – in my case four saddled horses, my weapons and luggage, decorations etc. – were lost I need hardly mention and since our enemies give us neither food nor money we would in fact, were it not for the kindness of the inhabitants of Querétaro, who send most of us food three times a day, and the fact that one or other of us still has some money, have had to die of sheer hunger. I could give you enough deplorable and sad details of these days that have recently passed if, on the one hand, distaste at speaking of it and, on the other, the inadvisability of committing all this to paper did not prevent me from doing so.

If I am not shot, I will certainly come home in a very short time and will then relate everything in the fullest manner. If the opposite happens, others of my comrades will be able to give sufficient information.

Although in no way tired of life, I believe and hope to be able to approach this last issue in complete composure, since it is after all only a question of nerves and my nerves are not of the weak kind.

In any case, dearest Mother, do not fear too much for me, for at present I am assured from different quarters that we foreigners have nothing to fear and that they will simply send us to Europe.

Since, however, the saying 'consider whom you can trust' is more applicable in Mexico than anywhere else, I hold it to be my duty to discuss such an eventuality so that, should such a thing after all happen to me, you, my dear Mother, will not be struck by the blow too unprepared.

---

* Except Salm, who held the rank of brigadier.

The United States as well as the European powers have, so we hear, energetically demanded treatment conforming to the practices of civilised peoples for the emperor and his compatriots who have followed him, in the anticipated event of their capture.

Unfortunately, however, the practices of civilized nations are a little difficult to apply to the Mexicans, the more so since they at present believe themselves to be able to challenge the whole universe.

The behaviour of the emperor and of the two generals, Miramón and Mejía, who are chiefly in danger, compete in reciprocal nobility. While the emperor says that as he was the head and alone responsible, one should shoot him, but spare his generals and officers, the two above-named generals, for their part, say that they alone persuaded the emperor to stay in the country and to place himself at the head of the army, instead of leaving from Orizaba, and theirs alone was the responsibility of having induced the emperor to continue the struggle. They alone, therefore, wish to be considered as the guilty ones and be judged. Unfortunately, nobility is here an unrewarding attribute – a virtue largely unknown even by name; and, unless a miracle occurs, I greatly fear for the lives of the three persons in question. In any case, you will already know the emperor's fate through the telegraphic channel many weeks before you receive my letter and if no harm has still been done to him by then he can be considered saved.

Let me, my good, dearest Mother, kiss and embrace you again many thousand times. Let us hope that it will soon be granted to me to press you to my heart.

In any case the telegraph will tell you in passing before the arrival of these lines whether you can expect the wish I have just expressed to be realized or not.

If you hear of a larger number of prisoners of war being shot, then consider me dead. In the contrary event, expect me soon.

Be sure that my last thought remains devoted to you – receive once more the thanks coming from my whole heart for the warm motherly love you have always kept for me and forgive me the many worries and the distress which I have caused you, particularly in earlier years. Kiss my good brother Franz, little Max, then Marie, Ludwig, their child, Adolf's family, Uncle Ernst, the Landges, Astens and Uncle François a thousand times. Give my regards to the Schmerlings, Perins, Thorens, Herzigs and all the rest and think of me and remember me, all of you, once in a while.

I embrace you once more in spirit and beg God to preserve you for many more years for your grateful son,

Ernst Pitner,
Lieutenant

Final Solution

After their capture, Maximilian and his officers were treated for the most part in a harsh and often humiliating manner. This had not been the original intention of General Escobedo, who had promised that they would be treated as prisoners of war. But instructions came from Juárez that they were to be dealt with as common criminals. When Maximilian was moved to the Capuchin convent, he was made by his guard to spend the first night among the tombs in the crypt, 'so that you realize that the end is near'. For most of his remaining days he had to endure the indignity of being stared at by a curious rabble through the open door of a small cell. Conditions for the prisoners would, however, have been much worse had it not been for the support they received from the inhabitants of Querétaro, who provided them with food, clothing, linen and money.

Despite their tribulations, morale among the captives remained remarkably high. Maximilian never lost his sense of humour and he and his officers often played cards together. Refusing to be intimidated by their captors, the Austrians gave grotesque nicknames to some of their guards. Salm records an occasion when

Lieutenant-Colonel Pitner and Major Malburg joked about a sentinel at their door whose thin, hungry figure and ragged state amused them. Colonel Doria, a man known in the Liberal army as a bloodhound, noticed it and said: 'Laugh on, gentlemen: these fellows are still good enough to shoot you'.

Salm comments: 'This observation damped a little the merriment of these officers'.

Basch records that one of Escobedo's adjutants, Colonel Palacios, recognized Ernst as one of those taken prisoner at Santa
Gertrudis and gave him the assurance that he would not get off so
lightly this time. Ernst explained how he had come to take up
arms again, but finally told the sneering Palacios: 'I can die no
more honourable death than in the company of the emperor.'

Soon after the fall of the city, Escobedo received orders that all
the top officers were to be shot out of hand, but the general
objected that this should not be done without a trial, in view of
the difficulties likely to arise with foreign governments, particularly that of the United States. Thereupon the order was given
that Maximilian and all his generals should be brought before a
court martial under the Republican law of 2 January 1862, under
which anyone captured bearing arms was punishable by death.
For any person convicted on this charge the death sentence was
automatic and there was no appeal. As well as the generals,
Escobedo was instructed to pick out other officers against whom
there were particular charges and bring them to trial: these
included Prince Salm and Ernst.* Other officers were sentenced
to terms of imprisonment in different parts of the country and had
to leave the city before the trials.

The treatment to which these prisoners were subjected was
harsh. Salm describes the departure of the first group of field-
officers:

Fifty field-officers, who stood in the yard of the casino, were to be
transported to Morelia: amongst them were Pradillo and Ormachea. It
was very hard to me to part from these faithful companions in arms,
and the more so as all of us had a very dark future before us. The
manner in which the Republican government treated these field-officers

* An American correspondent present in Querétaro reported to his newspaper in
New York:

The burly, well-built Austrian . . . is Lieutenant-Colonel Pitner, who fought at
Magenta and Solferino and has never ceased fighting since. He has more wounds than
he has lived years and has been taken prisoner almost as often as he has been
wounded. On the last occasion of his capture he was exchanged by Escobedo with the
express understanding that he would leave the country. But the *cacoëthes* for fighting
was strong upon him and instead of quitting Mexico he rejoined Maximilian.
Lieutenant-Colonel Pitner's fate is therefore sealed and he knows it, but not one whit
does that knowledge diminish his appetite or his flow of spirits – both considerable.
(*New York Herald*, July 1867).

was revolting, but was characteristic of the spirit of this government. These officers (amongst whom were many old men, and others who were disabled or weakened by their wounds) had to march on foot, in the heat of a Mexican summer, and each with his bundle on his back, for sixteen days to Morelia, escorted by a detachment of cavalry.

All these officers had been always on horseback, they were not used to march on foot in the heat of the sun, and on sandy roads, and the consequence was that many of them suffered from sore feet and other marching complaints. After the second day they therefore declared that they could not walk any longer, but preferred to be shot.

The citizens of Celaya received these unfortunate men with great kindness. They offered them not only all kinds of victuals and refreshments, but even mules, and requested permission to sell them on their arrival, and to buy with the money some commodities for themselves. Similar to this was their reception in other places.

Fifty of the captains were sent to Guanajuato, fifty to Zacatecas and seventy-two to San Luis Potosí. Amongst the latter were also the foreign lieutenants. All these prisoners were not treated as prisoners of war, but to the disgrace of Escobedo, who broke his word, were placed on a level with robbers and thieves.

There is some reason to believe that the traitor López (possibly with Escobedo's tacit approval) intended Maximilian to escape when he let the Liberals into the city; but Maximilian rejected his invitation to do so, as well as his offer of a safe haven in Querétaro. Subsequently, two attempts were made by the devoted and indefatigable Salm to organize Maximilian's escape. The first, though complicated by Maximilian's insistence that Miramón and Mejía should go with him, could well have succeeded. But the arrangements had to be called off at the last moment when Maximilian refused to leave because of the poor impression which he felt his departure would have made upon the foreign envoys whom he had asked to visit him in Querétaro and whose impending arrival had just become known. This well illustrates the indecisiveness as well as the quixotic high-mindedness which characterized so much of Maximilian's behaviour. The second attempt failed when an officer of the guard resisted the princess's offer of a large sum of money – as well as her own favours – in return for his co-operation.

Appeals for clemency were made to Juárez by many governments and individuals. Even the United States government made representations on Maximilian's behalf. Garibaldi sent a telegram in which, after congratulating Juárez on his victory, he asked him to spare Maximilian's life. And Princess Salm, who saw Juárez several times in support of Maximilian, went on her knees before him, begging him to show mercy. But all appeals were turned down on the grounds that Maximilian was a usurper who had caused much suffering to the country and that the good of the Mexican people required his death.

Maximilian, Miramón and Mejía were tried by a military tribunal of young officers convened on 12 June (Maximilian had refused to be present in person). The death sentence was a foregone conclusion and the three were shot together on 19 June on a hill outside the city named Cerro de las Campanas (Hill of the Bells).

Whatever weaknesses and shortcomings may have marked Maximilian's career, he behaved at the end with a dignity and composure which aroused general admiration. Before the fall of Querétaro he endeared himself to its inhabitants and to his own soldiers with his concern for their welfare. He retained his sense of humour to the last and it can fairly be said of him that 'nothing in his life became him like the leaving it'. Lord Acton wrote of him:

> His worst crime was in accepting the treacherous gift of Empire, but his misfortune was greater than his fault. I think he was well-nigh the noblest of his race, and fulfilled the promise of his words 'The fame of my ancestors will not degenerate in me'.

Second only to the nobility shown by Maximilian was that of some of his companions in misfortune. Mejía was offered his life by Escobedo, but refused the offer unless Maximilian was also spared. And, rather than be sent away to imprisonment as a colonel, Prince Salm insisted that he should be classified as a general so that he could stay with Maximilian, even though this meant that he would be court martialled, with every likelihood of being shot.

Message from Maximilian to his officers:

Querétaro, Prison of the Capuchins, 17 June 1867
To the generals and staff officers who are prisoners in this city: At this
solemn moment I address these lines to you, both as a mark of my
appreciation of the loyalty with which you served me as well as proof
of the sincere regard entertained for you by

your affectionate,
Maximilian

The text of a letter addressed by the Emperor Maximilian of
Mexico to the Emperor of Austria, dictated to Dr Basch on 18
June 1867:

Dear Brother,
Compelled by the dispensation of Providence, through no fault of
mine, to suffer an undeserved death, I send you these last lines in
order to thank you with all my heart for your brotherly love and
friendship.

May God reward you for it in abundance with happiness, peace and
prosperity for yourself, the empress and the dear children.

For errors I have committed, for distress and annoyance I have
caused you in my life I beg your forgiveness with all my heart. One last
request I make of you, that you lovingly remember the faithful
Austrians who have served me with devotion and self-sacrifice to the
end of my life's span, the more so since I have to recognize with deep
sorrow that this country has done nothing for them.

As I embrace you with heartfelt love, send warmest greetings to the
empress and the dear children and beseech you always to remember
my poor soul in your prayers I remain, to the end of my life

your eternally faithful brother,
Maximilian
Querétaro, 18 June 1867

Ernst wrote to his mother from Querétaro on 2 August:

Dear, precious Mother,
A strange feeling always impels me to write to you on my birthday
because I know and am convinced that you too think of me often and
a great deal today.

I have recently been somewhat neglectful in my writing and that for
a variety of reasons. In the first place, my situation to begin with was
rather critical and I did not want to alarm you unnecessarily; secondly
our – and particularly my – frame of mind was such that it became

almost impossible for me to commit a rational sentence to paper. Our whole attention, our only hopes were devoted to the person of the unfortunate emperor and our despair over his terrible end was indescribable. Our present prison is the one in which the emperor spent his last moments and from which he was taken to the place where the greatest political murder of our century was carried out.

I have spent the last month in the constant hope of being set free every day and even today I am almost certain that I will be able to bid this unfortunate country farewell in August; however, I must not delay any longer to tell you that there is no more danger at all for me and that General Escobedo has personally promised me my release.

Unfortunately we are in a country where there is neither word nor justice. The Austrians who were taken prisoner in the capital have already been free for three weeks* and we are still not let out of the prison.

I could tell you an enormous amount of my latest experiences, but they are too extensive to find room in this letter; and I have recorded them fully in my diary† and ask you to remain patient for a short time yet.

I think I wrote to Franz that I became a lieutenant-colonel during the siege, served first on the emperor's general staff and later had command of our elite battalion Cazadores del Emperador. Twice wounded, I with my battalion captured ten pieces of artillery from the enemy and for this received the Order of the Eagle. The poor emperor overwhelmed me with favours. Almost every day I was with him alone for one or two hours. We sat in his room, he questioned me about all and everything, had me tell him what I thought etc., etc. If he had survived, I am certain that through his favour I would have been outstandingly well placed in the army in Austria. But even as it is I do not propose to exchange the rank of lieutenant-colonel, which I have earned here with my blood, for the position of a lieutenant. I am taking excellent testimonials from the imperial minister of war here with me to Austria. Even before his death the poor emperor recommended me to General Escobedo, conveyed his embrace to me and sent me a memento‡ from among the little things he had had in use up to the last moment. Furthermore, I am the only officer belonging to the active Austrian army who was at the poor emperor's side in

---

* Under the terms of the surrender negotiated by Count Khevenhüller with Porfirio Díaz.
† Unfortunately, this part of the diary, as also a number of letters, has not been preserved.
‡ It is not known what this was. Basch however records that Ernst was one of those to whom Maximilian sent personal valedictory greetings before his execution.

Querétaro up to the hour of his death. The second Austrian officer who was also here as well as me is Major Malburg, but he was in fact moved from Querétaro to Morelia before the emperor's death. This is the same officer who, when I travelled with you from Brunnsee to Vienna at the beginning of October 1864, entered our compartment at Graz and travelled with us to Vienna, though sleeping and snoring most of the time. All the other Austrians had remained behind in the capital, Mexico, and none of them can on their return give the emperor of Austria those details which I am in a position to provide.

Although we are given neither a penny's worth of pay nor food here, we are nevertheless still not too badly off materially, for the population of Querétaro has the warmest sympathies for us and provides us all with food. Besides, I still had about 150 thaler in my pocket when I was taken prisoner and I can borrow money when this is used up. My room-mates are two Germans, Major von Görbitz, former ADC to General Miramón, who was shot at the emperor's side, and General Prince zu Salm-Salm, formerly principal ADC and master of the household of the lamented emperor. We are the only senior foreign officers and amidst the xenophobia prevailing here, which surpasses all belief, experience various small and large forms of harassment, both from the enemy officers guarding us as also even from the Mexicans of our own side. Fortunately I myself have the greatest aptitude for getting on with these people and not minding about anything – not so my two companions, who, firstly, are much more violent than I and, secondly, have only been in the country a short time and so have no idea of the people here and their customs and habits.

I cannot tell you how terrible it is for me to have had no news of you and my kinsfolk for one and a half years, only the hope of seeing you very soon gives me some consolation. I will not say anything about political matters and the future dawning for this country. Let us hope that the time will soon come when these people will harvest what they have sown.

Give a hug to Maxl and my best wishes for his sixteenth birthday. Were I not myself surprised to be entering my thirtieth year, I would hardly believe that the rascal is already so big. Affectionate kisses to Franz, Marie, Ludwig, their children, Adolf and the other relations. Warm greetings and regards to the Schmerlings and Thorens and you, my good, dearly beloved Mother, I hope to be able to hold personally to my heart in two months. Until then be embraced a thousand times in spirit by

Your grateful son,
Ernst

Disengagement

Although Maximilian was personally popular in Austria – to an extent which disturbed Franz Joseph, who was glad to see him removed from the European scene – Austrian opinion had always been critical of the Mexican affair. This was partly out of dislike for Louis Napoleon, whose armies had so recently defeated the Austrians in Italy, causing the loss of Lombardy. It was also felt, not without reason, that Maximilian was merely being used as a tool to further Louis Napoleon's imperial ambitions. The appearance in Vienna in 1863 of the Mexican delegation sent to offer the crown to Maximilian was subjected to a good deal of ridicule in the Austrian press. And, more seriously, a discerning article in one of the satirical journals pointed out that the offer could not have the support of the Mexican people and that the emperor would only be kept on his throne by French arms.* Once the enterprise had got under way there was general sympathy for

---

* An article in *Der g'rade Michel*, quoted by Hamann, *Mit Kaiser Max in Mexiko* (Vienna, 1983). This reads in translation:

> The Mexican people are not offering the crown and the Mexican people are altogether not in a position now to have a will of their own. By force, without a semblance of legality, the French have invaded Mexico, without a semblance of legality they call upon the clerical party to rule and it is now this party which is changing the country's constitution and creating an imperial throne. It is Napoleon who gives away the Mexican crown and the Mexican Assembly of Notables is only an instrument of Napoleon's will, which is now all-powerful in Mexico. It is a passion of Napoleon's to enjoy giving away crowns . . . But what attraction can a crown from Napoleon's hands possess? How can one take pleasure in establishing oneself in a country which obeys a French general, in mounting a throne which is supported by French bayonets, in ruling with a party which is the most hated in the country? How can a prince, even if possessed of the best intentions, win the love of his subjects under such conditions?

Maximilian in his predicament, but comment on events tended to be realistic and critical, a fact which caused Ernst to complain in his letters about what he then considered to be the jaundiced view of events in Mexico taken by the Austrian newspapers.

When the volunteer corps came to be recruited, attitudes also tended to cool. The authorities did not care to see able-bodied men, for whom there was a need at home, shipped abroad on a foreign adventure* and some of their lack of enthusiasm transmitted itself to the general public. There were also occasions when the unruly behaviour of some of the men gave rise to unfavourable comment. The town council of Trieste objected to the volunteers being assembled at the port, and when the shipment of additional recruits was unexpectedly cancelled in 1866 after the men had been immured on board ship for a fortnight, their frustration vented itself in disorders which troops had to be brought in to deal with.

When the end came for the volunteers, the manner of their return was a disappointment to many. Those members of the corps who had elected to be repatriated with the French were brought back to Austria in April 1867, and the reception they received was decidedly unenthusiastic. Much had changed since their departure and the changes had not been good for Austria. Austrian opinion now tended to regard the volunteers as troops who had avoided the recent fighting in Europe, which had been so costly, without appreciating the gallantry and devotion with which they had served the emperor's brother in a distant and alien land or the extent of the hardships they had had to endure. Those arriving in Trieste were confined to barracks until they could be sent home. Officers opting for reinstatement in the Austrian army had to revert to the rank they held before enrolling in the corps, no account being taken of their Mexican service (Franz Josef turned down a request that this should be counted for promotion). And all ranks were unable to obtain the substantial arrears of pay due to them (for which Maximilian's government, by now virtually non-existent and in any case bankrupt, was responsible). This led to ugly scenes outside the Mexican embassy in Vienna.

The worst sufferers, however, were the sick and disabled. They

---

* cf. Ernst's complaint (p. 23) about the failure of the military commander in Trieste to be present at the departure of the first troop ship.

could expect nothing from the Mexican government and the Austrian army bore no responsibility for them. With a pittance of pocket money they would be returned to their homes, there for the majority to eke out a miserable existence to the end of their lives.

Regrettably, for a force many of whose members had gone out with high hopes and generous intentions, the experience had brought mostly hardship and disillusion. They were compelled to realize that their courage, dedication and sacrifices had not won the recognition they deserved. Impoverished, frustrated and unsettled, they now had to rebuild their lives after three years given to an enterprise that had ended in failure.

Meanwhile nearly all the Austrians who had chosen to enrol in the Mexican army under Maximilian were now in Mexico City, whither the remnants of Márquez's force had retreated after his catastrophic defeat before Puebla. The troops of General Porfirio Díaz surrounded the capital, but had no intention of trying to capture it, since they expected it to fall into their hands without a fight once Querétaro had been taken. And the Austrian units in the city – particularly Khevenhüller's redoubtable hussars – were more than a match for any Liberal force that might oppose them.

But even after Querétaro had fallen and the emperor been taken prisoner, the unfortunate garrison continued to hold out because Márquez prevented news of what had happened from becoming known to those around him. Finally, on 16 June, a message was received from the Austrian chargé d'affaires confirming that the emperor was a prisoner and conveying his order to the Austrians to lay down their arms. Terms of surrender were then negotiated with Porfirio Díaz under which the Austrians were able to leave the city and embark at Veracruz to return to Austria.

Meanwhile Salm and Ernst (the only Austrian now left in Querétaro) remained in captivity, awaiting trial and possible execution (Salm put no trust in the assurances Juárez had given his wife that he would not be shot). And indeed, Salm, together with a number of Mexican generals, was tried and sentenced to death, but the execution was postponed at the last moment and they were eventually reprieved, Salm being condemned to seven years' imprisonment. After being deported to Veracruz he was eventually pardoned and returned to Europe in December. In the event Ernst, holding a rank below that of general, was not brought to trial and was also eventually pardoned. He left for Austria a little later than Salm.

Ernst wrote to his mother from Querétaro on 28 August:

My good, precious Mother,

Although there has still been no occurrence of note since my last letter of the 2nd of this month and I, together with my companions in misfortune, who are also prisoners, look forward impatiently to a final resolution of our affairs, I must nevertheless turn to you today without being able to inform you of any particular piece of news regarding myself, namely with a request, which you will surely not take amiss, but find understandable. As you know, it is already the fourth month that they have been keeping us locked up here, without bothering either about our means of subsistence or about us in any way at all. It is solely thanks to the Querétaro families, who send us food, that it is possible for us to exist at all; but it is left entirely to us to see to our laundry, clothing etc. Still worse off are my two comrades, Major Count Pachta and Major Malburg, who are prisoners in the town of Morelia; they are locked up in the public prison there and do not know a soul. The latter wrote me a letter describing his sad situation a few days ago and asked me, if this was possible for me with my extensive connections, to raise some money and send it to him, which I then also did with the firm of Bahnsen in San Luis, with which I had friendly relations, borrowing 100 thaler for myself and sharing this sum with him – and sending his share to Morelia. I have made out an order for this to your account and I ask you, on receiving it, to pay the sum amounting to 500 francs or 100 thaler for the time being and either to borrow the money for this or to sell one of your few shares, as I shall again be sending a remittance for the same sum to Vienna within fifteen or twenty days. For Malburg's father is a very rich man and is happy to know of a way of helping his son in any way in his troubled situation. He lives at Seilerstrasse 16, first floor. In sending the aforementioned 50 thaler to Major Malburg I am writing to ask him immediately to send me an order of 100 thaler on his father and I will send it to you and you will then be so good as to cash this money for yourself. I am sure that I do not need to tell you that, firstly, I am only troubling you with this request because I am really in distress through no fault of my own and, secondly, because I know for certain and assure you on my word of honour that you will get the sum you have spent back immediately after the arrival of my next letter and the presentation of Major Malburg's remittance. And now I pass to other matters, knowing full well that even if my request is temporarily irksome for you, it does not disturb you, since I do not doubt that you are convinced of the certainty of what I have written to you about the money being refunded and that assuredly you cannot believe that at my age and with my experience I would ever wish to become a burden to you again even in a monetary connection. The money order says: 'Three days after the presentation of this order 5,000 frs. in gold or 200 gulden in paper money with the appropriate silver are to be paid to the presenter'.

As I have already told you at the beginning, nothing much that is new is happening here. We are treated pretty badly – we are not allowed any visits and the mean and coarse duty officers let no opportunity pass of annoying us with petty harassments.

I have taken all steps to be freed soon and have even written to Juárez in the last few days, drawing his attention to the injustice and lack of justification for the fact that all the Austrians who were captured when the capital surrendered – eighty-four officers and 700 men, among them Colonels Khevenhüller and Kodolitsch – were set free and we are still not released, merely because we were at the emperor's side in Querétaro and although we were already taken prisoner five weeks previously. I wrote as the senior staff officer on behalf of the eighteen Austrian officers who are still held prisoner in various places. I also wrote in the same way to Vice-Admiral Tegetthoff,* so that he should concern himself for us on his arrival in Veracruz.

Incidentally, they are expecting an amnesty for 16 September, the anniversary of the declaration of Mexico's independence. *Vedremo que succede.* Unfortunately, I am the only Austrian here. My two room-mates – Prince Salm and another major – are Prussians and, moreover, endowed with all their bad national qualities. As a result, the life of the three of us together is not very pleasant and our conversation is somewhat laconic. You can imagine that after so many sad events and the frequent disappointments I have recently suffered my sense of humour and mood are nothing to write home about. This, too, is perhaps the reason why I write my letters in a more laconic style than appears to be justified by the circumstances. But if, on the other hand, you will bear in mind that it is impossible for me to give you pleasant and amusing pieces of news and that I certainly do not see the point of useless lamentation, I shall prefer to leave the recital of the interesting things I have experienced until the happy moment when, after an absence of more than three years and so many dangers more or less happily overcome, I can again fold you in my arms.

---

* Wilhelm von Tegetthoff, the victorious commander of the Austrian fleet at the battle of Lissa, who came to recover Maximilian's body and take it back to Austria.

Recently the articles in the American and European press have caused not a little excitement, not to say alarm, in this country. It is true that the government pretends not to care about it – it even had the captured imperial general O'Horan shot on the 21st of this month – but nevertheless, as I believe, is not a little embarrassed.

The poor emperor's corpse is still in Querétaro, the coffin lying like a bit of old junk in a corner of a dark and dirty room in the government building. *Sic transit gloria mundi.* One could shed tears of anger over the brutality and inhumanity of these barbarians, who do not even respect greatness in death.

I embrace you a thousand times, my good, precious Mother . . . and again express the hope to be able to press you to my heart very soon.

Your Ernst

Ernst wrote to his mother again from Querétaro on 20 September:

Most precious Mother,
Again a month has passed since I last wrote to you and still absolutely nothing in our situation has changed. We are still held prisoner here in the convent de las Capuchinas, while all the other Austrians who were in the capital, Mexico, are probably at this moment already at home, although they only surrendered five weeks after the fall of Querétaro. Much as I rejoice at my compatriots' freedom, I am outraged at the infamous injustice of this Republican government, which now makes us pay for having held out by the side of our unhappy monarch and compatriot until the last moment, when he was delivered into the enemy's hands by shameful treachery. We hoped with certainty for an act of grace by the government for the 16th of this month, the feast day of Mexican independence, but today is already the 20th and our hopes have almost entirely vanished. From Escobedo, who assured me of his decisive advocacy almost three months ago, there is also no further utterance and so one has to submit to the inevitable with patience and resignation and wait until some revolution or the change of government foreshadowed for the beginning of December brings the longed-for freedom. Add to this outlook the further circumstance that we do not receive a farthing for our subsistence and are entirely dependent on the charity of the inhabitants here, who send us our food, and that I am in unbearable company, and you will then understand that my mood is just not a happy one and that my patience is near its end.

For three weeks Vice-Admiral Tegetthoff has been in the capital to negotiate for the handing over of the body of the poor emperor. But over this, too, they are making difficulties and demanding either an official endorsement of his mission by the Austrian government or a private letter from the Austrian emperor in which the latter, as head of the family, asks President Juárez for the delivery of his brother's body. Both requirements are another humiliation for Austria and I do not see in what way this matter can be settled without detracting from our country's dignity in some degree.

Of course I wrote to Tegetthoff to get him to concern himself with the Austrians, eighteen in number, who are still kept back here in captivity, but to this hour have had no reply to my letter.

I enclose a written instruction from Major Malburg to his father, through which the 500 francs which you disbursed for me will be refunded to you by this gentleman. The family live at 16 Seilerstrasse, first floor. I don't know whether it is better for you first to send the letter in question there or perhaps to go there yourself at a convenient opportunity. In any case I would be pleased if you became acquainted with this family. Major Malburg, who knew only that I was the son of a state official and did not have the time from Morelia to inform himself of the rank of my poor father referred to you in his letter simply as 'Hofräthin',* but this will not impede the payment of the said 100 thaler.

I simply cannot tell you how terribly monotonous our life is here. Our apartments are dirty, gloomy convent cells without doors or windows, since these were used for firewood by the soldiers. It is comforting for us that our noble master occupied an exactly similar cell a few steps from my lodging, never complained about it, but kept his gaiety and dignity up to his last moment and referred to all the unaccustomed discomfort only in jokes. We have a passage thirty paces long for exercise and can communicate with the servants who bring us our food, but may not receive any other visits. Only those who are married may see their families.

You can imagine from all this that it is just not very amusing here with us, the more so as we are now enjoying this existence for the fifth month. But with a little patience I hope to overcome this too and, God willing, still to be home by Christmas. Until then, be embraced many thousand times . . .

your faithful son
Ernst

PS It seems quite extraordinary to me to be enquiring after the health of one or the other person when I, of course, know that I shall get no answer. It is now twenty months since I have had definite news of you all. Is this not frightful?

---

* Privy Counsellor's wife.

Telegram addressed to Thérèse Pitner, c/o Frau von Laudyn, Saybusch, Galicia, via Bielitz:

Through Baron Lago*. Ernst lives. Was sentenced, has been pardoned – Moritz.

Ernst wrote to his mother from Querétaro on 12 October:

Most precious Mother,
Another month will soon again have passed since I last wrote to you and it is still not granted to me to announce anything pleasing to you about my fate. Despite the most varied rumours, which have now been repeating themselves periodically for as long as three and a half months concerning our early release, none has so far been fulfilled and by the time this letter has reached you I shall already have been a prisoner for six and a half months.

About a week ago we were unofficially given the news that we should hold ourselves in readiness for departure, to be transported as prisoners to different places in the country. Two or three days later this information was altered to the effect that it only concerned the generals; and indeed the latter went off on the 10th to various destinations – namely, Monterey, Oaxaca and Veracruz, to begin the sentence imposed by court martial in these three towns. At this juncture I also had to part company with General Prince Salm-Salm, my room-mate and companion in misfortune hitherto, who went to Oaxaca. Those of us staying behind, who had not been brought to trial, were promised our early release on this occasion but, having already been disappointed so often, I cannot believe it and am resigning myself to sitting here until the congress assembles in December.

Admiral Tegetthoff has behaved in a not very nice way towards all of us. Not only did he personally not concern himself at all about those who faithfully had stood at the side of his former chief† until his last breath, but he did not even find it worth while to answer one of the three letters which I addressed to him as the highest in rank of the Austrian officers kept prisoner in the country on behalf of all of them and in which I merely asked him to exert himself for us indirectly, through third persons and in a private manner since, I said, I well knew that his delicate mission did not permit him to do this officially. I would greatly welcome it if the manner of this gentleman's behaviour towards us became known in Austria. That Tegetthoff knows me from

---

* Baron Eduard Lago, Austrian chargé d'Affaires.
† i.e., Maximilian, who had been head of the Austrian navy 1854–9.

the navy and that he is a friend of Max* and Eduard† I will only
mention quite in passing, since these are things which concern me
alone.

And now that I have given vent to this annoyance I must pass to
another matter, which is no less disagreeable to me. Although it was
only in my last letter that I sent you back the 100 thaler, or rather the
order for them, which I asked you to disburse for me, I must again
trouble you today with the same request. For when we learnt of the
departure order mentioned on the first page of this letter, I had to ask
for money from Mexico by telegram in order not perhaps to be dragged
through the country for 300 leguas on foot, with my belongings on my
back, escorted by brutal soldiers – and also without any money – but
in order to be able to buy myself at least a bad horse, like all the
others, and to keep a few thaler in my pocket. Herr Bahnsen, who is
in Mexico just now, was again so obliging as to agree immediately to
my request and I will refund you the money in question – 100 thaler –
in the same way as the last time and at the latest two months after
payment of the order. You cannot imagine how embarrassing it is for
me to bother you with such things, but I am sure that you will not
judge me wrongly. My situation compels me to this. If I only had a
quarter of the 200 thaler which the fallen government owes me in
arrears of pay and loss compensation, I could look to the future with
reassurance, also as regards my journey home.

Today is the anniversary [name day] of our poor emperor as well as
of my brother Max. Kiss him warmly from me. I will surely hardly
recognize him any more, for meanwhile he has almost become a man.
I too have changed considerably. My good humour is gone, perhaps
never to return, and now nobody takes me for younger than I am, as
used to happen to me so often before. My long twisted moustache and
a few crow's feet on my face make the approach of thirty very visible,
which anyhow does not bother me at all.

Although I have already sent you, in my last letter, heartfelt
felicitations for 15 October, nevertheless I again wish you all the good
that can be imagined for this day. It is three years now since we last
saw each other. Let us hope that this is the last of your anniversaries
which will find me out of Austria.

Kiss and embrace the brothers and sisters and relations, commend me
to our acquaintances and think often and much of your faithful son . . .

Ernst

Ernst wrote to his mother from Mexico City on 10 November:

---

* See note p. 6.
†One of Max Pitner's brothers.

Most precious Mother,
Just in a few lines I want to tell you that I am free at last and will be
leaving for Austria either at the end of November or in the middle of
December.

I arrived here yesterday from Querétaro and in two minutes the mail
closes for the courier who is going to Veracruz for the French mail-
boat. I must therefore close at once and I have no alternative but to
end, embracing you a thousand times. I shall be in Vienna at the end
of January. Greetings and kisses to all relations from

your faithful son,
Ernst.

Postscript

The years immediately following his return to Austria were a time of some difficulty for Ernst. He had no money and, although he had risen to the rank of lieutenant-colonel in Mexico, he had to be content with reinstatement in the Austrian army in his old rank of second-lieutenant. In 1869, after promotion to first-lieutenant, he saw service in the Italian campaign. He received various decorations, but although the emperor had personally promised him, in an audience after his return from Mexico, that he would be given employment in the consular service, it was some years before a post could be found for him. Eventually, in 1874, he was appointed to the embassy in St Petersburg, where he remained for fiteen years. Here he met and married a Russian princess, Eugénie Engalitscheff. In 1889 he was made consul-general in Tunis and in 1893 his knowledge of Russian affairs caused him to be appointed consul-general in Warsaw, which was then the capital of the Russian province of Poland. After two years in Warsaw, however, his health began to fail and a move to a milder climate was considered advisable. He was accordingly appointed consul-general in Barcelona and was also knighted. But he died soon after taking up his new appointment.

Unlike most of the other Austrians (including Ernst), Count (later Prince) Khevenhüller developed – and retained to the end of his life – a particular love for Mexico and its people. After Khevenhüller, who negotiated the surrender of Mexico City with Porfirio Díaz, had become acquainted with the general, a warm friendship developed between the two men which (Díaz having meanwhile become president of Mexico) played an important part in restoring relations – so severely embittered by the Maximilian episode – between the two countries. It was at Khevenhüller's suggestion that a memorial chapel was built, at Mexican expense, on the site of Maximilian's execution and Khevenhüller attended its consecration in 1901 as unofficial Austrian representative. Soon afterwards diplomatic relations were established and a treaty of friendship and commerce was concluded. When Khevenhüller died in 1905, the only wreath on his coffin bore an inscription which read: 'From General Porfirio Díaz, President of Mexico, to his dear friend, Prince Khevenhüller'.

After Prince Salm-Salm's return to Europe in 1868, he was successful in obtaining a commission in the Prussian army. He was killed leading his troops against the French in the Franco-Prussian War. He had just written a love letter to his wife (ending with the postscript 'Kiss little Jimmy').

The following notes were attached to Ernst's diary:

10 [March]: In the morning, skirmishing of the advance posts of both sides. Colonel Quiroga goes out with 600 horses and brings in 200 head of cattle.

50 men go for forage in the direction of Canada; are, however, attacked by 150 enemy horsemen and compelled as a result to abandon their design and to withdraw again to S Cruz, where they in fact arrive again without loss of men or transport.

In the afternoon the enemy is seen drawn up for parade. Their strength at that time can be put at 10,000 men, so far as the marshalled troops were visible.

Soldiers of the empress's regiment set fire to the vegetation on both sides of the town on General Mejía's orders in order to deny the enemy supplies of fodder and animals.

The enemy cuts the aqueduct to deny water to the city.

One enemy deserter arrives.

In the evening, skirmishing of the outposts. Council of war.

11 [March]: Skirmishing of the outposts. At 11 a.m. General Méndez advances with the regiment of the empress and other cavalry for reconnaissance.

12 [March]: Reconnaissance engagement under command of General Castillo.

13 [March]: Nothing special.

14 [March]: Enemy attack on the town from four sides – repulsed.

15 [March]: Nothing new.

16 [March]: Preparations to attack the enemy in San Gregorio: are not however proceeded with.

17–18 [March]: Nothing.

20–21 [March]: Nothing special.

22 [March]: Skirmishing engagement near San Inanico; in the evening Márquez leaves the town with 1,100 men.

23 [March]: Nothing new.

24 [March]: Enemy attack on the side of the Alameda – repulsed.

25–26 [March]: Enemy attacks three times near the bridge at 10, 12 and 2 o'clock at night.

27–31 [March]: Nothing new.

1 April: Attack on San Gregorio with two cannon. Lieutenant Rauf dead, Gunon wounded, twenty men lost. I am wounded.

2–10 [April]: Nothing new. On the 10th I receive the emperor's bronze medal for valour of the army.

11 [April]: Attack on Garita de Mexico. I am wounded, likewise Lieutenant Larache; we are thrown back.

12–26 [April]: Nothing special except for an attempted breakthrough by Messrs Moret and Salm and an attack by the empress's regiment and Salm in which we took twenty-three prisoners from the Supremos Poderes battalion.

27 [April]: Attack on the *cimatario*. We capture twenty-one guns and 546 prisoners. Lieutenant Volz dead; Lavergne slightly wounded.

26–31 [April]: Nothing new.

1 May: Attack on Garita Mepio and Hacienda Calleja. Colonel Rodríguez dead; Lieutenant Lavergne and Lieutenant Gieron dead; Captain Montero wounded.

2 [May]: Nothing new.

3 [May]: Attack on San Gregorio. Considerable losses on our side.

5 [May]: Night attack on the bridge, enemy repulsed.

15 [May]: Treachery. Enemy in the town. All captured.

19 [May]: General Méndez is shot.

We change our lodgings six times; nothing new until the end of May. On 1 June the prisoners are sent in different directions. The generals, a few *guerrilleros*, Salm and I remain here to be brought before a court martial.

Today, the 19th, at 7 in the morning H. M. the Emperor and Generals Miramón and Mejía were shot at the Cerro de las Campanas. Peace to their ashes.

The poor martyr, our noble emperor, died the death of a hero.

Standing and with eyes unbound he awaited the six shots in his breast. Immediately before he cried, 'Long Live Mexican Independence! . . . And I again remember Miramón's proclamation and its ending 'Woe to the vanquished'.

Bibliography

Acton, Lord: *Historical Essays and Studies* (London, 1907).

Alvensleben, Max, Baron von: *With Maximilian in Mexico* (London, 1867).

Basch, Samuel: *Erinnerungen aus Mexiko* (Leipzig, 1883).

Bazant, Jan: *Concise History of Mexico from Hidalgo to Cardenas 1805–1940* (Cambridge University Press, 1977).

Blasio, José: *Maximilian, Emperor of Mexico* (Yale University Press, 1934).

Cheetham, Nicolas: *History of Mexico* (London, 1971).

Corti, Egon Cesar, Conte: *Die Tragödie eines Kaisers* (Vienna, 1949).

Daniek, Edmund: *Sie zogen nach Mexiko* (Vienna, 1973).

Gamillscheg, Felix: *Kaiseradler über Mexiko* (Graz, 1964).

Hamann, Brigitte: *Mit Kaiser Max in Mexiko* (Vienna, 1983).

Haslip, Joan: *Imperial Adventurer* (London, 1971).

O'Connor, Richard: *Cactus Throne: Tragedy of Maximilian and Carlotta* (London, 1971).

Ratz, Konrad: *Das Militärgerichtsverfahren gegen Maximilian von Mexiko* (Vienna, 1985).

Salm-Salm, Prince Felix: *My Diary in Mexico* (London, 1868).

Salm-Salm, Princess Felix: *Ten Years of my Life* (London, 1875–6).

Smith, Gene: *Maximilian and Carlota; the Habsburg Tragedy in Mexico* (London, 1974).

Stichler, Gerlinde: *Der Anteil Oesterreichs an der Unternehmung Erzherzog Maximilians in Mexiko (Das Oesterreichische Freiwilligenkorps)* (Dissertation, University of Vienna, 1963).

Tavera, Schmidt Ritter von: *Die Mexikanische Kaisertragödie* (Vienna, 1903).

Index